SINGER
Creative Gifts & Projects Step-by-Step

CY DeCOSSE
INCORPORATED
MINNETONKA, MINNESOTA USA

SINGER
Creative Gifts & Projects
Step-by-Step

Contents

Singer Creative Gifts & Projects Step-by-Step draws pages from the individual titles of the Singer Reference Library. Individual titles are also available from the publisher and in bookstores and fabric stores:
Sewing Essentials, Sewing for the Home, Clothing Care & Repair, Sewing for Style, Sewing Specialty Fabrics, Sewing Activewear, The Perfect Fit, Timesaving Sewing, More Sewing for the Home, Tailoring, Sewing for Children, Sewing with an Overlock, 101 Sewing Secrets, Sewing Pants That Fit, Quilting by Machine, Decorative Machine Stitching, Creative Sewing Ideas, Sewing Lingerie, Sewing Projects for the Home, Sewing with Knits, More Creative Sewing Ideas, Quilt Projects by Machine, Creating Fashion Accessories

Pages 102 and 103 previously appeared in *Singer Home Decorating Projects Step-by-Step.*

Creating Fabrics 139

Embellishments 223

Creative Projects 275

Creative Details 181

Fiber Art 249

Library of Congress
Cataloging-in-Publication Data

Singer Creative Gifts & Projects Step-by-Step.
     p. cm.
     Includes index.
     ISBN 0-86573-290-6
     1. Handicraft. 2. Machine sewing.
     I. Title: Singer creative gifts and projects
     step-by-step.
TT157.S524   1993
746 – dc20   93-17642

Published in the U.S.A. in 1993
and distributed in the U.S.A. by:
Cy DeCosse Incorporated
5900 Green Oak Drive
Minnetonka, MN 55343

CY DECOSSE INCORPORATED
Chairman: Cy DeCosse
President: James B. Maus
Executive Vice President: William B. Jones

Created by: The Editors of Cy DeCosse
  Incorporated, in cooperation with the
  Sewing Education Department, Singer
  Sewing Company. Singer is a trademark of
  the Singer Company and is used under
  license.
Printed on American paper by:
  Quebecor Graphics (0195)

How to Use This Book

Sewing is more than making a garment or project. It is creating something unique for yourself or as a gift. *Creative Gifts & Projects Step-by-Step* gives you both the techniques and the inspiration to make many creative projects. This volume contains unlimited ideas for gift giving as well as for personalized garments and fashion accessories.

Just for Fun shows you how to decorate sunglasses, gloves, and shoes just for the fun of it. Unusual details such as buttons, frog closures, or buttons and zippers used in unexpected ways can make your sewing projects unique. This section also includes making silk flower appliqués and perforating paper for stationery.

Decorative Machine Stitching can personalize any project or garment. This section presents techniques for perfect stitching and also teaches couching, hemstitching, pintucks, using decorative thread in the bobbin, and French machine sewing.

In the Appliqués section of the book, you will learn how to sew several types of appliqués. The type you select will depend on the look you want to create and the fabrics you are using. There are also tips for perfecting the satin stitch and designing and embellishing your own appliqué.

In the Free-motion Sewing section, you will learn how to guide the fabric by hand, without the use of the presser foot and feed dogs. Use the basic free-motion techniques for thread painting, thread sketching, or making Battenberg lace, and go beyond the basics of machine stitching.

Create your own fabrics by hand-dyeing solids or by tie-dyeing, marbling, or using discharge dyeing techniques. Change the appearance, texture, or design of a fabric by twisting silk for a crinkled appearance or acid-washing it for the feel of suede. Or make felted wool from wool fabric for your projects.

The Creative Details section presents several techniques for sewing decorative seams, including edgestitching, fringing, fraying, and binding. Double or triple piping can outline and highlight seamlines and edges. Other details that make a garment truly unique include triangular pockets and buttonholes, bias-cut sleeves, and channel-stitched cuffs. Plus learn to copy design details.

In the Embellishments section, learn to make and add slentre braid, beadwork, and ribbonwork, and make suede lace.

The next section, Fiber Art, shows you how to work with fibers to make a variety of projects, such as rag baskets and braided rugs. Or try other fiber art techniques, such as hand appliqués for quilting, slashing, and a variety of piecing and patchwork techniques for your projects.

The Creative Projects section suggests projects and ideas that utilize your many new skills. Try your hand at some basic accessories that complete a special outfit, or make a hair ornament as a gift. Follow the complete instructions for simple zippered bags, handbags, portfolios, scarves, and a variety of belts. Other projects include ponytail wraps, headbands, beaded barrettes, chiffon hair bows, fabric-wrapped bracelets, and smocked Christmas ornaments.

Step-by-Step Guidance

From beginning to end, the step-by-step instructions in this book will make your sewing projects easy, understandable, and fun. Whether you are an experienced sewer or a beginner, you will find this book to be a help and an inspiration. Use it as your guide for making many creative gifts and unique sewing projects.

Fun Button Ideas

Sewers usually have a supply of buttons, because they save extra buttons from a project and salvage others from discarded garments. There are many creative ways of using these buttons.

To make button bracelets, choose elastic in the desired width and color. For a close fit, cut it the circumference of the arm plus allowance for overlap. Form the elastic into a loop, and stitch the ends together. Stitch buttons close together so they overlap, covering the elastic.

Cloth shoes and hair ornaments can be accented with buttons to coordinate with your outfit.

Earrings can be designed with a combination of buttons in various shapes and textures, using a color scheme to complement your clothing. Findings for making earrings are available at craft or jewelry supply stores.

Sunglasses

Create your own designer frames by embellishing inexpensive sunglasses. Sunglasses can become a fun, flashy accessory or a finishing touch for a special ensemble. Use items such as buttons, beads, rhinestones, decorative threads, and strips of leather. A few items are usually all that is necessary.

When applying embellishments with glue, make sure the base of the item rests flat on the surface of the frame, to ensure good adhesion. Use a jewelry glue intended for plastics and metals, working carefully to avoid excess glue on the frames. You may want to work with a tweezers and apply the glue using a toothpick.

Buttons add a simple embellishment to sunglasses. Remove the shanks from the buttons, using a wire cutter, and apply the buttons with glue.

Beads, gems, and painted designs are easy-to-add accents for sunglasses.

13

Gloves

Gloves can be fashionable accessories, not simply functional apparel. Whether you choose vivid, colorful gloves or opt for the ever-popular basic colors, a few embellishments can add style.

Decorative braid trims can be machine-stitched in place along the upper edge of the gloves. When attaching trims to knit gloves, make sure that the embellished gloves retain enough stretch to be

pulled on and off easily. For leather gloves, machine-stitch the trim in place, using a leather needle, or secure it with a glue intended for leather.

Buttons add a whimsical look to a glove. Choose buttons that will lie flat. Stitch them in place, one at a time, without carrying threads between them, to prevent catching the threads when putting on the gloves. This also ensures the necessary give between buttons.

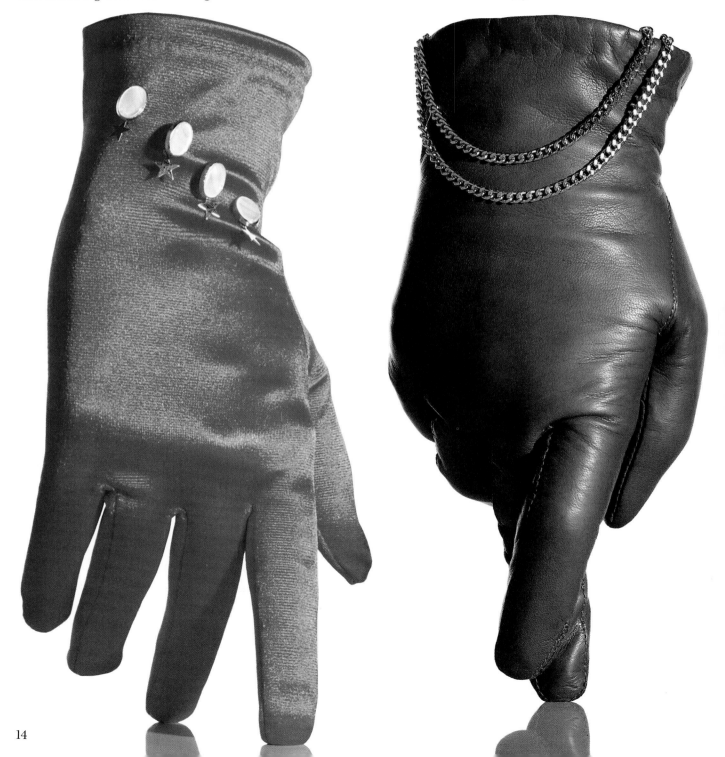

Shown left to right:

Small, charm-style buttons are stitched to stretch-knit gloves in a diagonal row.

Gold chains drape softly at the wrist like bracelets. The chains are simply hand-tacked in place to the inside of the glove at the upper edge.

Three large buttons are an elegant embellishment for a simple pair of stretch-knit gloves. Select buttons that will lie flat against the gloves.

Braid and gimp trims, machine-stitched in place at the upper edge, complement a pair of classic leather gloves. The small tassel, hand-stitched at the side of the glove, adds a final touch.

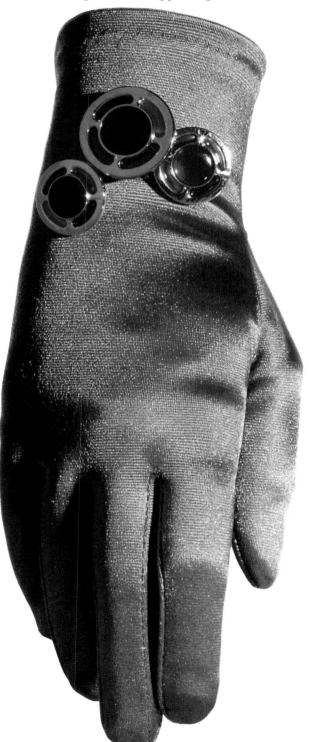

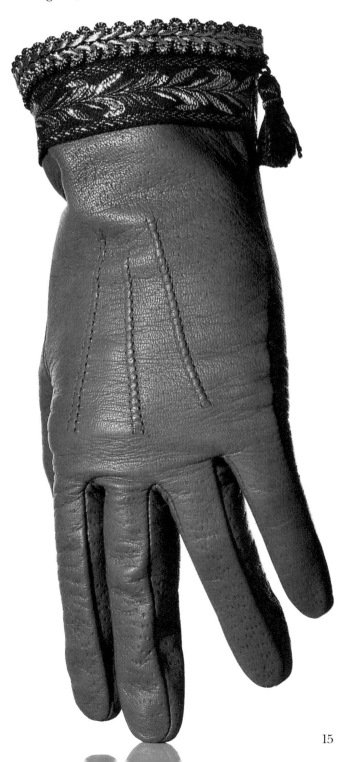

Beaded appliqués or decorative buttons can become shoe clips by simply stitching covered coat hooks to the underside of the appliqués or buttons.

Shoes

Use your creativity to embellish shoes so they coordinate with special outfits. Elegant appliqués can adorn the toe areas, or rhinestones can add unexpected glitz at the heels. Many decorations are easy to add, but you may prefer to have some embellishments stitched or stapled in place by a shoe repair service.

For special occasions, use shoe clips as temporary shoe decorations. They can be made using the hook portion of large covered hooks and eyes, called coat hooks. When attaching the shoe clips to the shoes, squeeze the hooks as necessary to hold the clips in place. To temporarily secure lightweight items, such as sequined appliqués, use double-stick tape.

When using glue to attach embellishments, select a glue that will dry clear and flexible, such as Tacky® glue. Avoid gluing embellishments to an area where they are apt to be rubbed off, or to areas where the shoes will flex when worn.

Paints can add a decorative flourish of color to shoes. When painting shoes, it is important that the paint remain flexible on the shoe. For this reason, textile paints are recommended for fabric shoes; heat-set the paint with a hair dryer. Acrylic paints are recommended for leather shoes. You may want to test a small amount of the paint in an inconspicuous area, because paint may not adhere to some highly waxed leathers.

Sequined appliqués can be held in place with double-stick tape to provide a temporary shoe decoration for a special occasion.

Textile paints are applied to canvas shoes in a color-blocked design. Using tape, mask off any areas of the shoe that will not be painted.

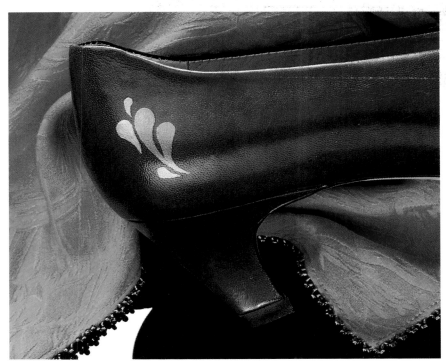

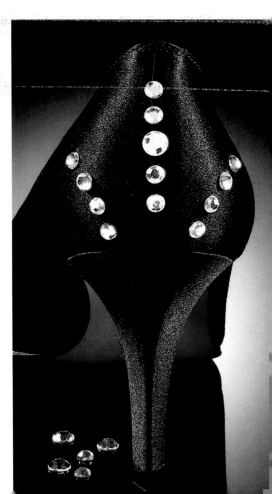

Painted accents add a splash of color at the outside heel area. For leather shoes, acrylic paints are recommended.

Rhinestones, glued in place, dress up a pair of basic pumps, as shown at right.

Buttons & Bows

Buttons and bows add interest to an otherwise plain garment. They can be functional or decorative.

Buttons can be stitched to the edge of a sleeve for an attractive cuff, below, or they can cover a design area such as the bow shape, left. Interface the design area to strengthen it for supporting the buttons. They can be sewn on quickly by machine before assembling a garment, or applied by hand to a ready-made garment. Use four strands of thread to secure buttons with just two stitches.

For centuries, bows have been used to decorate apparel. An easy method to tie a bow is shown, opposite. To keep the fabric or ribbon fresh, handle it as little as possible.

Buttons add a decorative touch, giving a basic garment a one-of-a-kind look.

How to Tie Quick Bows

1) Form two equal loops, about 1" (2.5 cm) apart.

2) Cross one loop in front of other.

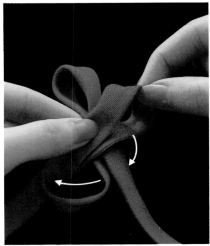

3) Wrap loop around back, and through center opening (arrow). Pull loops to adjust.

Chrysanthemums can be used to coordinate fabric shoes with a purse. For shoe ornaments, attach a large hook from a hook and eye set to the back of the chrysanthemum, and slide hook over edge of shoe. For purse ornaments, stitch the chrysanthemum directly to the purse flap.

Chrysanthemum Buttons

Chrysanthemum buttons are maneuvered through buttonholes by holding loops snugly together, then fluffing petals for a full, blooming appearance.

Fabric flowers add a finishing touch to an outfit when used as buttons or ornaments. Machine-made or bound buttonholes can be used with chrysanthemum buttons. Make test buttonholes in various sizes to find the size that works and looks best.

Use ¼" (6 mm) self-filled bias tubing to make these bowlike ornaments. To make the tubing, cut a bias strip of lightweight fabric 1 yard (.95 m) long and 1" (2.5 cm) wide for each chrysanthemum button. Fold the strip in half lengthwise, right sides together, and stitch a ¼" (6 mm) seam. Turn the tubing right side out, using a loop turner.

How to Make a Chrysanthemum Button

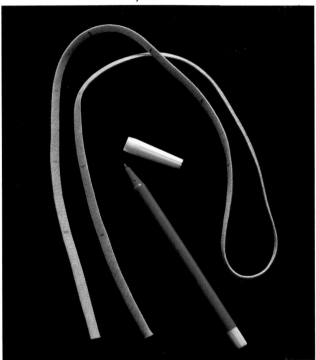

1) Mark 1 yd. (.95 m) of bias tubing every 2" (5 cm), beginning and ending 3" (7.5 cm) from each end of the tubing.

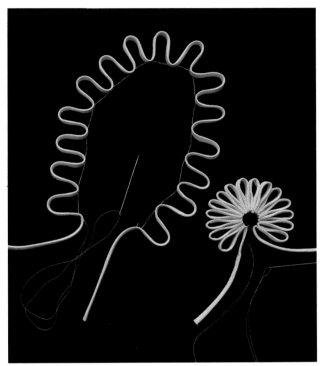

2) Stitch through each mark on tubing, using two strands of thread. Draw up tightly; arrange loops.

3) Gather all loops together, and secure with rubber band. Stitch loops in desired position, using two strands of thread.

4) Cut one end of tubing to within ⅜" (1 cm) of loops. Turn raw edge to inside; whipstitch to back of button. Cut other end to within 1" (2.5 cm) of loops. Turn raw edge to inside and whipstitch closed; make a shank by folding in half. Stitch securely to back of button.

Buttons & Buttonholes

The choice of buttons is a major consideration on any garment or project. A customized look can be achieved by creating Chinese ball buttons (pages 24 and 25) or chrysanthemum buttons (pages 20 and 21). Covered buttons, opposite, can be made in a variety of sizes and shapes.

To determine placement of buttons and buttonholes on a blouse or bodice front, mark the placement for one buttonhole at the fullest part of the bustline. Space others evenly from that position. Check the guidelines below to determine whether buttonholes should be vertical or horizontal.

Tips for Vertical or Horizontal Buttonhole Placement

Vertical buttonholes work well with lightweight fabrics and small buttons. They are commonly used for shirt plackets, shirt or blouse front bands, or pocket flaps.

Horizontal buttonholes are used for stability in areas of stress, such as on cuffs, neck bands or waistbands. Buttonholes on jackets and coats are usually horizontal.

Tips for Making Covered Buttons

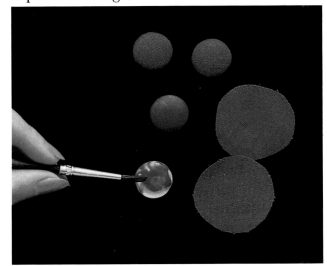

Paint metal button to match fabric color to prevent show-through of metal when using sheer or loosely woven fabric. Or use two layers of sheer fabric.

Wet washable fabric, and stretch it over metal button for a smooth fit when covering a button.

Chinese Ball Buttons

Chinese ball buttons can be used with buttonholes, button loops, or frog closures (pages 26 and 27).

Cord-filled bias tubing is used to make the buttons, because it has body and shapes well. Chinese ball buttons can be made from one or more strands of bias tubing. Select lightweight fabrics for smooth knots.

Two strands of ⅛" (3 mm) cord-filled bias tubing make a ¾" (2 cm) ball button; one strand makes a ½" (1.3 cm) button. To make the tubing, you will need two 24" (61 cm) lengths of ³⁄₃₂" cording and two 1" × 12" (2.5 × 30.5 cm) bias strips of lightweight fabric.

How to Make Cord-filled Bias Tubing

Fold bias strip around cord, right sides together and raw edges even. Using zipper foot, stitch loosely along cord. Stitch across strip and cord at middle of the length of cord; trim seam allowances. Slide strip over exposed cord, turning right side out. Cut off stitched end of fabric and excess cord.

How to Make Chinese Ball Buttons

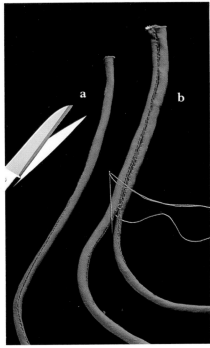

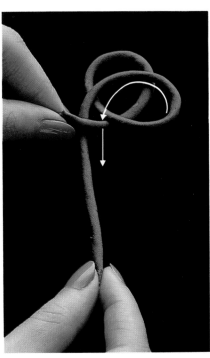

1) Make cord-filled bias tubing, opposite. Use one 12" (30.5 cm) piece **(a)** for each single-strand button. Or use two 12" (30.5 cm) pieces **(b)** for each double-strand button; slipstitch loosely together.

2) Loop the long end of the tubing as shown. (It may be helpful to pin end of tubing to a padded surface.)

3) Loop tubing a second time, over first loop and under tail.

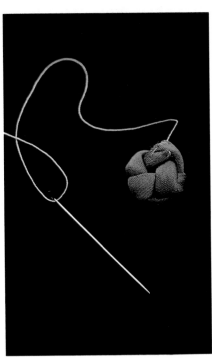

4) Weave the loose end of the tubing over and under previous loops.

5) Pull on both ends of the tubing, gently easing knot into a ball.

6) Cut ends of tubing so they overlap under the button; whipstitch. Make thread shank, covering it with closely spaced blanket stitch.

Frog Closures

Frog closures are often used with Chinese ball buttons for a traditional Oriental appearance. Although there are some ready-made frogs available, the selection is limited, so you may want to make your own.

Frog closures can be made from purchased braid or cord-filled bias tubing to match or contrast with the garment. The cording or braid can be knotted or arranged in many ways for a variety of styles. The

choice of fabric, the diameter of the cording, and the size of the loops add further variety.

To make your own cord-filled bias tubing (page 24), cut a bias strip for each frog about 60" (152.5 cm) long; for a frog with a Chinese ball button, cut a bias strip about 72" (183 cm) long. The length of bias tubing required depends on the diameter of the tubing.

How to Make Frog Closures

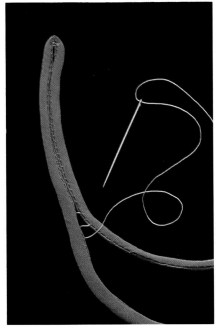

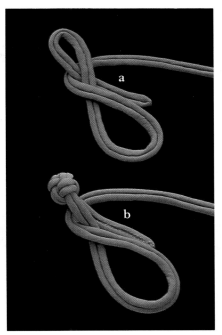

1) Cut bias strips, left. Make cord-filled bias tubing (page 24). Fold tubing in half, and slipstitch strands together from the back. Work with tubing face up when making frogs.

2) Form one end of tubing into a small top loop and a large button loop. Bring other end around small loop to back (**a**). For a frog with a Chinese ball button (**b**), make button (pages 24 and 25), starting 4" (10 cm) from one end of tubing; position button at top of small loop.

3) Bring long end around to front, and form another loop to fit inside large bottom loop, following the direction of the original loop.

4) Carry long end up and around small top loop, below previous loop; bring end around to front, and form a loop to fit inside other large bottom loops.

5) Carry long end up and around the small top loop, below previous loops; bring end down to center of large bottom loops, and insert in center. Pull through to secure.

6) Adjust small loop to size of ball button. Trim loose ends of tubing; slipstitch ends and loops in place on wrong side.

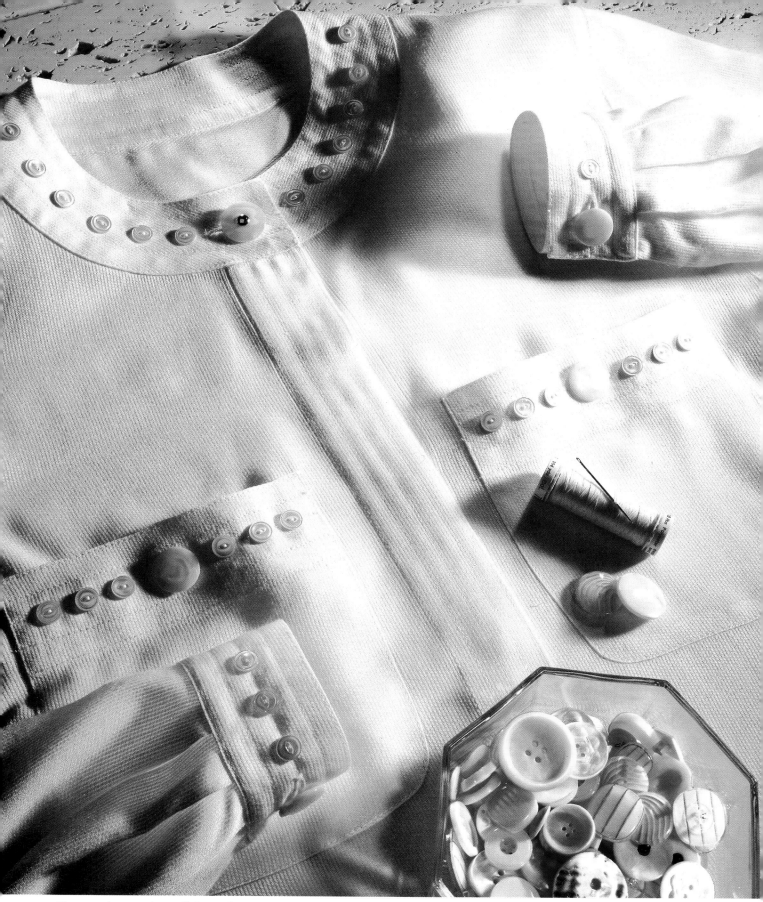

Buttons in a variety of sizes, shapes, or colors can be used as a decorative detail.

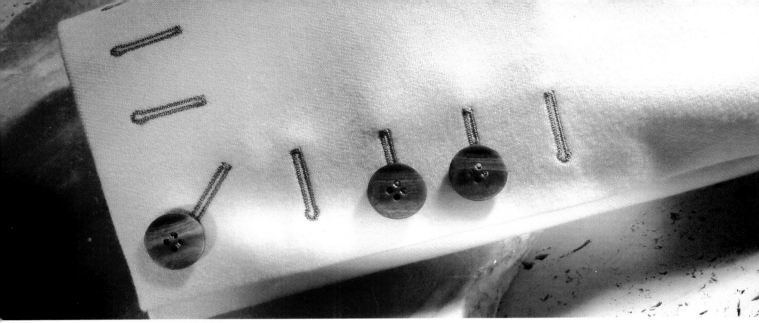

Buttonholes do not have to be functional. They can be stitched along a placket or any garment edge as a design detail.

Unexpected Creative Details

Doing the unexpected can offer many possibilities for creativity. Although most notions have been invented to serve a specific purpose, they can also be used in unconventional ways. For example, tassel fringe or gimp cord, designed as home decorating trims, can be used to accent the design details of a garment. Zipper tapes can be inserted into seams so the zipper teeth create an interesting piping, or the zipper tapes can be topstitched to a garment as a decorative, colorful trim. Buttons and buttonholes can be purely decorative rather than being used as closures.

Tassel fringe can be used to accent the lapel or neckline of a garment.

Zipper teeth can become a decorative piping to accent the edges or details of a garment; insert the zipper tape into the seam as for beaded piping (page 233).

Perforating Paper

The decorative stitches on the sewing machine can be used to create unusual greeting cards or stationery. Use firm paper, a large needle, and a long stitch length.

Practice stitching designs on typing paper with and without thread in the machine. Some designs may be lost without the use of thread to connect the holes; others may be too complex and simply destroy the paper. When using thread, use any machine embroidery thread, or experiment with different kinds of threads, such as metallics. When thread is not used, it is possible to stack and perforate paper in layers.

Test designs, using different needles. A wing needle makes a slit in the paper; twin needles duplicate designs side by side.

Ways to Use Perforated Paper

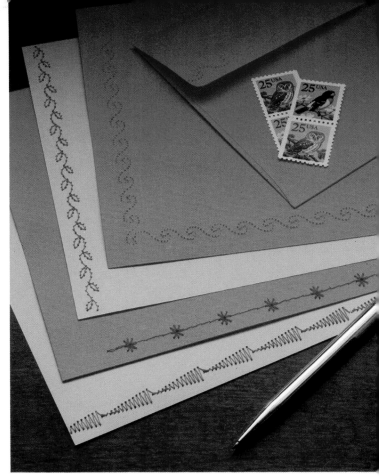

Business cards can be decorated with a stitched border to add a creative touch.

Stationery sheets and the flaps of envelopes can be perforated or stitched with thread.

Place cards can be embellished by stitching over decorative ribbon for a festive touch.

Ruching

Ruches may be either applied to the fabric surface or inset; they will add surface relief and bulk. Entire sections of a garment can also be ruched. Choose fabrics that enhance the technique itself. They should reflect light, because the play of light on the folded or gathered surfaces is part of the effect. Fabrics like taffeta, satin, metallics, or iridescents are dramatic. Transparent fabrics like organza, chiffons, or voiles used in certain areas of a gown can create an interesting detail. Your imagination is the only limit to applying this technique to your projects.

Applied Ruches

For applied ruches, strips of ruched fabric or ribbon are attached to the surface of a garment. Most often with this technique, the ruched strip is applied by stitching down the middle. This allows the sides to lift up, giving an opportunity to finish the edges in a variety of ways.

Edge finishes may include decorative stitching by machine or by hand; "feathering," raveling the edges for a fringe; or a rolled hem stitched with a serger.

Applied ruched strips (left) can add fullness to a hemline, emphasize a sleeve, or even cover an entire evening gown for a stunning effect. Snail-shirred ruches (top three) add a soft, scalloped effect to a garment. Box-pleated ruches (bottom two) can be embellished by joining pleats together with beading or embroidery.

Ruched garment section (page 35) adds texture and surface interest to a princess-style knit dress.

Tips for Sewing Ruches

Sew a test sample to determine the amount of fullness suitable for your fabric. Experiment to achieve the look you want.

Cut ruches on the bias if raveling or shaping around curves is a problem. Cutting on the bias also lessens the need for pressing.

Add a flat piece of fabric as a stabilizer to the wrong side of a ruched strip if the shape of the garment might shift.

Gathered inset ruche (page 36) accents the design line of a jacket.

Box-pleated applied ruche (page 34) adds flair to the sleeve edge on an evening dress. Snail-shirred applied ruches are a softer alternative.

Triangle-tipped inset ruche (page 37) adds a sophisticated note to evening pants.

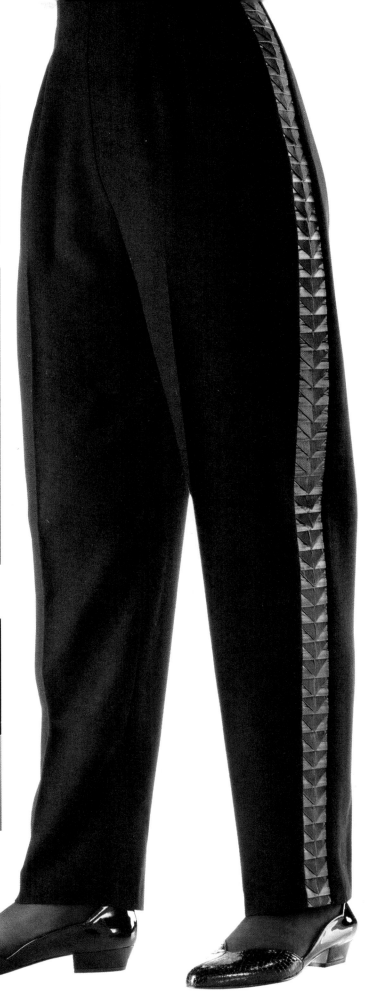

How to Make a Snail-shirred Applied Ruche

1) **Cut** fabric strip on lengthwise grain to desired width and two to three times finished length. Finish edges as desired. Fold strip on true bias lines; press folds.

2) **Stitch** a continuous gathering line, following bias folds. Draw threads to gather. Apply to the garment, sewing by hand or by machine along gathering stitches.

How to Make a Box-pleated Applied Ruche

1) **Cut** fabric strip on straight grain to the desired width and three times the finished length. Cut cardboard template the desired depth of each pleat and two times as wide as strip. Mark center line of template.

2) **Finish** edges of fabric strip as desired. Fold strip over template, forming pleat; finger-press. Remove template and stitch along center of strip to secure pleat. Repeat to end of fabric strip.

3) **Pinch** opposite sides of each box pleat together. Tack at center of upper edge by hand or by machine. Stitch a bead at the center of each pleat when tacking, if desired.

Ruched Garment Sections

A commercial pattern may be adapted to create a garment with a ruched section, such as the dress pictured on page 32. Use this method for ruching an entire garment section, or just a portion of it. Depending on the pattern and the fabric, it may be necessary to stabilize the ruched area with a backing fabric, so the garment retains its shape when worn. A soft, lightweight fabric, such as chiffon or tricot, may be used for the stabilizer. For more body in the ruched area, use a firmer, crisp stabilizer, such as taffeta or organdy.

How to Ruche a Garment Section

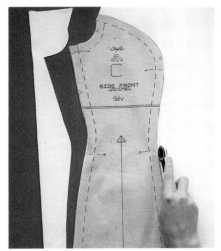

1) Cut fabric for stabilizer, if desired, from the section of pattern piece to be ruched.

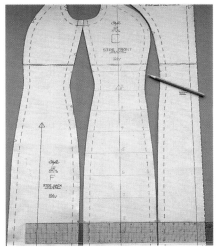

2) Mark where ruche begins and ends on the pattern piece to be ruched, and on adjacent pieces. Extend grainline to length of pattern piece. Draw parallel lines 2" to 3" (5 to 7.5 cm) apart in area to be ruched. Number sections.

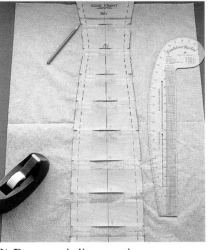

3) Draw grainline on tissue paper; lay pattern on top. Cut pattern on marked lines. Expand ruched section one and one-half to three times in length, distributing extra length evenly. Draw cutting lines and seamlines. Mark ends of ruched area.

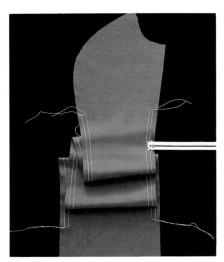

4) Cut out garment; transfer the pattern markings. Stitch two rows of gathering stitches ¼" (6 mm) apart on edges to be ruched, with first row just inside seamline.

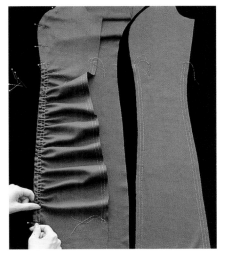

5) Match ruched section to garment section, pulling up gathers evenly and aligning markings; pin. Baste stabilizer, if used, to wrong side of ruched section. Stitch seams with ruched section up.

6) Trim seam allowances of ruched section. Finish seam allowances separately. Press seam allowances toward flat section.

Inset Ruches

Ruches may be inserted into a seamline to accent a design line on the pattern. Or, add your own design line to a garment by cutting a garment section apart and inserting a ruche.

Inset ruches may either be gathered or pleated. Gathered inset ruches may be gathered equally on both sides and inserted in a straight seamline, or unequally, to follow a curved seamline. Pleated inset ruches, such as triangle-tipped ruches, are inserted only in straight seams. Stabilize inset ruches with a lightweight backing fabric applied to the wrong side of the ruche, if necessary.

How to Adjust a Pattern for an Inset Ruche

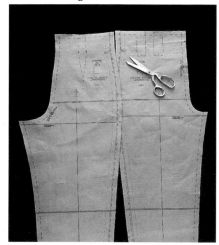
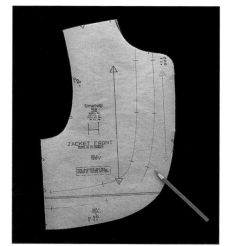
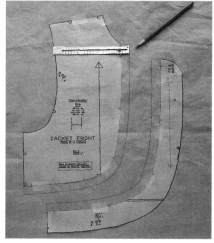

Add ruche centered on seamline.
Draw new cutting lines (red) one-half the finished width of ruche from edge on both pattern pieces. Draw the new seamlines (blue); transfer the pattern markings.

Add ruche to garment section.
1) Mark desired finished width of ruche on pattern. Add markings for alignment. Draw a grainline on outer piece.

2) Cut pattern apart on marked design lines; add 5⁄8" (1.5 cm) seam allowances.

How to Sew a Gathered Inset Ruche

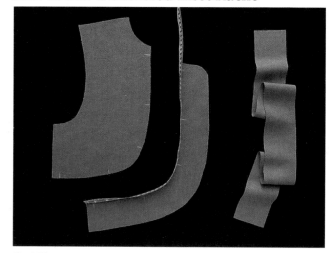
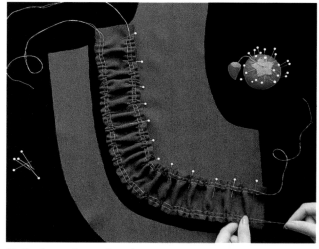

1) Adjust pattern, above. Cut out garment. Measure seamline where ruche will be inserted; on curved seamlines, measure longest edge. Cut fabric strip for ruche one and one-half to three times the length of seamline by the desired finished width plus 1¼" (3.2 cm) for seam allowances.

2) Gather edges of ruche, and pin, right sides together, to fit garment edges. On curved ruches, gathers will be tighter on inside curve. Stitch to garment, gathered side up. Grade seam allowance of ruched strip before finishing edges. Press the seam allowances toward the unruched sections.

How to Sew a Triangle-tipped Inset Ruche

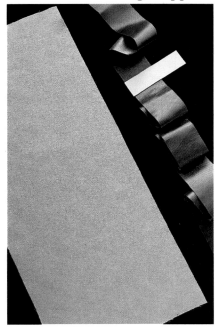

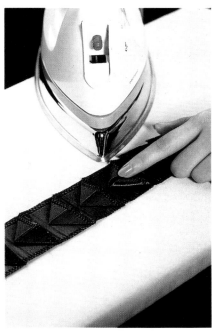

1) Adjust pattern, opposite. Cut out garment. Cut fabric strip for ruche five to six times the finished length by desired width plus ½" (1.3 cm) for seam allowances. Cut cardboard template one-half the width of strip plus ⅛" (3 mm) by two times the width of strip.

2) Finish edges of fabric strip by serging or zigzag stitching. Fold fabric strip over the cardboard template and press into pleats; space pleats ¼" (6 mm) apart.

3) Fold each pleat again so corners meet in center; press. Continue to fold and press, forming a series of triangles.

4) Fold fabric between triangles to form narrow pleat, so each triangle slightly overlaps the preceding one, covering raw edges. Press edges sharply. Tack invisibly along center back, catching underlayer only.

5) Finish seam allowances of garment. Pin ruche to garment, right sides together; match seamlines and align markings across ruche. [Ruche has ¼" (6 mm) seam allowances.] Stitch, ruche side up. Press seam allowances toward unruched sections.

Braided Ribbon Belt

A single ribbon can be a subtle statement of color on a garment; several ribbons, braided, can add yet another dimension.

Braided ribbons can be used as a belt. The width of the belt varies, depending on the width of the ribbon. A belt made from ⅝" (1.5 cm) ribbon will be about 1½" (3.8 cm) wide.

To make a braided ribbon belt, measure the waistline over the garment and add 1½" (3.8 cm) for finishing ends; ribbons will be braided to this length. Cut four lengths of double-faced ribbon, each length one-third longer than the desired length of braid. For example, if the braid will be 27" (68.5 cm), cut 36" (91.5 cm) of each ribbon.

Grosgrain ribbon is used for finishing the ends of the belt, because it is a durable ribbon. You will need a length of grosgrain ribbon ten times the width of the double-faced ribbon.

How to Make a Braided Ribbon Belt

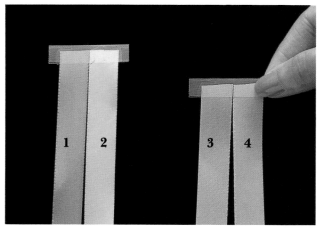

1) **Join** ribbons in two sets of two ribbons. Ribbons are now referred to as ribbon 1, ribbon 2, ribbon 3, and ribbon 4.

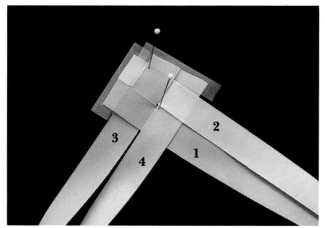

2) **Pin** ends of ribbons to a long, padded surface. Weave ribbon 2 under ribbon 3 and over ribbon 4. Weave ribbon 3 over ribbon 2 and under ribbon 1; weave ribbon 4 under ribbon 2 and over ribbon 1.

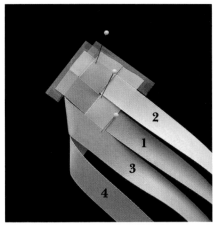

3) Fold ribbon 3 and ribbon 4 up and over to align them with ribbons 1 and 2.

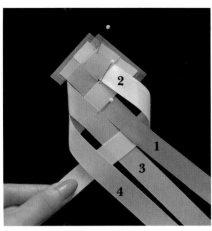

4) Fold ribbon 2 to the back; weave under ribbon 1, over ribbon 3, and under ribbon 4.

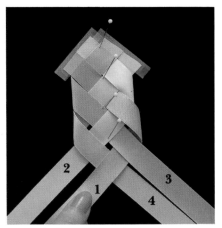

5) Fold ribbon 1 to the back, and weave under ribbon 3 and over ribbon 4.

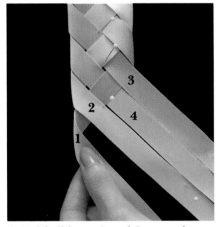

6) Fold ribbons 1 and 2 up and over to align them with ribbons 3 and 4.

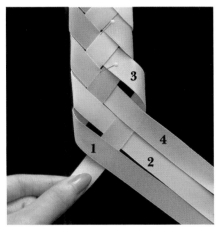

7) Fold ribbon 3 to the back; weave under ribbon 4, over ribbon 2, and under ribbon 1.

8) Fold ribbon 4 to the back; weave under ribbon 2 and over ribbon 1. Repeat steps 3 through 8 until braid is desired length.

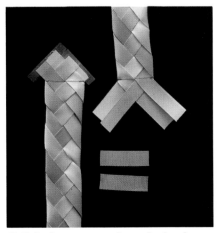

9) Stitch across ends at desired finished length of belt. Cut two strips of ⅝" (1.5 cm) grosgrain ribbon, each ½" (1.3 cm) longer than width of braid.

10) Turn under ends of grosgrain strips ¼" (6 mm). Place one long edge of strips on stitching lines, one on right side, one on wrong side. Stitch along edge of ribbon.

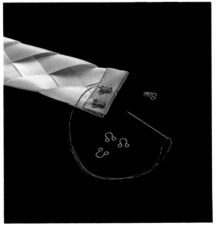

11) Trim braid seam allowance to ¼" (6 mm). Fold back strips, enclosing ends of braid; handstitch into place. Apply fasteners.

Silk Flower Appliqués

Silk flowers can be used to make attractive appliqués. They can embellish garments, including evening gowns and casual wear, or they can be used to make a shadow box picture.

If you intend to wash the project, test the flowers for colorfastness by dipping them in soapy water and rinsing them. This is especially important for red or dark colors.

To appliqué silk flowers on a garment, take the flowers apart and remove any wires or florist tape. Then shape the petals into new flowers, and stitch them to the garment (pages 41 to 43). Petals from two flowers can be combined into one to vary the look.

When using silk flowers in a shadow box, it is not necessary to remove all the wires from the petals and stems; they may be helpful in shaping the flowers. The flowers may be glued, instead of stitched, into the shadow box.

Plan the placement of the flowers on your project before you begin, marking the placement line for the stem and the general spacing of the main flowers.

Use lightweight monofilament nylon thread to apply silk flowers; it is invisible and does not detract from the flowers. All-purpose thread may be used to stitch the stems. (Contrasting thread is used to show detail in the photos that follow.)

Tips for Appliquéing Silk Flowers

Layer two or more single-layer flowers. Stitch to project through center of flower. Hand-stitch pearl, seed pearls, or button to flower.

Pinch two or more layers of petals at center, and gather by hand to create a full blossom; stitch through layers at base of flower. Stitch in place on project.

Place tear-away stabilizer under fabric in stem area. Zigzag over yarn to make stem; remove stabilizer. Attach leaves to project by stitching along center vein.

How to Shape Petals to Form a Flower

1) **Strip** petals from stem; remove wires and stamens.

2) **Roll** petal into bud shape and stitch through layers; use as a bud or as center petal of a flower. To start shaping flower, wrap another petal around center petal, ¼" (6 mm) higher than center petal.

3) **Continue** wrapping desired number of petals around center petal.

4) **Stitch** back and forth through base of flower, by machine or by hand, to secure petals.

5) Fold petals back to achieve desired shape. Tack one petal to another, as necessary, to shape flower; work from center of flower outward.

6) Trim off base of flower next to stitching. Stitch trimmed base to garment at desired location, stitching over previous stitches.

7) Fold back one or two outer petals at the top of flower, and stitch them to garment to prevent flower from drooping.

8) Fold back one or two outer petals at the bottom of flower, and stitch them to garment, covering trimmed base of flower.

Decorative Machine Stitching

Guide to Decorative Stitching

There are many types of decorative stitching, offering a wide variety of decorative effects. Use this guide to quickly identify each type of stitching and to determine the correct stitches and accessories to use. Specialty presser feet (page 49) and unique sewing machine needles (page 50) are used for some of the stitching techniques.

Thread sketching and thread painting (pages 122 and 123) both use free-motion stitching techniques (pages 116 to 121) to resemble hand embroidery stitches.

Stitch type: Straight and zigzag
Presser foot: None
Needle: Regular

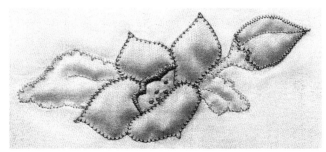

Appliqués, shadow (pages 104 to 109), are designs made up of small pieces of fabrics placed under a sheer overlay and outlined with decorative stitching.

Stitch type: Straight, zigzag, blindstitch, or blanket
Presser foot: Special-purpose or open-toe
Needle: Regular

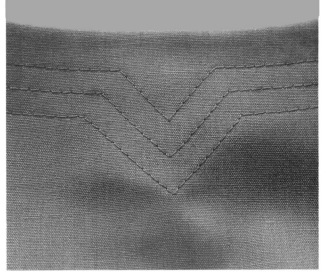

Topstitching (page 59) is used to emphasize the edge of a garment or other design lines, such as seamlines, or to add new design lines.

Stitch type: Straight
Presser foot: Straight-stitch, blindstitch, or topstitching
Needle: Regular

Appliqués (pages 84 to 113) are designs made up of small pieces of fabrics outlined with satin stitching.

Stitch type: Straight and zigzag
Presser foot: Special-purpose or open-toe
Needle: Regular

Battenberg lace (pages 127 to 137) is made by shaping Battenberg tape and embellishing the open areas with free-motion stitching.

Stitch type: Straight and zigzag
Presser foot: None
Needle: Regular

Hemstitching (pages 65 to 69) creates the look of entredeux when sewing hems and attaching lace.

Stitch type: Zigzag, blanket, or other
Presser foot: Special-purpose or open-toe
Needle: Single-wing or double-wing

French machine sewing (pages 72 to 81) consists of strips of fabrics and trims joined together. The fabric strips are embellished using several decorative techniques.

Stitch type: Depends on method
Presser foot: Depends on method
Needle: Depends on method

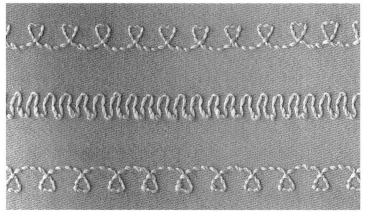

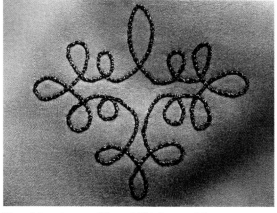

Bobbin thread, decorative (pages 62 and 63), creates a special effect by using specialty thread in the bobbin and stitching with fabric placed right side down.

Stitch type: Straight, zigzag, or other
Presser foot: Special-purpose or open-toe
Needle: Regular

Couching (pages 60 and 61) is attaching narrow trims or heavy threads by stitching over them with decorative stitches.

Stitch type: Zigzag, blanket, blindstitch, or other
Presser foot: Cording or special-purpose
Needle: Regular

Pintucks, decorative (pages 70 and 71), are formed by stitching near a fold, using a decorative stitch.

Stitch type: Narrow decorative
Presser foot: Special-purpose or open-toe
Needle: Regular

Pintucks, traditional (pages 70 and 71), are formed by stitching near a fold, using straight stitching.

Stitch type: Straight
Presser foot: Straight-stitch
Needle: Regular

Pintucks, twisted (pages 70 and 71), are formed by stitching across traditional pintucks to twist them.

Stitch type: Straight
Presser foot: Straight-stitch
Needle: Regular

Specialty Threads

Specialty threads can enhance decorative stitching. Several types of thread, ranging from fine machine embroidery threads to heavier pearl cottons and topstitching threads, can be used successfully in the needle and bobbin of the machine.

Not all specialty threads work well in all sewing machines. You may need to do some testing to see which threads give the best results. It may be necessary to adjust the needle and bobbin tensions of the machine (pages 52 and 53) when using a specialty thread.

Topstitching thread (1) is a heavier thread, used to make the stitches more noticeable. As the name implies, it is frequently used for topstitching.

Metallic thread (2) is available in several weights. The finer metallic threads can be used for machine embroidery; the heavier weights can be used as the cord for couching.

Pearl thread (3) may be cotton or rayon, and it is available in several weights. Depending on the weight, one or more strands can be couched over, or used as the cord for corded satin stitching.

Fine monofilament nylon thread (4) can be used in the bobbin of the machine, so the bobbin thread will not show on the right side. It can also be used for couching over decorative trims, so it does not detract from the trim.

Ribbon thread (5), a flat, lightweight ribbon, can be used in the bobbin of the machine; for decorative stitching, the fabric is placed right side down on the machine. Ribbon thread can also be used as the cord for couching.

Machine embroidery thread (6) is used for smooth, even satin stitching and machine embroidery. Cotton machine embroidery thread, available in weights ranging from 30-weight to 60-weight, gives a matte finish with only a subtle sheen; rayon thread, in 30-weight or 40-weight, has a shiny appearance. Select a fine, lightweight thread for sewing on lightweight fabric and to prevent thread buildup. A heavier thread may be used to achieve good coverage with fewer stitches.

Cotton basting thread (7), a lightweight, inexpensive thread, may be used in the bobbin, when machine embroidery thread is used in the needle. (Photo shows cotton basting thread on wrong side of fabric.)

Presser Feet

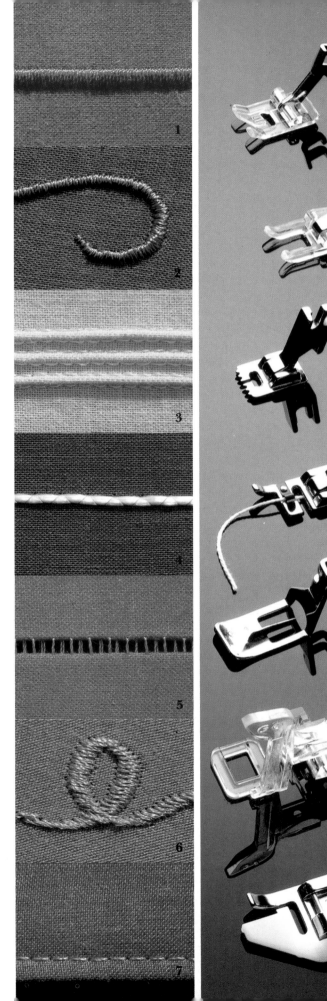

Several presser feet are available, each designed for a specific purpose. Some of these presser feet come with the sewing machine; others may need to be purchased separately.

Special-purpose foot (1), or embroidery foot, is used for satin stitching and machine embroidery. The foot has a wide groove on the bottom, which allows the fabric to feed through the machine smoothly, even with the buildup of heavy decorative stitching. The bar between the toes of the presser foot keeps the fabric smooth as it is fed under the needle.

Open-toe foot (2) is used for sewing intricate design details with corners or curves. The space between the toes of the presser foot allows you to see stitching lines more clearly. The open-toe foot has a groove on the bottom, so it can be used for satin stitching and machine embroidery.

Pintuck foot (3) is used for twin-needle pintucks. There are several grooves on the bottom of the pintuck foot, which keep multiple rows of pintucks an equal distance apart.

Cording foot (4) is used for applying a cord to fabric. The cord is threaded through a hole in the cording foot and feeds automatically during stitching.

Tacking foot (5) is used to make the looped stitches that create fagoting.

Darning foot (6) is used for free-motion machine embroidery, including monogramming and thread painting. Although free-motion embroidery can be done without a presser foot, the darning foot makes it easier to follow the curves of the design.

Blindstitch foot (7), sometimes called a topstitching foot, can be used as a guide for topstitching.

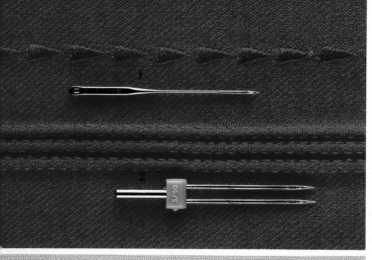

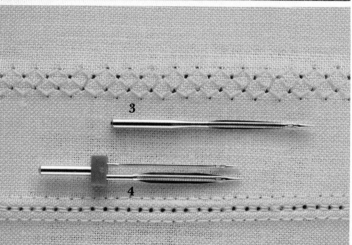

Specialty Needles

For decorative stitching, it is important to use a sharp, new needle. A slightly damaged or a dull needle can cause broken threads and skipped stitches.

A regular needle (1) in size 70/9 or 80/11 is used for sewing with fine fabric and thread. To prevent strip-back when using rayon machine embroidery thread, it may be necessary to use a needle one size larger. Strip-back is frayed thread that bunches up at the eye of the needle; it usually occurs when sewing fast.

A twin needle (2), or double needle, is used for sewing two parallel rows of topstitching. When combined with the pintuck foot (page 49), a twin needle is also used for pintucks and corded decorative sewing.

Single-wing (3) and double-wing (4) needles are used for hemstitching to produce the characteristic "holes" of hemstitched fabric. The double-wing needle features a wing needle and a regular needle on one shank.

Embroidery Hoops

For many types of decorative sewing, it is helpful to place the fabric in an embroidery hoop. The hoop holds the fabric taut so it does not pucker when it is stitched. A 5" to 7" (12.5 to 18 cm) hoop is a good size for most projects.

A wooden hoop with a fixing screw works best for free-motion embroidery because it can be tightened firmly. Select a hoop that is 1/4" (6 mm) thick so it will slide easily under the sewing machine needle. The hoop should be very smooth, with beveled edges, so it does not snag the fabric or scratch the bed of the sewing machine.

To prevent the fabric from slipping or loosening up while stitching, wrap the inner ring of the embroidery hoop with twill tape, or glue 1/4" (6 mm) velvet ribbon to the outside edge of the inner ring (page 118). The inner ring will then grip the fabric, so it can be held more tightly in the hoop.

A spring-loaded hoop works very well for most decorative machine sewing. It holds the fabric securely without distorting the grainline or damaging the fabric. Always use a spring-loaded hoop for securing lightweight fabrics that can be easily damaged.

Stabilizers

Stabilizers are used for decorative stitching, to prevent puckering, stitch distortion, thread breakage, and skipped stitches. Stabilizers are especially helpful for appliqué, cutwork, machine embroidery, and monogramming.

Tear-away stabilizer is a nonwoven product that is either basted or pinned to the fabric; when pressed with an iron, some will temporarily adhere to the wrong side of the fabric. Tear-away stabilizer can easily be removed after the stitching is completed, by tearing it next to the stitches.

Water-soluble stabilizer is a translucent plastic film that is either basted or pinned to washable fabric. It is easily removed with water after the stitching is completed.

Tear-away stabilizer. Tear stabilizer close to stitches, taking care not to distort stitches. Use tweezers to remove any small pieces remaining under stitches.

Water-soluble stabilizer. Trim stabilizer close to stitches. To remove any remaining stabilizer, soak fabric in cool water for about five minutes, or spray stabilizer with cool water.

Sewing Machine Tension

Poor stitch quality detracts from the appearance of decorative stitches. Stabilizer is frequently used while sewing decorative stitches to help improve the quality of the stitches; stabilizer prevents puckering, stitch distortion, and skipped stitches. In addition to using stabilizer, you may need to adjust the tension of the machine to achieve perfect stitches.

In some types of decorative stitching, such as satin stitching and machine embroidery, the bobbin thread tends to show on the upper side of the fabric unless the tension is adjusted. A tension adjustment may also be necessary for decorative bobbin thread sewing (pages 62 and 63), because heavier specialty threads are used in the bobbin.

To check the tension, test-sew, using the same fabric, thread, and stitch type you will be using for the project. If you intend to use stabilizer when sewing the project, place the stabilizer under the fabric before sewing the test stitches. Start with regular tension on the machine; if regular tension does not give a good stitch, follow the instructions, below, for adjusting the machine tension.

Sequence for Adjusting the Tension for Specialty Bobbin Thread

1) Test-sew with specialty thread in the bobbin, using regular tension on the machine; some specialty threads work well without any adjustment.

2) Loosen needle thread tension, if regular tension does not give a good stitch. This allows heavier bobbin threads to lie on the surface of the fabric; heavier threads cannot penetrate fabric, unless the fabric is loosely woven.

3) Bypass the tension, according to the manual for your sewing machine, if adjusting the needle thread tension does not give a good stitch; heavier bobbin threads may feed more easily through the machine if the tension is bypassed. Follow the instructions, opposite, for bypassing the tension on wind-in-place bobbins.

4) Adjust the bobbin case tension screw, only as a last resort, according to the manual for your sewing machine. Do not attempt to adjust the tension screw if the manual does not include instructions.

How to Adjust the Tension for Satin Stitching and Machine Embroidery

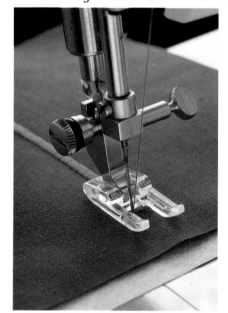

1) Thread machine with desired thread; set stitch width and stitch length. Place tear-away or water-soluble stabilizer under fabric scrap; stitch a row of satin stitching or machine embroidery.

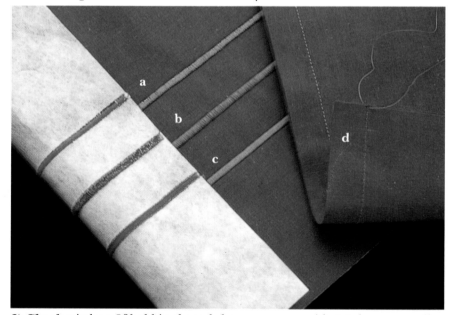

2) Check stitches. If bobbin thread shows on upper side **(a),** loosen needle thread tension. If needle thread is slack **(b),** tighten needle thread tension. Perfect tension on satin stitches and machine embroidery **(c)** does not cause puckering, and bobbin thread does not show on upper side; threads lock on underside of fabric. Perfectly balanced tension for regular sewing **(d)** does not cause puckering; threads draw equally into the fabric.

How to Bypass the Bobbin Thread Tension for Wind-in-place Bobbins

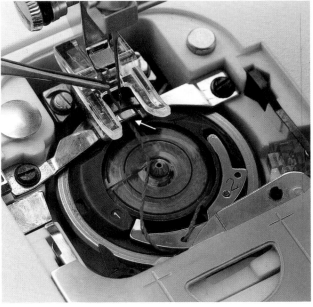

1) Wind bobbin by hand (page 63); insert bobbin. Remove needle plate. Bring bobbin thread through hole in bobbin case (arrow); for easier threading, apply liquid fray preventer to end of thread. Use tweezers to grasp end of thread.

2) Place bobbin thread under bobbin case retaining bridge (arrow). Replace needle plate, pulling bobbin thread through hole in plate. It may be necessary to loosen needle thread tension slightly to prevent thread from jamming.

Utility Stitch Patterns

The utility stitch patterns on a sewing machine were designed primarily to serve specific functions, such as blindstitching a hem or overcasting a seam; however, they can also be used as decorative stitching.

A twin needle can be used with utility stitches for a decorative look, following the guidelines in your manual for twin-needle stitching. You can also vary utility stitches by changing the stitch width or stitch length. Or change the look of the stitches by aligning or staggering the stitch patterns in two or more rows of stitching.

Straight stitch pattern can be stitched using a twin needle for two parallel rows of stitching in one step.

Zigzag stitch pattern or other utility stitch patterns can also be stitched using twin needle for an echo effect.

Fagoting stitch pattern can be varied by changing the stitch width and stitch length.

Multistitch-zigzag stitch pattern can be varied by changing the stitch length.

Blindstitch stitch pattern forms a new design when two rows of stitching are aligned opposite each other.

Overedge stitch pattern forms a new design when two rows of stitching are staggered.

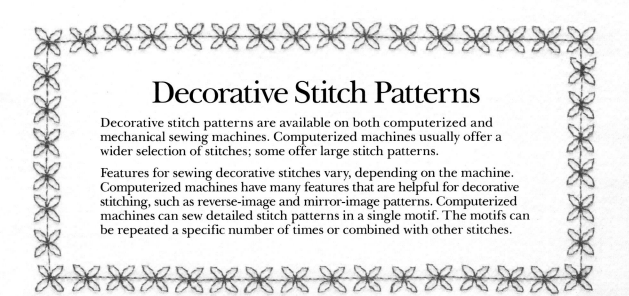

Decorative Stitch Patterns

Decorative stitch patterns are available on both computerized and mechanical sewing machines. Computerized machines usually offer a wider selection of stitches; some offer large stitch patterns.

Features for sewing decorative stitches vary, depending on the machine. Computerized machines have many features that are helpful for decorative stitching, such as reverse-image and mirror-image patterns. Computerized machines can sew detailed stitch patterns in a single motif. The motifs can be repeated a specific number of times or combined with other stitches.

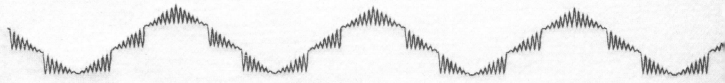

Continuous stitch patterns can be used as border designs.

Single-motif stitch patterns can be stitched one motif at a time.

Large stitch patterns of 25 mm width are available on some computerized machines.

Reverse-image stitch patterns are alternated so motifs face outward in opposite directions.

Mirror-image stitch patterns are alternated so motifs face each other.

Alphabet stitch pattern can be programmed to write words. Monograms, shown at right, are available on some computerized machines in various sizes and styles of lettering.

Using the Decorative Stitch Patterns

Accent a collar or cuffs with rows of decorative stitching. Mark placement lines and sew decorative stitches before assembling the collar or cuffs.

Decorative stitches can add just the right accent to a child's playsuit or an elegant blouse.

Deciding which of the many decorative stitches to use is the first step in planning a project. Whether you have a basic sewing machine with utility stitches or a top-of-the-line machine that also has automatic decorative stitches, there are several designs you can stitch (pages 54 and 55). On some machines, you can change the look of the stitches by varying the stitch length and stitch width.

Experiment with the stitches by sewing on fabric scraps, turning both left and right corners; some stitches may be attractive at both left and right corners, while others may look good only in one direction.

Also experiment with different types of thread. Changing from an all-purpose thread to a specialty thread, such as a shiny rayon, can change the effect of the stitching from sporty to dressy.

Sew the decorative stitches on the garment section before the seams are sewn, whenever possible, so the bulk of the seam allowances does not interfere with the stitching. It may be easier to sew the decorative stitches on the fabric before cutting out the garment piece.

Topstitch ribbed openings or hems of a T-shirt, using a utility stretch stitch instead of the straight stitch.

Make your own trim by sewing decorative stitches on a strip of contrasting fabric; then apply the trim with topstitching. You can also use rows of decorative stitching to add body to the brim of a hat.

Center a monogram on a turtleneck collar. Place tear-away stabilizer under the area to be monogrammed, to prevent the fabric from stretching.

Decorative Topstitching

Even the straight stitch can be decorative when it is used as topstitching. To make topstitching more noticeable, a heavier thread, such as topstitching thread or buttonhole twist, may be used in the needle; or use two strands of all-purpose thread. All-purpose thread is usually used in the bobbin.

Adjust the stitch length for topstitching according to the weight of the fabric. Short stitches are used on lightweight fabrics to prevent puckering, but longer stitches are more attractive on mediumweight to heavyweight fabrics. Check the stitch length and tension adjustments on a test sample, using the same thread, fabric, interfacing, and number of layers that you will use in the garment. Adjust the tension, if necessary, as on page 52.

To keep topstitching rows straight, it is helpful to use a guide, such as a blindstitch foot, quilting bar, or seam guide. A seam guide can also be made by placing layers of tape on the bed of the sewing machine. A thread tail can be used to guide fabric around corners without jamming.

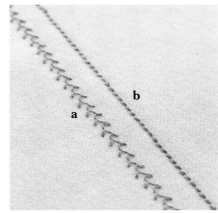

Feather stitch (a) can be set to a stitch width of 0 for the look of straight topstitching **(b)**. The sewing machine sews back and forth three times, creating a heavier stitch.

Three Ways to Guide Topstitching

Use blindstitch or topstitching foot to guide edgestitching; place edge of fabric against presser foot guide.

Use quilting bar to guide evenly spaced rows of topstitching; align the previous row with the end of quilting bar.

Make a seam guide for topstitching by building up a ridge on bed of machine with layers of tape.

How to Turn Corners

1) Take one stitch through corner of fabric, by hand or by machine, leaving long thread tails in fabric.

2) Topstitch to corner. Raise presser foot, leaving needle down in fabric; pivot. Lower presser foot, and hold onto thread tails as you continue to stitch.

Couching

Trims, such as pearl cotton, round cording, yarn, and braid, can be attached to a garment by couching over them with machine stitches. You can use specialty thread for decorative stitches or fine monofilament nylon thread for invisible stitches. To avoid flattening a rounded trim, select a stitch pattern on the machine that just catches the fabric on both sides of the trim, but does not pierce the trim itself.

If the design you are stitching has corners or tight curves, select a narrow, flexible trim. Wider trims can be couched successfully if the design has straight stitching lines or gradual curves.

Place tear-away stabilizer under the fabric during stitching to prevent puckering. If you are using a knit fabric or one that is lightweight or loosely woven, also apply fusible interfacing to the wrong side of the fabric before stitching.

It is helpful to use a cording foot for couching. The trim is threaded through the hole in the foot and is guided automatically, leaving your hands free to turn the fabric. The cording foot may also have a groove on the bottom, which allows narrow trims to feed smoothly. If a cording foot is not available, thread the trim through a piece of plastic tape applied to a presser foot, as shown opposite.

How to Couch Trims

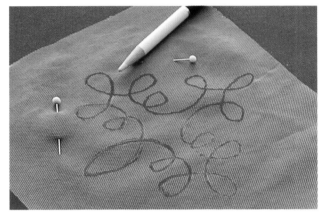

1) Trace design on nylon net. Position net over fabric; pin in place. Transfer design, using chalk or water-soluble marking pen.

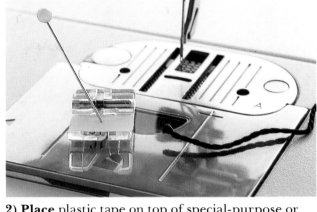

2) Place plastic tape on top of special-purpose or open-toe presser foot, if cording foot is not available. Puncture tape at center of needle hole opening in presser foot, making hole the width of trim.

3) Place trim from front to back down through hole in tape, or through cording foot. Attach presser foot. Adjust stitch width so stitches will catch fabric on both sides of trim.

4) Place tear-away stabilizer under fabric in design area. Stitch over trim, guiding fabric so stitching follows marked line; trim feeds by itself.

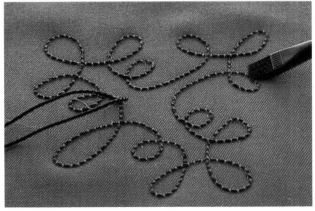

5) Remove stabilizer (page 51). Brush away chalk markings or blot water-soluble markings with a damp cloth. Press fabric lightly on padded surface, from wrong side of fabric, taking care not to flatten trim.

How to Finish the Ends of Couched Trims

Thread end of trim through a tapestry needle and pull to the wrong side **(a)**; clip thread, leaving short tail. Or seal trimmed end with liquid fray preventer **(b).** Or enclose end in seamline **(c).**

Decorative Bobbin Thread Sewing

Specialty threads can be used to create many beautiful decorative effects. Threads that do not fit through the eye of a sewing machine needle can be used in the bobbin of the machine. Stitch with the fabric right side down, so the decorative thread shows on the right side of the fabric.

Heavy threads, such as pearl cotton, pearl rayon, metallic thread, six-strand embroidery floss, and ribbon thread, can be used for decorative bobbin thread sewing. Wind the threads on the bobbin, using one of the methods opposite.

Experiment to determine the types of specialty threads and decorative stitches that work best in your sewing machine. Test-sew on a fabric scrap, adjusting the stitch length and stitch width until you achieve the desired effect; adjust the tension of the machine, if necessary (pages 52 and 53). Check the stitches frequently on the underside of the fabric to ensure that the stitching is consistent.

Two Ways to Wind the Bobbin with Specialty Thread

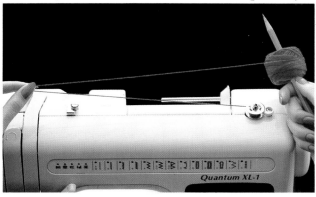

Wind bobbin slowly on the machine, leaving thread out of tension disc; control thread with hand, as necessary, to encourage even winding. If ball or cone does not fit on spool pin, place it over a pencil; hold pencil in hand while winding bobbin.

Wind bobbin evenly and firmly by hand, in same direction as it would be wound on the machine. This method can be used for all types of bobbins, but is always used for winding heavy threads on wind-in-place bobbins.

How to Sew with Decorative Bobbin Thread

1) Thread machine with all-purpose or lightweight monofilament nylon thread in needle. Wind bobbin with specialty thread, above. Attach open-toe presser foot. Test-sew, using regular tension. Adjust tension, if necessary (pages 52 and 53).

2) Mark design on tear-away or water-soluble stabilizer; if using an asymmetrical design, mark mirror image (pages 92 and 93). Baste or pin stabilizer to wrong side of fabric.

3) Stitch slowly, following design lines on stabilizer; hold needle and bobbin threads for the first few stitches to prevent jamming. Stitch continuously as much as possible; do not secure stitches at ends by backstitching or stitching in place.

4) Remove stabilizer (page 51). Thread the end of bobbin thread through tapestry needle, and pull to wrong side. Knot thread ends; trim ends ½" (1.3 cm) from knots.

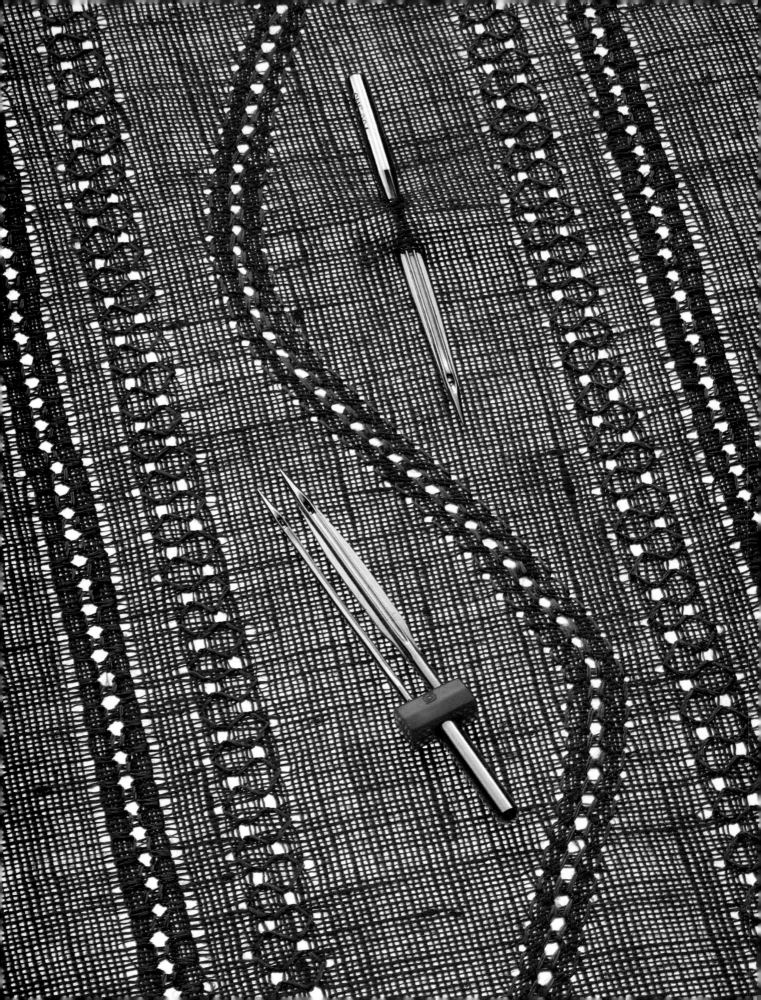

Hemstitching

Traditional hemstitching is done by drawing threads from the fabric and handstitching to produce a lacelike effect, but the same look is easy to duplicate on the conventional sewing machine without drawing threads. Wing needles push the threads aside to produce the characteristic "holes" in the hemstitched fabric. Hemstitching can be used to embellish fabric or to create the look of entredeux when sewing hems and attaching laces.

Two types of wing needles are available: single-wing and double-wing. Single-wing needles are used for sewing either straight, zigzag, or decorative stitches. Sizes range from 90/14 to 120/20; a 120/20 needle makes the largest holes. Double-wing needles are used only to sew straight stitches and feature a wing needle, size 100/16, and a standard needle, size 80/12, on one shank. It is helpful to use an open-toe presser foot when hemstitching.

When using a single-wing needle, test-sew various zigzag, utility, and decorative stitches on your sewing machine, varying the stitch length and stitch width as desired, to determine which stitch patterns you prefer. For more pronounced holes, choose a stitch pattern that allows the wing needle to pierce the same holes more than once. The holes may also be made more pronounced by tightening the tension of the machine slightly, but this may cause some fabrics to pucker.

Hemstitching is most successful on delicate, crisp, natural-fiber fabrics, such as handkerchief linen, organdy, and organza. The fabric must be woven loosely enough so the wing needle can push the threads aside without damaging them, yet must also have enough body so the hole made by the needle does not close immediately after it is pierced. Lightweight fabrics that are more closely woven, such as batiste, may be used, but they may tend to pucker. For best results, use a fine cotton or rayon machine embroidery thread.

To prevent puckering, spray the fabric thoroughly with spray starch and press it before stitching, and, if necessary, place a piece of water-soluble stabilizer under the fabric. Then hold the fabric taut while hemstitching.

If you hemstitch on the crosswise grainline or on the bias, the holes will be more pronounced than if you hemstitch on the lengthwise grainline. It may be necessary to place the pattern pieces on a different grainline when laying out the pattern.

How to Embellish Fabric Using a Single-Wing Needle

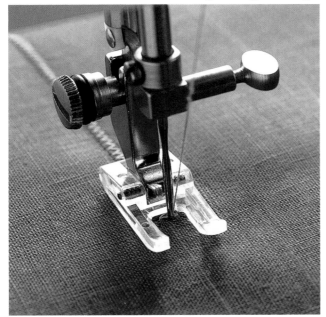

1) **Apply** spray starch to fabric; press. Mark desired stitching lines, using chalk or water-soluble marking pen. Stitch a row of zigzag, utility, or decorative stitches on marked line.

2) **Turn** fabric at end of stitching and stitch again, if desired, for more pronounced holes. Stitch slowly, making sure needle enters holes exactly on first line of hemstitching.

Hemstitched Laces

When lace trims are attached with hemstitching, the open work formed by the hemstitching enhances the open work of the lace. For a transparent effect, the fabric under the lace is trimmed away close to the hemstitching.

There are two methods for hemstitching laces. The first method is used in areas that will be subjected to stress. Hemstitching is done on a folded edge of fabric and provides extra strength as well as protection against raveling. The alternate method is used for attaching laces that must be eased to follow a curved design, but may also be used for attaching laces in a straight line.

Lightweight lace trims of 100 percent cotton, or of 90 percent cotton and 10 percent nylon, are easy to handle, and shape well. If insertion lace will be eased into curves, select a lace that has gathering threads in the headings, if available. If the lace does not have gathering threads, the edges of the lace can be gathered as on page 78. Apply spray starch to the lace and press it before applying the lace to the garment, to make the lace easier to handle and to prevent puckering.

If the lace is to be hemstitched on the straight of grain, it is recommended that you mark placement lines on the fabric by pulling threads. If the lace will be shaped to follow a curve, placement lines are marked, using a water-soluble marking pen or chalk.

How to Attach Lace Insertion Using Hemstitching

1) Mark placement line, above. Pin lace to fabric at marked line. Stitch lace to fabric, using regular needle and straight stitch; stitch along both headings of lace.

2) Cut down center of fabric under lace, taking care not to cut lace. Press fabric edge on each side away from lace. Change to a single-wing or double-wing needle.

3) Hemstitch, using single-wing needle and zigzag or decorative stitch, with one side of stitch on fabric and other side on lace. Or use double-wing needle and straight stitch, with wing needle on fabric and regular needle on lace.

4) Turn fabric at end of stitching and stitch again, if desired, for more pronounced holes; stitch slowly, making sure wing needle enters holes exactly on first line of hemstitching.

5) Repeat steps 3 and 4 for other edge of lace. Trim excess fabric from wrong side, close to stitches.

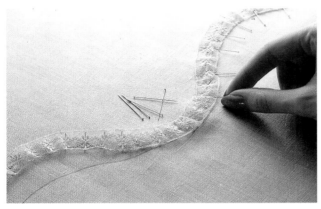

Alternate method. 1) Mark placement line, opposite. If lace requires shaping, pull up gathering threads in lace headings; ease lace to shape of design. Pin lace to fabric at marked line. Press lace flat.

2) Stitch as in steps 1, 3, and 4, on both edges of lace. Trim fabric under lace, from wrong side, close to stitches, taking care not to cut lace.

How to Attach Lace Edging Using Hemstitching

Trim off hem allowance. Place lace edging on right side of fabric, with lower edge of lace at raw edge. Stitch lace heading to fabric, using regular needle and straight stitch; press fabric edge away from lace. Follow steps 3 and 4. Trim excess fabric from wrong side, close to stitches.

Alternate method. Trim off hem allowance. Place lace edging on right side of fabric, with lower edge of lace at raw edge. Stitch lace heading to fabric, using regular needle and straight stitch. Follow steps 3 and 4. Trim excess fabric from wrong side, close to stitches.

Hemstitched Hems

Hemstitched hems may be either single-fold (top) or double-fold (bottom). For a soft hem with a more sheer appearance, use a single-fold hem. Double-fold hems have more body and appear more opaque.

The technique for single-fold hems can also be used to decoratively secure the raw edge of a facing so it stays neatly in place. Hemstitching also eliminates the need for a seam finish on the facing.

To sew a double-fold hem, double the hem allowance when laying out the pattern. This technique can also be used to hemstitch a cut-on band, such as a band at the center front of a blouse, without the need for interfacing.

How to Sew a Single-fold Hem

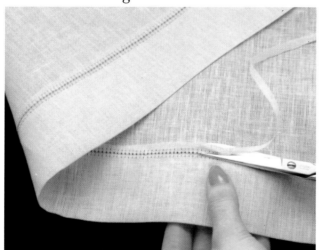

Single-wing needle. Press hem. Using single-wing needle and decorative stitch, stitch from right side ¼" (6 mm) from hem edge. Stitch a second row of stitching as in step 2, opposite, if desired. Trim fabric close to stitches from wrong side.

Double-wing needle. Press hem. Using double-wing needle and straight stitch, stitch from right side ¼" (6 mm) from hem edge. Stitch a second row of stitching as in step 2, opposite, if desired. Trim fabric close to stitches from wrong side.

How to Sew a Double-fold Hem Using a Single-wing Needle

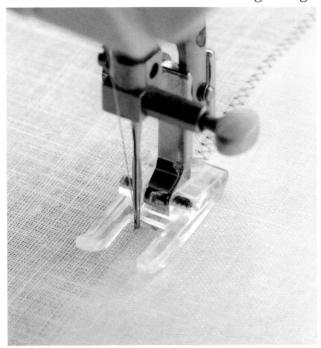

1) Press hem, folding twice. Stitch, using single-wing needle and zigzag or decorative stitch, so one side of stitch pierces hem allowance and other side of stitch pierces single layer of fabric.

2) Turn fabric at end of stitching and stitch again, if desired, for more pronounced holes. Stitch slowly, making sure wing needle enters holes exactly on first line of hemstitching.

How to Sew a Double-fold Hem Using a Double-wing Needle

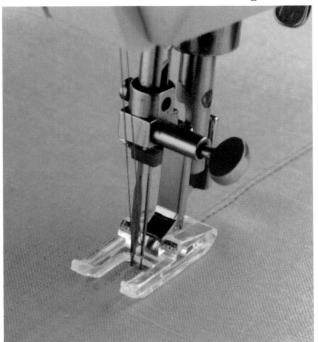

1) Press hem, folding twice. Stitch from right side, using double-wing needle and straight stitch so standard needle pierces hem allowance and wing needle pierces single layer of fabric.

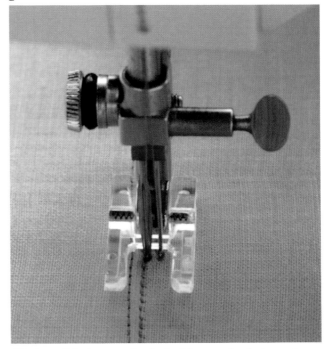

2) Turn fabric at end of stitching and stitch again, if desired, for more pronounced holes. Stitch slowly, making sure needle enters holes exactly on first line of hemstitching.

Pintucks

Pintucks are one of the most versatile decorative effects. They can be a demure accent on a feminine blouse or a tailored treatment on a crisp shirt. They can also add interest to pillows and table linens.

Traditionally stitched pintucks (top), are stitched near a folded edge and are suitable for lightweight to mediumweight even-weave fabrics. Two variations of the traditional pintuck are decoratively stitched pintucks (middle) and twisted pintucks (bottom).

Pintucks are less likely to pucker if they are stitched on the crosswise grain of the fabric. It is better to sew all the pintucks before cutting out the garment piece unless you are using a pattern that includes pintucks.

Pintucks can be as narrow as 1/16" (1.5 mm) on lightweight fabrics. On mediumweight fabrics, make the pintucks 1/8" (3 mm), so they will lie flat when pressed to one side. Depending on the width of the presser foot, you may be able to guide the foldline of the fabric along the inner edge of the presser foot for 1/8" (3 mm) pintucks. On some machines, you can move the needle to a right-needle position to guide a 1/16" (1.5 mm) pintuck.

How to Sew Traditionally Stitched Pintucks

1) Measure size and spacing of all pintucks on fabric; allow ⅛" (3 mm) to ¼" (6 mm) to be taken up by each tuck. Pull threads to mark foldlines of tucks, or mark foldlines with chalk.

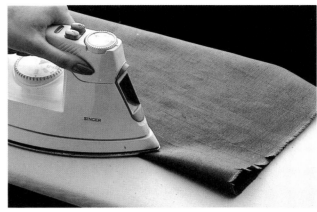

2) Fold and press fabric, wrong sides together, on foldline for each pintuck.

3) Stitch ¹⁄₁₆" to ⅛" (1.5 to 3 mm) from foldline of first pintuck, using straight stitches. Press pintuck with needle thread up.

4) Stitch remaining pintucks in same direction as first pintuck to prevent distortion; press.

How to Sew Decoratively Stitched Pintucks

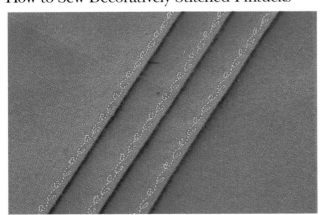

Stitch ⅛" (3 mm) traditionally stitched pintucks, above, using decorative stitch set at narrow stitch width, instead of straight stitch.

How to Sew Twisted Pintucks

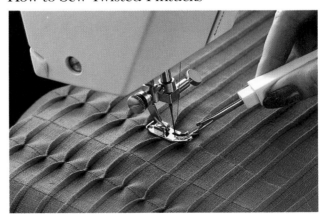

Stitch and press ⅛" (3 mm) traditionally stitched pintucks, above. Mark evenly spaced rows across pintucks; topstitch, reversing the direction of tucks with each row. Use seam ripper or screwdriver to change direction of pintucks as you stitch.

French Machine Sewing

French machine sewing consists of stitching strips of fabric and trims together. These strips may be placed either horizontally or vertically on the garment piece, and they may vary in width, as desired.

The fabric strips may be embellished with machine embroidery, pintucks, or hemstitching, or they may be gathered to make puffing strips. The strips are pieced together to create heirloom fabric before the pattern is laid out. Use French machine sewing to embellish areas such as a yoke, collar, blouse front, or skirt hem. The best styles to choose are those with few darts and seams.

All-cotton Swiss batiste, available in three weights, is the traditional fabric choice for French machine sewing; its wrinkles are merely part of its appeal. Other batistes and broadcloths in cotton or cotton blends are also suitable. Imperial® batiste, for example, is an economical polyester/cotton blend that is wrinkle-resistant.

Lace trims of 100 percent cotton, or of 90 percent cotton and 10 percent nylon, feel soft and are easy to handle. You may use insertion lace or lace edging. Lace beading, with double-faced satin ribbon woven through the beading, adds special detailing.

Entredeux is a trim that resembles hemstitching, with seam allowances on both sides. It is used between fabric strips and laces to reinforce seams decoratively.

For sewing lightweight fabrics and trims, use a 50-weight or 60-weight cotton machine embroidery thread, because it will not add bulk to the seams. Or if extra sheen is desired, fine rayon thread may be used. White thread is appropriate for sewing white, ecru, or pastel fabrics; the fine white thread blends into the fabric.

A sharp, new needle in size 70/9 is essential for machine heirloom sewing. Change the needle after every few hours of sewing, even if the point of the needle feels smooth.

You may want to practice the heirloom techniques on pages 74 to 78 before making your project.

Pillow of Swiss cotton features pintucks, puffing strips, decorative stitching, and delicate Swiss laces. Lace beading is accented with narrow satin ribbons.

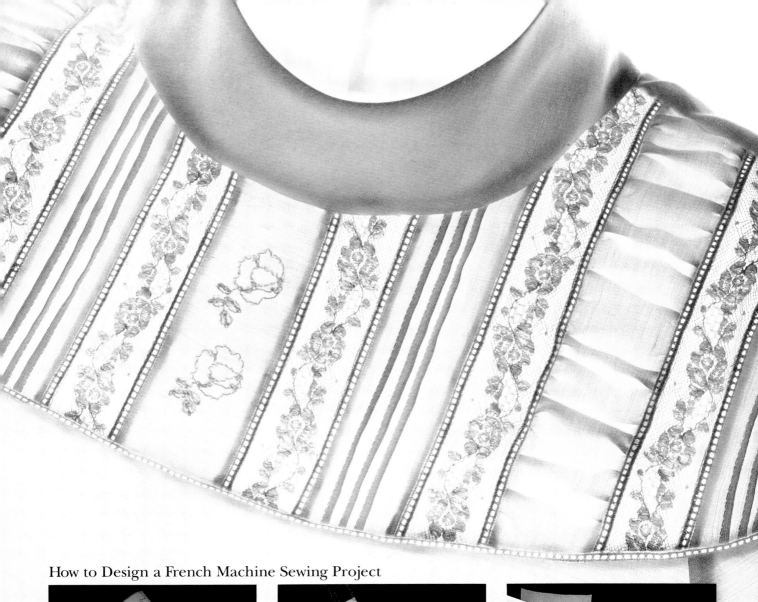

How to Design a French Machine Sewing Project

1) Make a full-size pattern piece from tissue; trace onto firm paper. Plan design, using entredeux, lace trims, and fabric strips. Entredeux should be between all strips of fabric and lace; fabric strips should be at ends, if edges are curved.

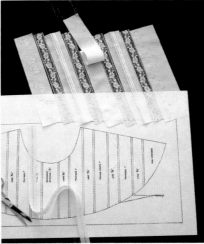

2) Measure pattern at its widest and longest points. Embellish and cut strips (page 74); finished length of the strips should be 1" (2.5 cm) longer than width or length of the pattern, depending on the direction of the strips.

3) Stitch entredeux, lace trims, and fabric strips together (pages 76 to 78) to form rectangle or square. Block fabric and cut out garment piece (page 79).

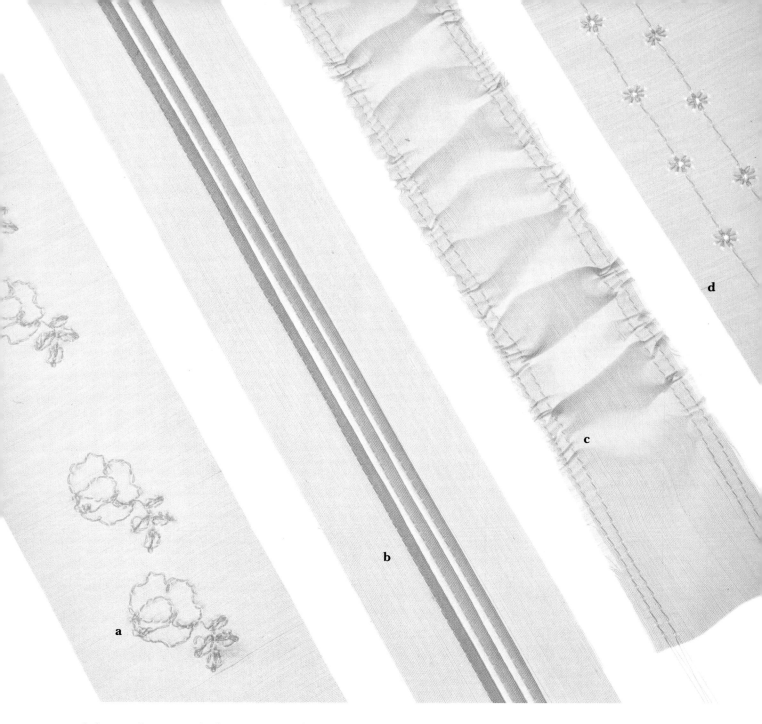

Making the Heirloom Strips

Make heirloom strips by embellishing strips of fabric with decorative machine stitching **(a),** pintucks **(b),** gathering or puffing **(c),** or hemstitching **(d).**

The fabric strips are cut or torn on the straight of grain; seams are less likely to pucker when strips are cut or torn on the crosswise grain. Each strip is cut ½" (1.3 cm) wider than the desired finished width to allow for seam allowances; allow additional width for pintucks. Cut puffing strips 1½ times longer than the

pattern piece to allow for gathering. Cut other strips 1" (2.5 cm) longer than the pattern piece.

Apply spray starch to all fabric strips, except puffing strips, to make the fabric easier to handle. To prevent scorching, spray the starch on the wrong side of the fabric and press from the right side. For puffing strips, press, but do not starch, the fabric strips before gathering them. To prevent flattening the gathers, puffing strips should not be pressed with an iron after they are sewn; they may be finger-pressed.

How to Prepare Straight-grain Fabric Strips

Swiss cotton. Clip into selvage. To straighten end of fabric, pull a thread across to other selvage; cut on pulled thread line. Clip again and pull a thread at desired width of each fabric strip, opposite; cut on pulled thread line.

Cotton/polyester batiste. Clip selvage and tear fabric to straighten end. Clip again and tear at desired width of each fabric strip, opposite; press flat. Trim torn edges, if desired, using rotary cutter and ruler.

How to Sew Puffing Strips

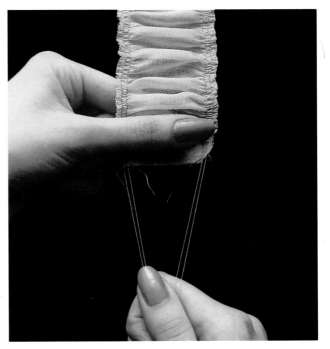

1) Cut fabric strips, above. Set stitch length to 12 stitches per inch (2.5 cm); loosen needle thread tension. Stitch two rows of gathering threads on each long side of strip, with rows ⅛" (3 mm) and a scant ¼" (6 mm) from edge.

2) Pull up gathering threads on each side of puffing strip, gathering strip evenly to desired length. Knot gathering threads at each end.

Joining the Heirloom Strips

Fabric strips, laces, and trims for French machine sewing are stitched together with narrow seams that are neat and durable. A technique called rolling and whipping is often used; the seam allowances actually roll or curl and are secured with zigzag stitches.

When flat lace edging or insertion lace is rolled and whipped to a fabric strip, the extended fabric rolls over the lace edge. When flat lace is applied at a hem edge, the rolled-and-whipped seam may be pressed toward the fabric and edgestitched through all layers.

Entredeux is frequently used between fabrics and laces to reinforce the seams. For a decorative effect, lace beading and entredeux can be embellished by weaving narrow ribbon or embroidery floss through the holes of the trim.

Gather flat lace, if desired, before stitching it to trimmed entredeux. If both edges of the entredeux are trimmed off, the gathered lace and entredeux can be used to highlight a yoke seam or neck edge.

How to Set the Machine Stitch Length

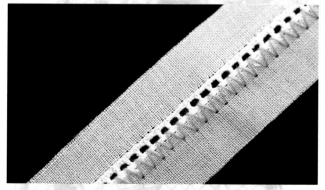

Cut a test strip of entredeux about 4" (10 cm) long. Set stitch width of zigzag stitch 3 mm wide; set stitch length for 16 to 18 stitches per inch (2.5 cm). Then adjust stitch length until needle stitches into each hole of the entredeux. This stitch length is used for the entire project.

How to Sew a Fabric Strip to Flat Lace Using Rolling and Whipping

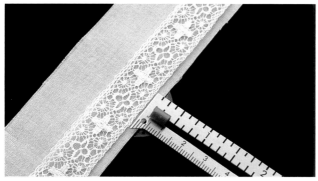

1) Place starched strips of fabric and flat lace, right sides together, with lace on top and fabric extending ⅛" (3 mm) to right of lace.

2) Set stitch width of zigzag stitch so left swing of needle stitches to the left of lace heading and right swing extends over raw edge of fabric strip. As needle moves to the left, edge of fabric rolls over lace; if fabric does not roll, adjust needle thread tension. Press seam toward fabric.

How to Sew a Fabric Strip to Entredeux Using Rolling and Whipping

1) Trim seam allowance of entredeux to ¼" (6 mm). Place starched strips of fabric and entredeux, right sides together, with raw edges even. Stitch next to entredeux holes; trim seam allowances to ⅛" (3 mm).

2) Set stitch width of zigzag stitch so left swing of needle stitches in ditch of entredeux and right swing extends over raw edges. As needle moves to the left, edges of strips roll; if fabric does not roll, adjust the needle thread tension. Press seam toward fabric.

How to Sew a Puffing Strip to Entredeux Using Rolling and Whipping

1) Trim seam allowance of entredeux to ¼" (6 mm). Place puffing strip and starched entredeux, right sides together, with raw edges even. Stitch next to entredeux holes; trim seam allowances to ⅛" (3 mm).

2) Set stitch width of zigzag stitch so left swing of needle stitches in ditch of entredeux and right swing extends over raw edges. As needle moves to the left, edges of strips roll slightly; if fabric does not roll, adjust needle thread tension. Press seam toward fabric, using tip of iron; do not press puffing strip flat.

How to Sew Flat Lace Trims Together

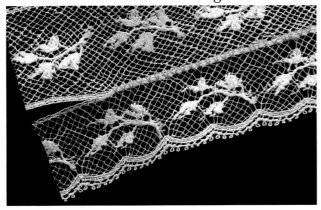

Butt edges of laces, right sides up. Set stitch length (page 76); zigzag, using a narrow stitch width.

How to Sew a Flat Lace Trim to Entredeux

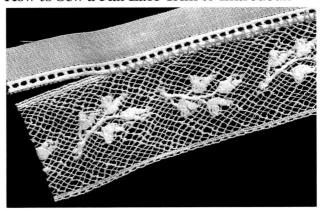

Trim away one seam allowance of entredeux. Butt trimmed edge of entredeux to edge of lace. Set stitch length (page 76); zigzag, using a narrow stitch width. Stitch into the center of entredeux holes.

How to Gather a Flat Lace Trim and Sew to Entredeux

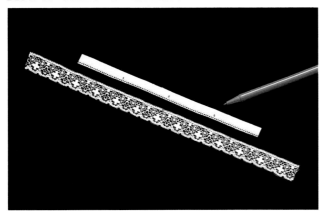

1) Cut entredeux 1" (2.5 cm) longer than needed; trim away one seam allowance. Cut flat lace 1½ times longer than entredeux. Divide lace and entredeux into fourths; mark.

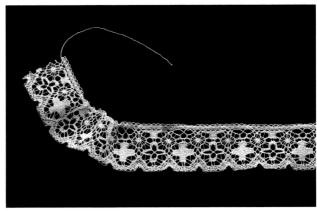

2a) Lace with gathering thread in heading. Pull the gathering thread in heading from both ends to gather lace; some laces have several gathering threads, in case of breakage. Match marks on lace and entredeux.

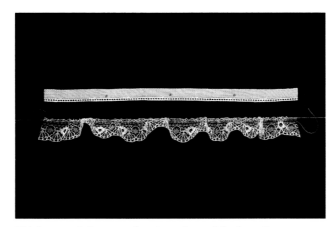

2b) Lace without gathering thread in heading. Stitch next to lace edge, using 10 to 12 stitches per inch (2.5 cm); pull bobbin thread to gather. Match marks on lace and entredeux.

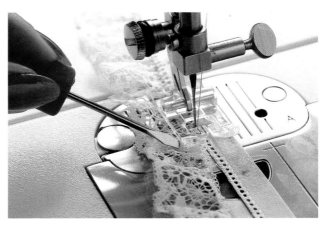

3) Butt trimmed edge of entredeux to lace. Set stitch length (page 76); zigzag, using a narrow stitch width. Guide gathers under presser foot, using a small screwdriver. Remove gathering thread.

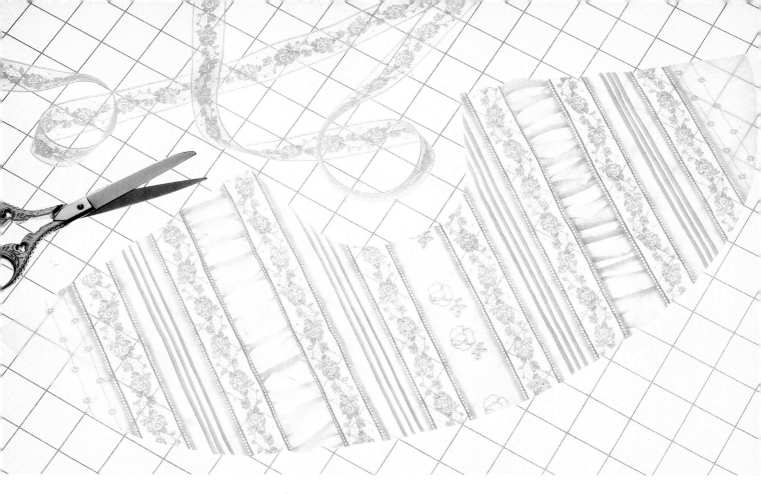

Cutting the Heirloom Fabric

Block the completed heirloom fabric to set the shape before cutting the garment pieces. The fabric is pinned to a padded surface, such as an ironing board, so the seams are straight. Then the fabric is steamed, taking care not to flatten any machine embroidery or puffing strips. After the blocked fabric has cooled, place the full-size pattern pieces on the fabric (page 73), matching the planned design as closely as possible.

How to Block and Cut the Heirloom Pieces

1) Pin heirloom fabric to padded surface so seams are straight.

2) Steam fabric to set shape, taking care not to flatten puffing strips or machine embroidery. Allow fabric to cool before removing pins.

3) Position pattern piece on fabric, centering it on middle strip; seams of strips may not match planned design exactly. Cut garment piece.

Finishing the Heirloom Garment

French seams and French bindings are used for seam finishes in delicate heirloom garments. French seams are used only for straight seams. French bindings are used for curved seams, such as armhole seams of set-in sleeves, opposite. They are also used for seams with gathers, such as gathered waistlines.

Eliminate facings whenever possible, and bind the edges of the neckline and sleeveless armholes with French binding. Or use lace and entredeux at the neckline as a pretty finish; attach the lace to the entredeux, as on page 78, and then sew the entredeux to the garment edge, as on page 77.

Rolling and whipping may be used for a narrow hem finish on a ruffle or at the lower edge of a garment.

How to Sew Narrow French Seams

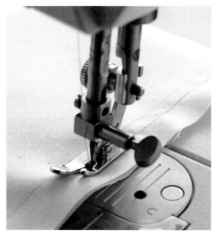

1) Place garment pieces with *wrong* sides together. Stitch seam, within the seam allowance, ³⁄₁₆" (4.5 mm) from the seamline, using 16 to 18 stitches per inch (2.5 cm).

2) Trim seam allowances to scant ⅛" (3 mm); press seam allowances to one side. Fold on stitching line, right sides together; press.

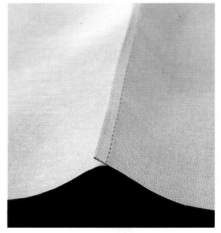

3) Stitch seam ⅛" (3 mm) from fold, encasing raw edges. Press seam allowance to one side.

How to Finish Seams and Edges with French Binding

Seams. 1) Cut 1¾" (4.5 cm) bias strip of lightweight fabric 1" (2.5 cm) longer than edge. Press the strip in half lengthwise, wrong sides together. Trim seam allowances on garment to scant ¼" (6 mm).

2) Pin binding to garment, raw edges even. Stitch, using ¼" (6 mm) seam; stretch binding slightly on inside curves. For continuous edge, tuck ½" (1.3 cm) to inside of binding at beginning of strip (arrow). For edge at garment opening, wrap ½" (1.3 cm) of binding around ends.

3) Press binding toward seam allowances. Fold the binding in half over raw edges; pin. Slipstitch folded edge of binding to previous stitching line. Press.

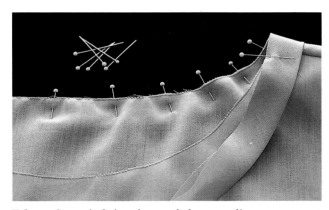

Edges. Staystitch just beyond the seamline to prevent stretching; trim at seamline. Cut and press bias strip, as in step 1. Pin binding to right side of garment, raw edges even; attach as in steps 2 and 3.

How to Sew a Narrow Hem Using Rolling and Whipping

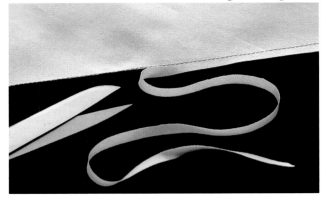

1) Staystitch bias edges ¼" (6 mm) from edge; then trim fabric close to stitching. It is not necessary to staystitch edges that are on the straight of grain.

2) Set stitch width to 12 to 16 stitches per inch (2.5 cm); set stitch width so left swing of needle stitches ⅛" (3 mm) from raw edge and right swing of needle extends over raw edge. As needle moves to the left, edge of fabric will roll.

Appliqués

Appliqués

Appliqués can be the focal point of a garment; they can also be used for other projects, such as framed artwork, wall hangings, and tablecloths. Appliqués can be made from one fabric or from a combination of fabrics in various colors and textures. They can be bright and bold, or soft and subtle. Satin appliqués can add the perfect touch to an evening gown; velour appliqués can embellish a towel. You may sew a transparent appliqué on a negligee or one that is softly padded on a toddler's playsuit. The direction of the grainline can be varied on appliqué pieces for an interesting effect.

Select a background fabric that has enough body to support the weight of the appliqué and that will not stretch out of shape. Then check that the background fabric does not show through any light-colored fabrics in the appliqué. Appliqué fabrics can be interfaced with fusible knit interfacing, if necessary, to prevent show-through or to add body to the appliqué. The fusible knit interfacing will not cause the appliqué to become stiff.

Garments can be dressed up with appliqués made from silky fabrics.

Appliqués can be creatively embellished with ribbons or other trims for added dimension.

Home decorating projects, such as curtains, can be enhanced with appliqués to complement any decorating scheme.

Appliqués are stitched to the garment using satin stitching. The width of the stitches depends on the size of the appliqué; use wider stitches for larger appliqués. Machine embroidery thread (page 48) is recommended for satin stitching, but all-purpose thread, which is available in a wider color selection, may be used. After threading the machine, adjust the tension (page 52) so the bobbin threads do not show on the right side of the fabric. The color of the thread may be changed, as desired, to blend or contrast with different areas of the appliqué.

There are several ways to apply an appliqué (pages 90 and 91), depending on the fabrics used and the effect you want to create. Tear-away stabilizer is used on the wrong side of the background fabric to prevent the stitches from puckering.

Appliquéd garments may be washed and dried by machine if the fabrics are washable. To prevent excessive abrasion of the appliqué, turn the garment wrong side out before washing.

Children's clothing can be brightened with a whimsical appliqué.

Dinnerware designs can be copied and used for appliqués on table linens.

Designing Appliqués

Greeting cards frequently have simple artwork to use as inspiration for appliqué designs.

Many designs can be adapted for appliqués. If the design is smaller or larger than you want, it can be enlarged or reduced, using a photocopy machine. Elaborate or detailed designs can be simplified to make the appliqué easier to sew.

Artwork, stencils, greeting cards, and children's drawings can be good sources of inspiration for appliqués. Or you may want to draw your own appliqué design; geometric designs are easy to draw and make interesting appliqué shapes that are also easy to sew.

When designing an appliqué, decide on the size and basic shape of the area you want to cover. Keep in mind that appliqués do not show up as well on areas of the garment that curve around the body.

Select a garment pattern that will work with the appliqué design you have chosen. It is usually best to select a pattern that has simple design lines, so the appliqué will be the center of interest on the garment.

Paintings and other forms of artwork can inspire an appliqué design. Simplify the shapes, because appliqués are easier to cut and stitch if they are not intricate.

Books, such as pictorial design books and children's coloring books, offer a wide selection of appliqué ideas.

Positioning the Appliqués

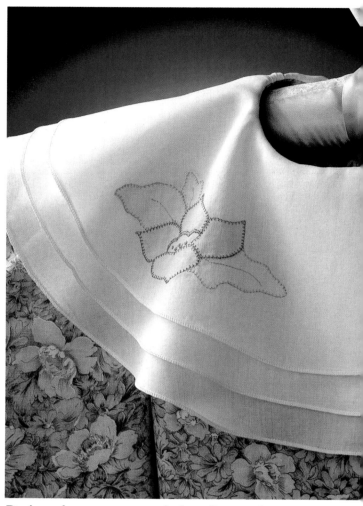

Appliqués can be used to add interest to nearly any section of a garment. For example, they can encircle a neckline or a hemline, accent one or both shoulders, or embellish the front and back of a garment.

To mark the placement of an appliqué, baste the seams of the garment so it can be tried on. If the appliqué will be positioned over a seamline, permanently stitch and press that seam. Try on the garment and position the appliqué, to ensure that the placement of the design is appropriate. Appliqués may wrap around the sides of a garment, but the focal point of an appliqué is usually positioned in the front or back, where it is most noticeable.

For vertical placement of an appliqué, mark a vertical center line on the appliqué and align it to the grainline of the garment. For centered symmetrical designs, align the center line of the appliqué to the center line of the garment.

Designs that are asymmetrical are frequently positioned to one side of the project.

How to Mark the Placement of an Appliqué

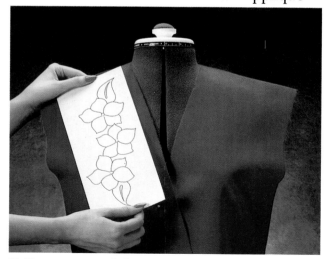

1) Baste seams; stitch any seams that will be under appliqué, using regular stitch length. Place pattern for appliqué design in desired position. Pin in place, using safety pins.

2) Remove basting so project lies flat. Place on cutting board or padded surface. Insert straight pins with small heads, straight down through pattern and fabric, marking placement points of appliqué.

Designs that are symmetrical usually look best when they are centered on the project.

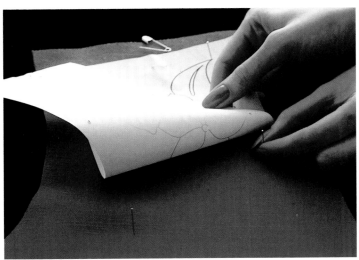

3) Remove safety pins, and carefully lift pattern, leaving straight pins in fabric.

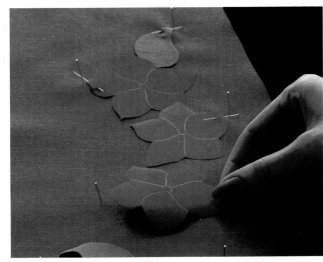

4) Position appliqué on project, matching appliqué to placement points.

Selecting an Appliqué Technique

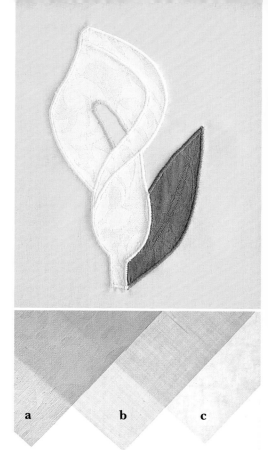

There are several ways to apply appliqués. The method you select depends on the look you want to create, the fabrics you are using, and whether you want a supple appliqué or one with more body.

Fused Appliqués

The appliqué fabric **(a)** is cut to shape and secured with fusible web **(b)** to the background fabric **(c).** Tear-away stabilizer **(d)** is placed under the background fabric; then satin stitching is done from the right side to cover the raw edges.

Considerations

Fusible web causes appliqué to become somewhat stiff.

Appliqué cannot shift or ripple during stitching, because it is fused to the background fabric.

Use basic fabrics, such as cotton broadcloth, poplin, or other lightweight to mediumweight fabrics that fuse securely.

Avoid using fabrics that will become too stiff when fusible web is applied, such as chintz, or those that will bubble when fused, such as some silky fabrics.

Reverse Appliqués

The appliqué fabric **(a)** is placed on the right side of the background fabric **(b);** the appliqué shape is not cut out. The design is marked on tear-away stabilizer **(c)** and the stabilizer is placed on the wrong side of the background fabric.

The design lines are stitched from the wrong side, using straight stitching. Then the appliqué fabric is trimmed close to the stitching, and satin stitching is done from the right side to cover the raw edges.

Considerations

Appliqué is supple, because fusible web is not used.

Appliqué fabric is secured to the background fabric by straight stitching from the wrong side of the project before cutting it to the shape of the design.

Use this method for satins and other fabrics that do not fuse well with fusible web. Use a hoop, if necessary, to keep silky fabrics smooth.

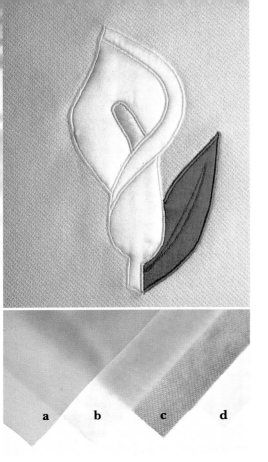

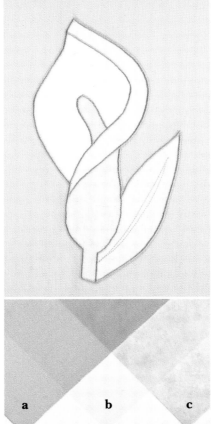

a   b   c   d

a   b   c

a   b   c

Padded Appliqués

The appliqué fabric **(a)** is placed over layers of polyester fleece or quilt batting **(b)** and background fabric **(c)**; the appliqué shape is not cut out. The design is marked on tear-away stabilizer **(d)** and the stabilizer is placed on the wrong side of the background fabric.

The design lines are stitched from the wrong side, using straight stitching. Then the appliqué fabric and fleece are trimmed close to the stitching, and satin stitching is done from the right side to cover the raw edges.

Considerations

Appliqué fabric and fleece are secured to the background fabric by straight stitching from the wrong side of the project before cutting them to the shape of the design.

Use lightweight to mediumweight appliqué fabrics. Because the polyester fleece or quilt batting adds bulk to the appliqué, avoid using bulky or stiff appliqué fabrics. Heavier background fabrics may be used with padded appliqués.

Transparent Appliqués

The appliqué fabrics **(a)** are layered under the background fabric **(b)**; the appliqué shapes are not cut out. The design is marked on tear-away stabilizer **(c)** and the stabilizer is then placed on the wrong side of the appliqué fabric.

The design lines are stitched from the wrong side, using straight stitching. Then one or more layers of fabric are trimmed from the right side close to the stitching to make transparent openings. Satin stitching is done from the right side to cover the raw edges.

Considerations

Appliqué is transparent in some areas of the design.

Multiple layers of sheer fabric give a more opaque appearance.

Several sheer or opaque fabrics can be used, including chiffon, sheer tricot, organza, and organdy.

Shadow Appliqués

The design is marked on the garment fabric **(a).** Water-soluble stabilizer **(b)** is placed under the garment fabric. The appliqué fabric **(c)** is placed under the stabilizer; the appliqué shape is not cut out.

The design lines are stitched from the right side, using decorative stitching. Then the appliqué fabric is trimmed close to the stitching.

Considerations

Appliqué is supple because no fusible web or interfacing is used.

Lightweight appliqué fabrics are layered under sheer or lightweight garment fabric, creating a shadow effect.

Several sheer or opaque fabrics can be used, including Swiss cotton, batiste, organdy, and lightweight broadcloth. Avoid using fabrics that ravel easily. Use washable fabric, because water-soluble stabilizer is used.

Fused Appliqués

Fused appliqués are the easiest to apply, because they are secured to the project with paper-backed fusible web. Although the fusible web adds some stiffness, it prevents the appliqué from shifting or rippling during stitching. Using this technique, it is possible to make appliqués in intricately shaped designs.

Fused appliqués work best with basic fabrics, such as cotton broadcloth or poplin, because they fuse well. Knit fabrics may also be used; apply fusible knit interfacing to knit fabrics to stabilize them before applying the fusible web. Sheer or light-colored fabrics should also be interfaced with fusible knit interfacing, to prevent background fabric from showing through the appliqué. Avoid using fabrics that bubble when fusible web is applied, such as some satin fabrics.

The appliqué is marked on the paper backing of the fusible web before it is applied. Because the fusible web is applied to the wrong side of the fabric, it is necessary to trace the mirror image of any asymmetrical appliqué design to prevent it from being reversed on the right side of the garment. To do this, hold the pattern up to a light source. A light table is helpful for tracing patterns; if you do not have a light table, a temporary one can be made by placing a light under a glass-top table. Or you can hold the pattern up to a window during daylight hours.

How to Sew an Appliqué Using Paper-backed Fusible Web

1) Hold the appliqué pattern up to a light if using an asymmetrical design, and trace the mirror image of the design onto back of pattern.

2) Use mirror image of design to trace pieces of the appliqué onto paper side of paper-backed fusible web, using lead pencil; add ¼" (6 mm) to sides of any pieces that will underlap another piece.

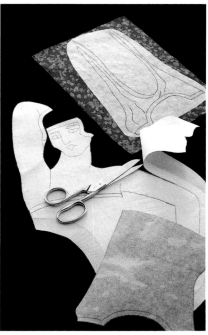

3) Cut around design, leaving a margin. Place the fusible web on the wrong side of appliqué fabric, with paper backing up. Press with a hot, dry iron for a few seconds. Allow fabric to cool. Cut out the appliqué pieces.

4) Transfer any additional design lines to the *right* side of fabric by holding appliqué piece up to light. Remove paper from paper-backed fusible web.

5) Mark placement of appliqué on garment (pages 88 and 89). Position appliqué pieces; fuse to right side of garment following manufacturer's directions.

6) Cut tear-away stabilizer at least 2" (5 cm) larger than the appliqué. Place stabilizer under the appliqué area on wrong side of garment; pin in place from right side.

(Continued on next page)

How to Sew an Appliqué Using Paper-backed Fusible Web (continued)

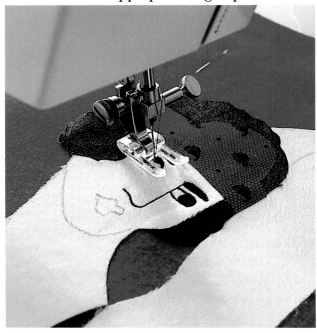

7) Set machine for short, straight stitches. Stitch on marked lines, outlining any fine design details, such as facial features. Fill in design areas, as desired, by stitching several rows close together.

8) Set machine for closely spaced zigzag stitches; set stitch width, as desired. Loosen needle thread tension, if necessary, so bobbin thread will not show on right side of fabric. Satin stitch around appliqué and any remaining design lines (pages 96 and 97). Remove tear-away stabilizer (page 51).

How to Sew a Gathered Appliqué Using Fusible Web

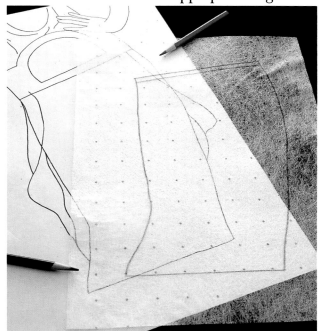

1) Place tissue paper over mirror-image side of the appliqué pattern; tape or pin in place. Trace outline of appliqué piece to be gathered; add ¼" (6 mm) seam allowance on edge to be gathered. Remove tissue.

2) Slash tissue pattern at several places, from edge to be gathered to, but not through, opposite edge. Place paper under tissue pattern. Spread tissue on slashed lines so edge to be gathered measures 1¼ times original length; tape in place.

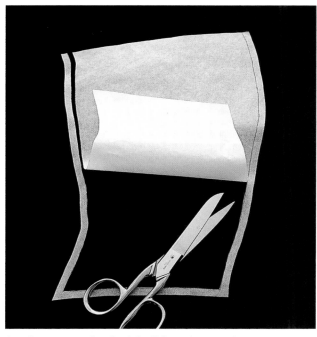

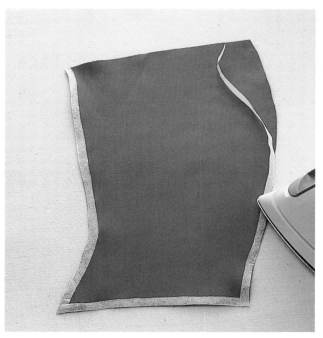

3) Place paper-backed fusible web over tissue pattern; trace outline. Draw lines ¼" (6 mm) inside traced outline on sides that will not be gathered; cut fusible web on marked lines to make ¼" (6 mm) strip.

4) Place tissue pattern on wrong side of fabric; cut appliqué piece. Place fusible web on wrong side of appliqué, with paper backing up; press with hot, dry iron for a few seconds. Allow fabric to cool.

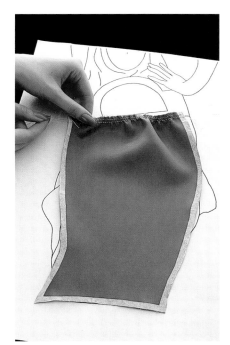

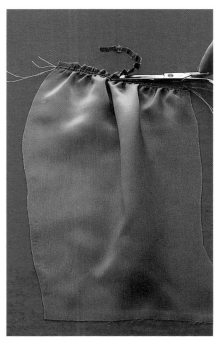

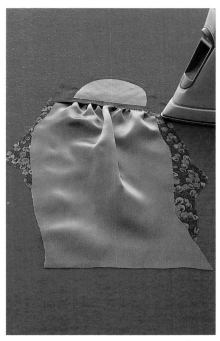

5) Stitch two rows of gathering stitches on side of appliqué to be gathered. Pull up gathers to original length of appliqué pattern. Remove paper backing from fusible web.

6) Mark placement on garment (pages 88 and 89). Fuse piece to garment, following manufacturer's directions. Straight-stitch gathered side in place ¼" (6 mm) from edge. Trim close to stitching.

7) Position adjacent appliqué piece so edge overlaps the gathered piece up to the stitching line; fuse. Fuse any remaining appliqué pieces, and complete appliqué (pages 93 and 94, steps 6 to 8).

How to Satin Stitch Corners and Curves of Appliqués

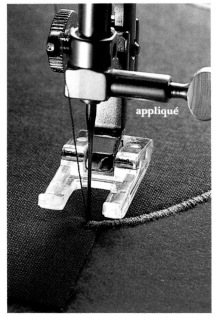

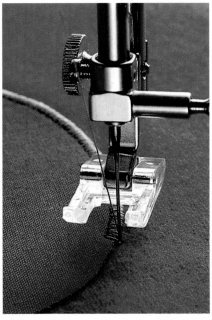

Inside corners. Stitch past corner a distance equal to width of satin stitch, stopping with needle down at the inner edge of satin stitching; raise presser foot. Pivot and satin stitch next side of appliqué, covering previous stitches at corner.

Outside corners. Stitch one stitch past corner, stopping with needle down at outer edge of satin stitching; raise presser foot. Pivot and satin stitch the next side of appliqué, covering previous stitches at corner.

Curves. Pivot fabric frequently, pivoting with needle down at longest edge of satin stitching.

How to Satin Stitch Outside Points of Appliqués

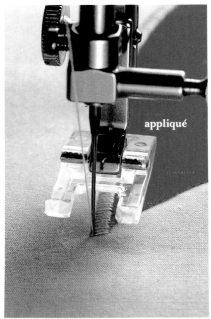

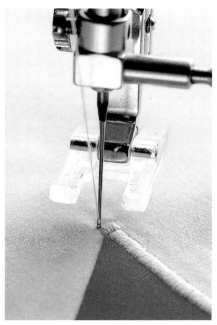

1) Stitch one stitch past the point, stopping with needle down at outer edge of satin stitching; raise the presser foot.

2) Pivot fabric to a 90° angle. Stitch two to four stitches, stopping when stitches just cover previous stitches; stop with needle down on outer edge of satin stitching. Raise the presser foot.

3) Pivot fabric; satin stitch next side of appliqué.

How to Satin Stitch Inside Points of Appliqués

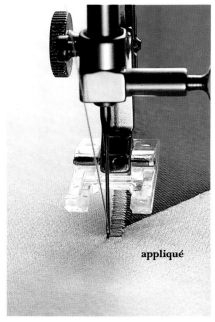

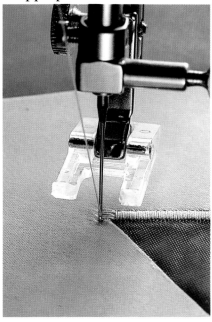

1) Stitch past the point a distance equal to the width of satin stitch, stopping with needle down at inner edge of the satin stitching; raise the presser foot.

2) Pivot fabric to a 90° angle. Stitch two to four stitches, stopping when stitches just cover previous stitches; stop with needle down on inner edge of satin stitching. Raise presser foot.

3) Pivot fabric; satin stitch next side of appliqué.

How to Satin Stitch Tapered Outside Points of Appliqués

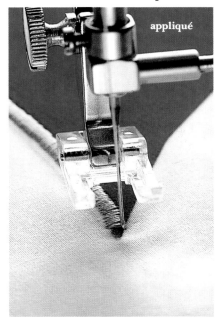

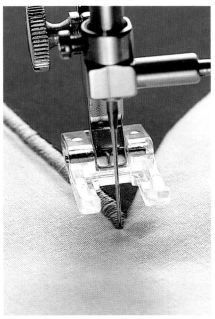

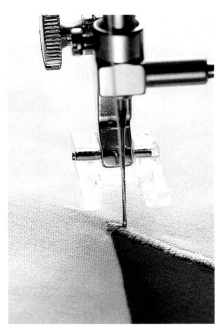

1) Stitch, stopping when inner edge of satin stitching meets other side of appliqué. Raise presser foot.

2) Pivot fabric slightly. Continue stitching, gradually narrowing stitch width to 0 and stopping at point. Raise presser foot.

3) Pivot fabric and stitch back over the previous stitches, gradually widening stitch width to original width. Pivot fabric slightly and stitch next side of appliqué.

Reverse Appliqués

Reverse appliqués are used when you want a supple appliqué, because they are not stiffened with fusible web. The appliqué shapes are not cut until after the outline of the design is stitched to the background fabric. When sewing appliqués from satin, challis, or other fabrics that are either silky or lack body, it may be necessary to secure the fabric layers in an embroidery hoop to prevent rippling while the

design outline is being stitched. The appliqué design is marked on tear-away stabilizer, and the stabilizer is placed on the wrong side of the fabric; because of this, it is necessary to trace the mirror image of any asymmetrical appliqué design to prevent it from being reversed on the right side of the garment (pages 92 and 93).

How to Apply a Reverse Appliqué

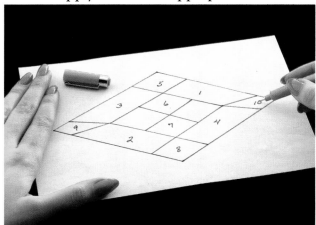

1) Decide sequence for stitching the appliqué pieces, starting with those that should appear to be under other pieces; number areas in sequence of stitching.

2) Cut tear-away stabilizer at least 2" (5 cm) larger than entire design area. Trace design onto stabilizer; if using an asymmetrical design, trace mirror image (pages 92 and 93).

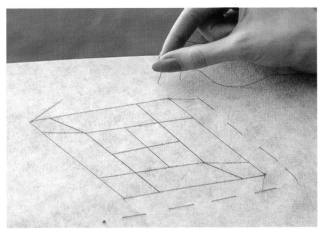

3) Mark placement of appliqué on garment, as on pages 88 and 89, steps 1 to 3. Position stabilizer on wrong side of garment, matching placement points of design to pins. Pin or baste stabilizer to garment.

4) Cut fabric larger than first piece to be appliquéd; do not cut out appliqué shape. Place appliqué fabric, right side up, on right side of garment. Baste or pin; if pins are used, place pins on wrong side of garment.

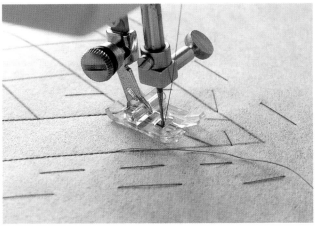

5) Stitch on design lines from wrong side, using straight stitches. Outline and fill in fine details, such as facial features, if any, as on page 94, step 7.

6) Remove basting or pins used in step 4. Trim excess appliqué fabric close to stitching from right side.

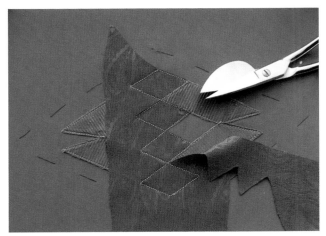

7) Repeat steps 4 to 6 for each piece in appliqué, applying pieces in sequence.

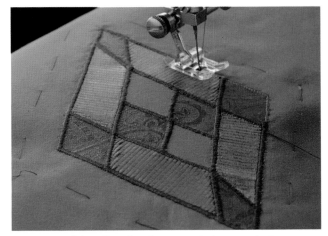

8) Set machine for closely spaced zigzag stitches; set stitch width as desired. Loosen needle thread tension, if necessary, so bobbin thread will not show on right side. Satin stitch on design lines. Remove stabilizer.

Padded Appliqués

A softly padded effect can be achieved
by placing low-loft quilt batting or polyester
fleece under the appliqué fabric. A padded
appliqué is stitched from the wrong side before
cutting the appliqué fabric and batting to the shape
of the design. This eliminates any concern about keeping
the layers even at the edges of the appliqué during stitching
and is especially helpful if you are sewing an appliqué from
lightweight or silky fabrics. If necessary, fabrics can be secured in an
embroidery hoop to prevent rippling while the design outline is stitched.

How to Apply a Padded Appliqué

1) Cut tear-away stabilizer at least 2" (5 cm) larger than entire area to be appliquéd. Trace design onto stabilizer; if using an asymmetrical design, trace the mirror image (pages 92 and 93).

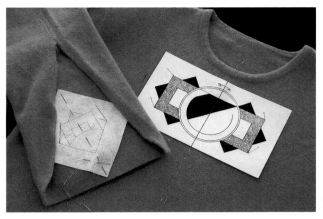

2) Mark placement of appliqué on garment, as on pages 88 and 89, steps 1 to 3. Position stabilizer on wrong side of garment, matching placement points of design to pins. Baste or pin stabilizer to garment.

3) Cut piece of low-loft quilt batting or polyester fleece larger than entire area to be appliquéd; place on right side of garment over design area.

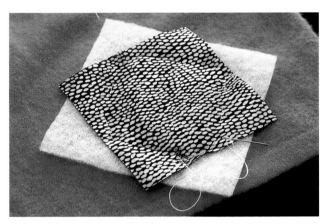

4) Cut fabric for appliqué piece larger than design area; do not cut out appliqué shape. Place appliqué fabric, right side up, over fleece. Baste or pin; if pins are used, place pins on wrong side of garment.

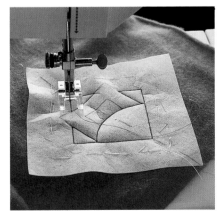

5) Stitch design lines on stabilizer, using short, straight stitches. Remove basting or pins used in step 4. Trim excess appliqué fabric close to the stitching from right side.

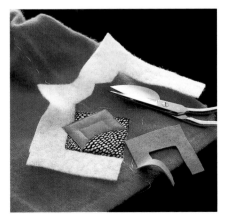

6) Repeat steps 4 and 5 for each appliqué piece. Trim fleece close to stitching.

7) Satin stitch from right side, as on page 94, step 8. Remove the stabilizer (page 51).

101

Transparent Appliqués

One or more layers of sheer fabric can be used to make an elegant transparent appliqué. The sheer fabric is placed on the wrong side of the background fabric; the layers are stitched together along the design lines, and the background fabric is trimmed away from the right side to create sheer openings.

If several layers of sheer fabric are used, you can trim just one or two layers in some of the design areas for an opaque effect and trim all but one layer in other areas for a more transparent effect.

How to Apply a Transparent Appliqué

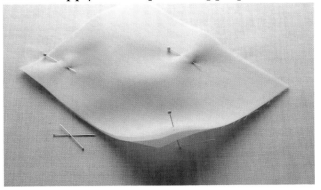

1) **Mark** placement of appliqué, as on pages 88 and 89, steps 1 to 3. Place background fabric right side down. Pin one or more layers of sheer fabric to background fabric, right side down, inserting pins at placement points of design. Remove pins from right side of fabric.

2) **Cut** tear-away stabilizer at least 2" (5 cm) larger than area to be appliquéd. Trace design onto stabilizer; if using an asymmetrical design, trace the mirror image (pages 92 and 93). Position stabilizer over sheer fabric layers, matching placement points of design; pin in place. Baste stabilizer to garment through all layers. Remove pins.

3) **Stitch** three rows of straight stitches on outer design lines from wrong side, using short stitch length. Trim background fabric within design areas close to stitching. Insert a pin into background fabric layer; lift and clip a few threads, making an opening that allows for easier trimming without cutting sheer fabric.

4) **Stitch** three rows of straight stitches on remaining design lines, from wrong side. Trim away one or more sheer layers from right side of fabric, within design areas, using a pin to separate sheer layers for easier trimming.

5) **Set** machine for closely spaced zigzag stitches; set stitch width, as desired. Loosen needle thread tension, if necessary, so bobbin thread will not show on right side. Satin stitch around appliqué.

6) **Remove** tear-away stabilizer (page 51). Trim excess sheer fabric outside design area, from wrong side, close to the stitching.

Shadow Appliqués

Shadow appliqué is a machine-stitched technique resembling shadow work embroidery. Lightweight appliqué fabrics are layered under a lightweight or sheer garment fabric, creating a shadow effect.

Batiste and broadcloth work well for appliqué fabrics. Select a garment fabric that is sheer enough to allow the color of the appliqué to show through, such as Swiss cotton, batiste, organdy, or handkerchief linen. Avoid using fabrics that ravel easily. It is important to preshrink fabrics before sewing, especially if using several types of fabric, because different fibers may shrink differently.

Select fabric and thread colors carefully, checking the colors, as shown at right, to see the actual effect of the fabrics and threads in the finished project. If the garment is to be lined, also check the color of the lining fabric. Appliqué and lining fabrics will appear to be somewhat lighter in color after they are layered,

depending on how sheer the garment fabric is. Select thread colors that are the same as or slightly darker than the colors of the appliqué fabrics.

Use a fine 60-weight cotton machine embroidery thread or a 40-weight rayon thread in the needle of the machine. Use a fine 60-weight cotton machine embroidery thread in the bobbin.

Use a sharp, new size 70/9 sewing machine needle when sewing shadow appliqués, because lightweight fabrics and fine threads are used.

Select decorative machine stitches, shown at right, that will highlight the design without overpowering it. The settings for stitch width and stitch length will vary, depending on the stitch pattern you select and the size of the appliqué piece.

It is important that you practice shadow appliqué techniques before beginning a project. Use the

Selecting Fabric and Thread Colors

Layer small swatches of appliqué fabrics under the garment fabric to see how colors will appear when applied. For lined garments, check lining color by placing it under appliqué swatches. Check each thread color to be used by placing one strand of thread on layered appliqué fabric.

Selecting Decorative Stitches

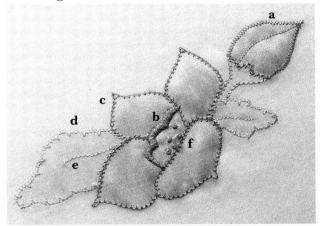

Select decorative stitches that highlight the design without overpowering it, such as zigzag **(a)**, satin **(b)**, blanket **(c)**, and blindstitch **(d)**. The straight stitch **(e)** can be used to stitch design details within the appliqué areas; do not use it for the outer edges of appliqué pieces, because it does not secure appliqués well and fabric will ravel. Machine-stitched French knots **(f)** can also be used.

selected fabrics and threads, to become familiar with the techniques and to check the selection of stitches, fabrics, and threads.

Apply spray starch to the right side of the garment fabric; then trace the design on the right side, using a slightly dull No. 2 lead pencil. Pencil marks will wash out easily with mild soap if spray starch has been applied to the fabric.

Place water-soluble stabilizer under the appliqué area and place the layered fabrics in a 5" to 7" (12.5 to 18 cm) embroidery hoop. Spring-loaded hoops are recommended for securing the lightweight fabrics, because they hold the fabrics taut without distorting the grainline and damaging the fabrics.

When pressing shadow appliqués, place the appliqué face down on two or three layers of velour towels and press the appliqué from the wrong side. The padded surface prevents the stitching from being flattened.

How to Apply a Shadow Appliqué

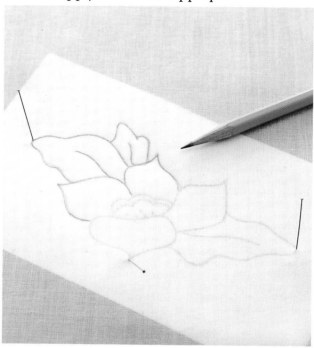

1) Starch garment fabric on right side in design area, using spray starch; press. Mark placement of the appliqué on garment, as on pages 88 and 89, steps 1 to 3. Position pattern for appliqué on wrong side of fabric; match placement points of design to pins. Trace design on right side of fabric, using dull No. 2 pencil.

2) Cut water-soluble stabilizer larger than embroidery hoop. Place stabilizer on wrong side of fabric.

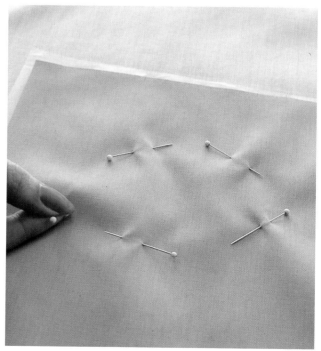

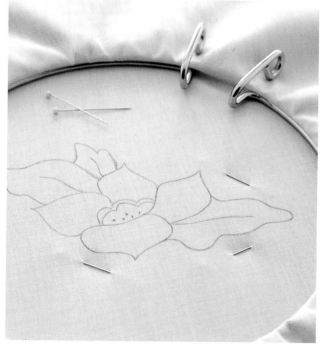

3) Cut appliqué fabric larger than entire design area for the fabric color. Place appliqué fabric, right side down, on stabilizer; pin.

4) Position fabrics, right side up, in embroidery hoop (page 119). Remove pins, or repin fabric from right side if appliqué fabric is not secured in hoop.

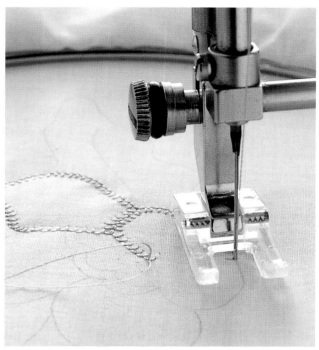

5) Set straight stitch length for 20 to 25 stitches per inch (2.5 cm). Draw up bobbin thread on design line; do not start at a corner. Stitch in place a few times to secure stitches. Stitch along outer design lines, using decorative stitches, so right swing of needle is on the line and left swing of needle is within design area. Stitch corners, curves, and dividing lines, as on page 109.

6) Stitch in place a few times at end of design area, to secure stitches. Raise presser foot and pull threads to next design area of same fabric color. Stitch all designs for same fabric color, securing threads at beginning and end of stitching. Clip thread tails.

7) Trim excess appliqué fabric close to stitching from the wrong side.

8) Repeat steps 3 to 7 for each appliqué fabric color, changing thread color and decorative stitch pattern, as desired.

(Continued on next page)

How to Apply a Shadow Appliqué (continued)

9) Set machine for straight stitches of 14 to 16 stitches per inch (2.5 cm) to sew outline stitching. Stitch on design lines in center areas of appliqués. Stitch French knots, opposite, if included in design.

10) Satin stitch areas as desired, with closely spaced zigzag stitches. Draw up bobbin thread; stitch in place a few times to secure stitches. Starting with stitch width at 0, gradually widen stitch width as you sew, following shape of area. Taper the stitching, as necessary, by narrowing stitch width.

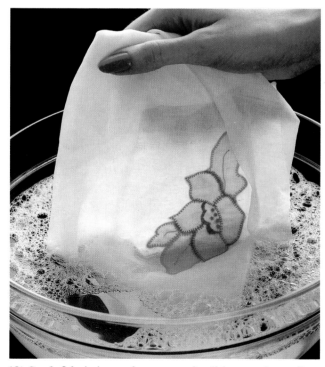

11) Trim excess water-soluble stabilizer around the appliqué design.

12) Soak fabric in cool water and mild soap about five minutes to remove the stabilizer between fabric layers, and the pencil markings.

How to Stitch Corners, Curves, and Dividing Lines of Shadow Appliqués

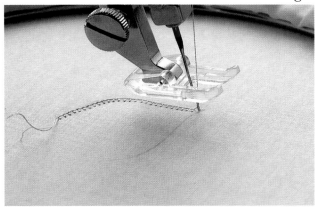

Corners. 1) Stitch to corner, stopping with needle down at right swing of stitch; it may be necessary to turn corner, slightly before or beyond marked design line. Raise presser foot.

2) Turn hoop to pivot; the first stitch around corner (arrow) is stitched inside the design area. Pivot and stitch next side of appliqué.

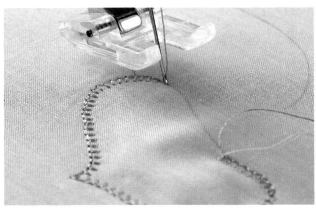

Curves. Pivot fabric frequently, with needle down on design line, turning hoop slightly; stitches should point to center of design.

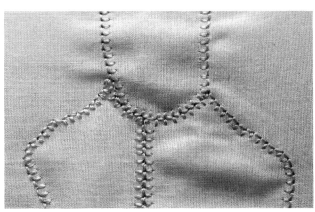

Dividing lines. Butt stitches together where two areas of design share a common design line; align stitches so they meet directly opposite each other.

How to Make Machine-stitched French Knots

1) Cover feed dogs with cover plate or lower them. Draw up bobbin thread. Stitch in place a few times to secure stitches; clip thread tails. Set machine for zigzag stitches, setting stitch width according to size of French knot desired. Stitch 10 complete zigzag stitches, or until threads begin to round over sides, forming a ball.

2) Set machine for straight stitches. Take two stitches in center of knot **(a)**. Raise presser foot. Take one stitch in front of knot, close to ball of thread **(b)**. Take two stitches in center of knot again, to secure threads **(a)**. Pull gently on tail; clip threads close to stitching.

Piecing the Background Fabric

To create an overall effect for an appliquéd project, the background may be pieced, providing a setting or backdrop for the appliqué. For example, you can create a landscape effect if the lower portion of the garment is green and the upper portion, blue. Or add textural interest to a project by using a combination of smooth and textured fabrics for the background.

The background is pieced before the appliqué is applied. To plan the placement of the design, draw the background and appliqué design lines on a full-size pattern piece. If sewing a garment, pin-fit the pattern to check the placement lines for the background fabrics; the exact position of the appliqué itself can be planned after the main garment seams are basted (pages 88 and 89).

Stitch the design lines on the background fabric, using satin stitches, to match the stitching on the appliqué.

How to Piece the Background of the Appliqué

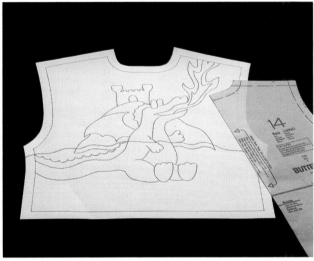

1) Make a full-size pattern piece for the garment section. Draw appliqué design, including background design lines, on pattern. Pin-fit the pattern to check placement of design lines for background fabric.

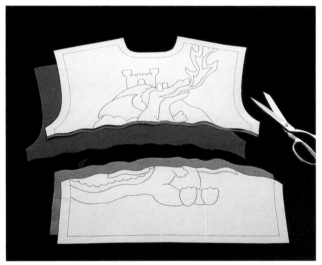

2) Cut pattern apart on design lines. Add ¼" (6 mm) seam allowance for underlap to one pattern piece at design line, using tissue paper. Cut garment pieces from fabric.

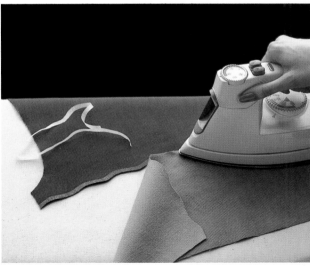

3) Cut paper-backed fusible web to size and shape of seam allowance; fuse in place on underlap of garment piece. Remove paper backing from fusible web. Overlap adjoining garment piece; fuse.

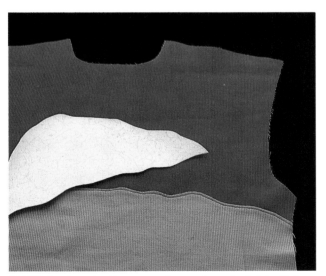

4) Stitch close to the raw edge, using straight stitch. Apply appliqué; satin stitch over the raw edge of the background when satin stitching appliqué (pages 96 and 97).

Embellishing Appliqués

To add interest and dimension to an appliqué design, appliqués can be embellished with trims. For example, a pom-pom can be used as a decorative nose for a clown or teddy bear, a buckle can be added to an appliquéd belt, or ribbons can be tied to the string of an appliquéd kite.

The fabrics used in the appliqué can be embellished with decorative machine stitches. Or hemstitching, machine embroidery, and cutwork can be used to embellish some pieces of an appliqué.

Ribbons or cords can be tacked in place or inserted under edge of appliqué before satin stitching to secure them.

Notions, such as pearls, pom-poms, or bells, can be stitched on appliqués or glued in place with permanent fabric glue.

Decorative stitching can embellish some of the appliqué pieces and add detail to the appliqué.

Movable eyes can be stitched or glued in place. Buttons can also be used for eyes.

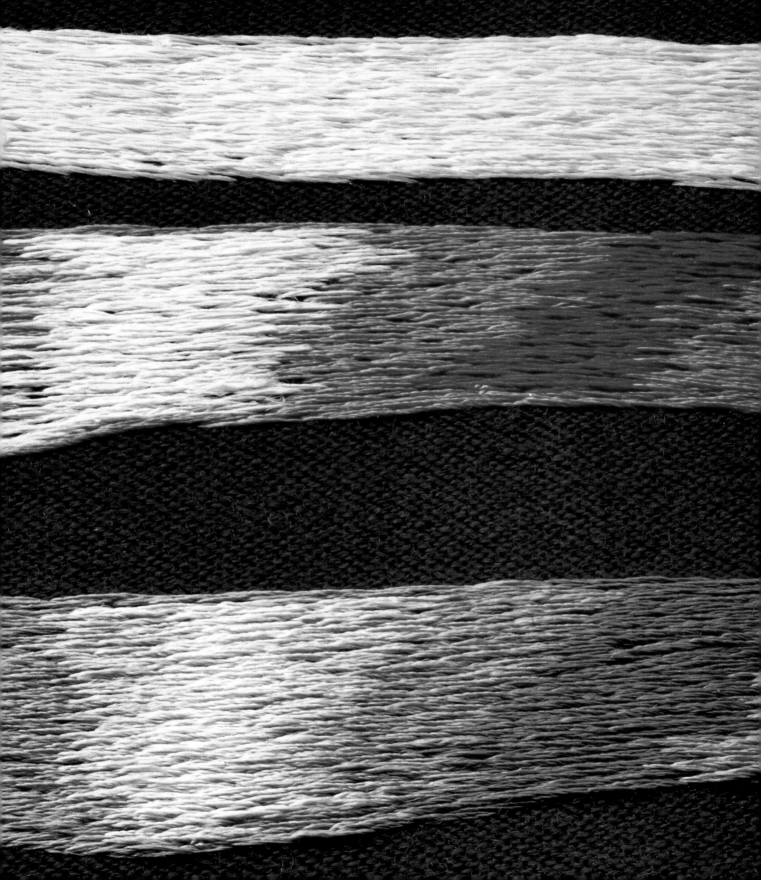

Free-motion Sewing

Free-motion Machine Embroidery

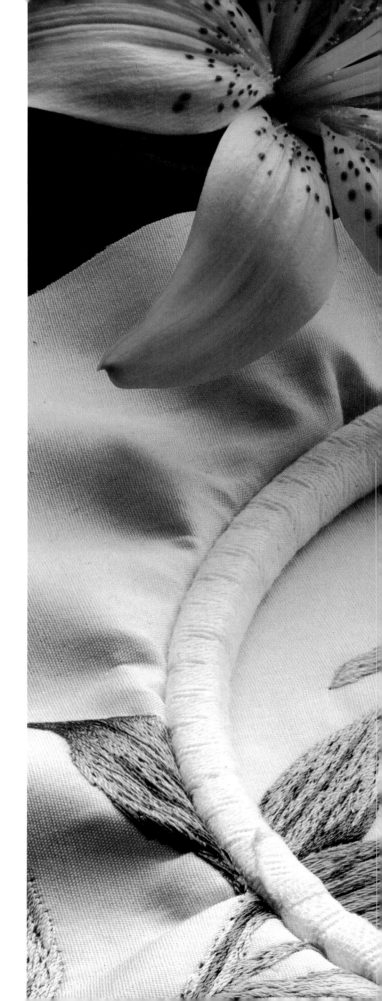

Free-motion machine embroidery offers opportunities for creativity that are not possible with the decorative stitches on your sewing machine. Use free-motion embroidery for thread painting on garments and home decorating projects, for monogramming on towels and garments, and for making Battenberg lace.

In free-motion sewing, the presser foot is removed and the feed dogs are covered with a cover plate, or lowered. The fabric is moved freely under the sewing machine needle to create a design. At first, you may feel awkward, because you feed the fabric through the machine manually instead of using the feed dog system. With practice, you will be able to slide the fabric smoothly as you stitch. You control the stitch length. Create stitches that are close together by moving the fabric slowly as you stitch.

The fabric is held taut in a 5" to 7" (12.5 to 18 cm) embroidery hoop. A wooden hoop with a fixing screw works best because it can be tightened firmly. Select a hoop that is ¼" (6 mm) thick so it will slide easily under the sewing machine needle. The hoop should also be smooth, with beveled edges, so it does not snag the fabric or scratch the bed of the sewing machine.

For best results, use machine embroidery thread (page 48). It is available in cotton, rayon, and metallic, in weights ranging from 30-weight to 60-weight. Larger design areas are filled in more quickly when heavier, 30-weight, thread is used. Finer threads fill in areas more smoothly, without thread buildup, and reduce fabric puckering. Cotton basting thread or fine monofilament nylon thread may be used in the bobbin instead of machine embroidery thread. It is not necessary for the bobbin thread to match the color of the needle thread.

You may find it necessary to use tear-away stabilizer under the fabric to prevent puckering, especially if the embroidery design area is large. Stabilizers also help prevent thread breakage and skipped stitches. It is not necessary to place the stabilizer in the hoop with the fabric; it can be placed under the hoop as you stitch.

Use a sharp, new needle for machine embroidery. Even a slightly damaged or dull needle can cause broken threads or skipped stitches. For sewing with cotton machine embroidery thread, use a fine needle in size 70/9 or 80/11. Use a size 80/11 or 90/14 with rayon machine embroidery thread.

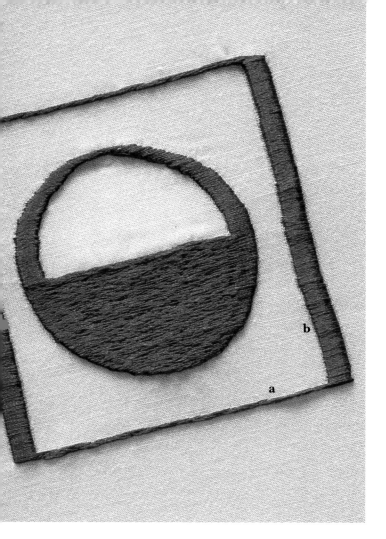

Getting Ready to Sew

To prevent the fabric from loosening or slipping while stitching, wrap the inner ring of the embroidery hoop with cotton twill tape, or glue velvet ribbon to the outside edge of the inner ring. Then position the fabric firmly in the hoop.

To become familiar with the techniques of free-motion embroidery, it is helpful to practice sewing the side stitch **(a)** and satin stitch **(b).** The side stitch is formed as you move the fabric sideways; the width of the side stitches is determined by the stitch width setting and the density of the embroidery. The satin stitch is sewn as you move the fabric slowly toward you or away from you; the width of the satin stitches is determined by the stitch width setting.

The circle and square design is helpful for learning the basic techniques. Use machine embroidery thread (page 48) when you are practicing and adjust the tension of the machine, if necessary, so the bobbin thread does not show on the right side of the fabric (page 52).

It is easier to sew in free motion if you are relaxed. Rest your hands comfortably on the sides of the embroidery hoop; do not grip the hoop. Run the machine at a moderate to fast speed, but move the hoop slowly as you stitch, so the stitches will be close together and filled in.

How to Prepare the Embroidery Hoop

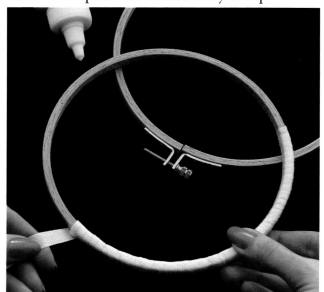

Twill tape method. Secure one end of narrow, cotton twill tape to inner ring of hoop with fabric glue. Wrap ring in diagonal direction, overlapping tape by half its width; pull firmly while wrapping. Secure other end of tape with glue. Allow glue to dry before using the hoop.

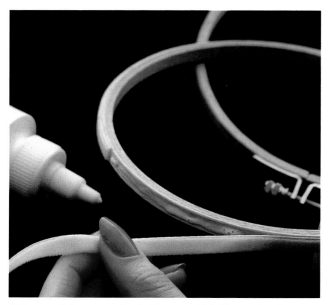

Velvet ribbon method. Secure ¼" (6 mm) velvet ribbon with fabric glue to outside edge of inner ring. Allow glue to dry before using hoop.

How to Prepare the Practice Fabric

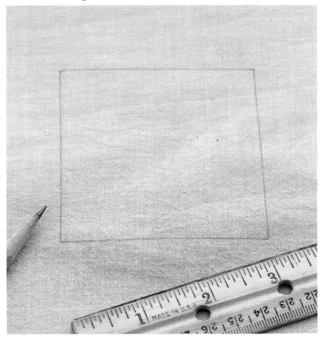

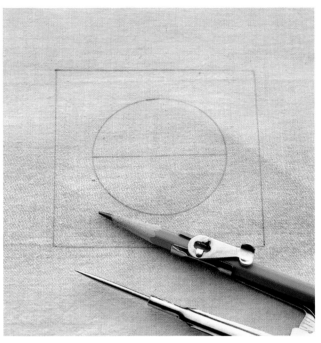

1) Cut 12" (30.5 cm) square of muslin or organdy. In center of fabric, draw a 3" (7.5 cm) square, using a lead pencil or water-soluble or fine-tip permanent marking pen.

2) Draw 2" (5 cm) diameter circle inside the square; draw horizon line through center of circle; this line must be kept horizontal at all times as you sew.

How to Position the Fabric in the Embroidery Hoop

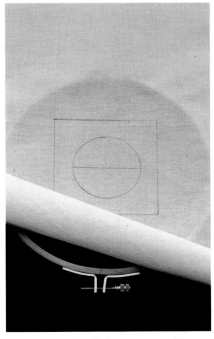

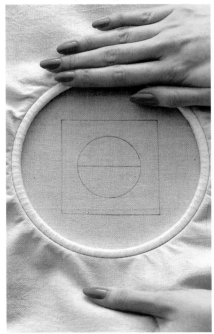

1) Loosen the fixing screw of hoop slightly with screwdriver to separate rings. Place outer ring on table, with screw facing toward you. Place the fabric over the hoop, right side up, centering design.

2) Push inner ring into outer ring with heels of your palms, making sure fabric is taut. Partially tighten screw and gently pull fabric edges evenly until fabric is very taut; do not distort grainline.

3) Push inner ring to underside about ⅛" (3 mm); this helps to tighten fabric. Tighten screw with screwdriver to prevent fabric from slipping or loosening as you stitch.

How to Practice Free-motion Embroidery

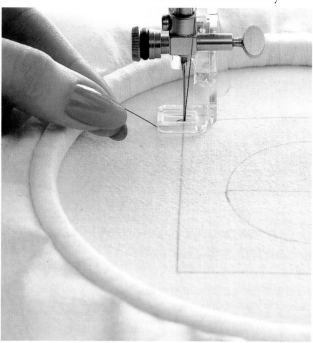

1) Adjust tension (page 52). Cover feed dogs with cover plate or lower them. Attach darning foot. Set stitch width to 0. Draw up bobbin thread at upper left corner of square. Holding threads, stitch in place a few times to secure stitches.

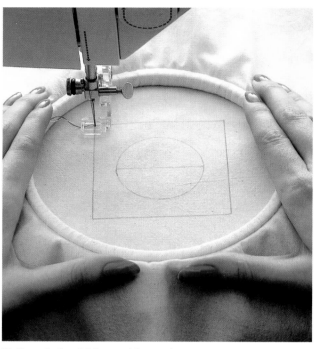

2) Set stitch width to wide setting. Rest hands on sides of hoop; do not grip hoop. Sit comfortably, directly in front of needle.

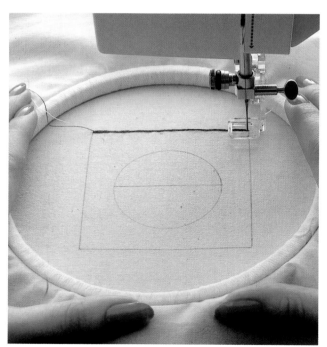

3) Stitch at moderately fast speed, moving hoop sideways slowly to sew side stitch. Clip thread tails from starting point.

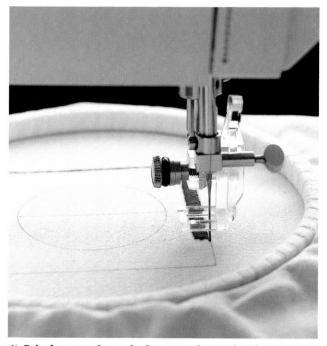

4) Stitch at moderately fast speed, moving hoop away from you to sew satin stitch. Practice stitching so fabric does not show between the stitches; stitch back over the previous stitches to fill in, as necessary. (Darning foot was raised to show detail.)

5) Continue around square, moving hoop sideways to sew side stitch. Then move hoop toward you to sew satin stitch on last line of square. Set stitch width to 0 and secure stitches.

6) Lift darning foot; pull threads to edge of circle near horizon line. Set stitch width to 0 and secure stitches; reset stitch width to wide setting. Move hoop smoothly sideways, forward, or backward as you stitch around circle. Do not turn hoop; keep horizon line horizontal. Set stitch width to 0 and secure stitches.

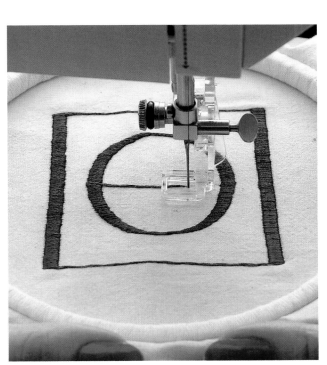

7) Clip needle thread carried from outer design area. Set stitch width to wide setting. Stitch across horizon line, using side stitch.

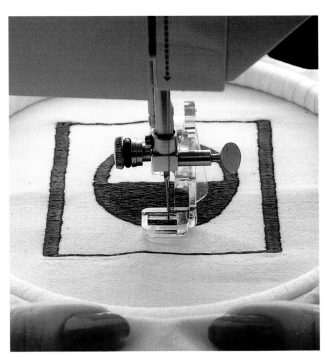

8) Continue stitching rows from side to side across circle, with each row next to the previous row, until one half of circle is filled in; allow stitches to run into outline of circle to prevent a line around circle. Stitch other half of circle.

Thread Sketching

Thread sketching is done by stitching with the needle as if you were using a pencil to draw lines. Use free-motion techniques and the straight stitch.

Thread painting looks similar to hand embroidery fill-in stitches. Free-motion machine embroidery techniques are used to fill in an entire design area with thread. For the fill-in stitches, use the zigzag stitch in a stitch width that is appropriate for each design area. Change the stitch width, as necessary, from one area to another.

Tips for Thread Sketching and Thread Painting

Use needle to thread-sketch marked design lines on fabric or to sketch free-form shapes.

Draw directional or horizon lines as a guide for filling in areas of the design with thread painting.

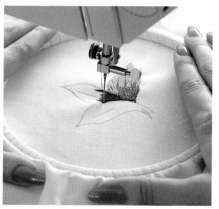

Start stitching on areas that are farthest away from you or those that appear to be under other areas.

Thread Painting

Both techniques can be used to embellish solid-color fabric or to emphasize the design of a printed fabric, adding texture and dimension to the fabric. The basic free-motion techniques on pages 116 to 121 are used for both thread painting and thread sketching. Set the stitch width to 0 and stitch in place a few times to secure the stitches when moving from one area to another, or when changing thread colors.

How to Shade Areas in Thread Painting

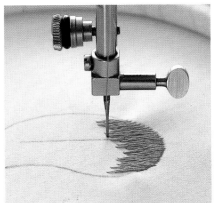

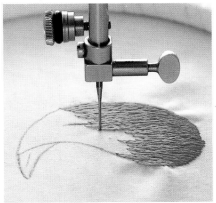

1) Stitch in place at edge of design area, such as base of petal or leaf. Outline and fill in portion of design for first thread color, working from base out; leave a jagged edge for blending in next color. Stitch in place at end to secure stitches.

2) Change thread color; stitch in place at jagged edge of design area. Using fill-in stitches, stitch second color, blending into jagged, open areas of first color. Continue blending new colors along edges of previous colors to complete design.

3) Use a dark, contrasting thread color to add accent stitching, if desired. Using narrow zigzag stitch or straight stitch, sew along edge of design and on design lines, such as veins in leaf.

Secrets of Lace Embroidery

Make a garment special by adding an inset yoke of delicate lace embroidery. Or create a lace collar that can be used with many different garments.

Lace can be embroidered on a conventional sewing machine, with the presser foot removed; on some machines, a darning foot may be used. Two layers of tulle are placed over water-soluble stabilizer and held firmly in an embroidery hoop.

The lace is stitched with a fine needle and machine embroidery thread. Or use silk or rayon thread to add luster to the embroidery stitches. Stitch over the design several times for more definition.

How to Make Embroidered Lace

1) Transfer embroidery design to the tulle, using a water-soluble marking pen.

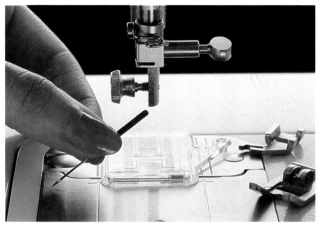

2) Remove presser foot. Cover feed dogs with feed cover plate, or lower them. Loosen tension, and release pressure on presser foot. Insert fine needle.

3) Place two layers of tulle, with a double layer of water-soluble stabilizer underneath, upside down in embroidery hoop. Place hoop under needle. Lower presser foot lifter to control tension on upper thread.

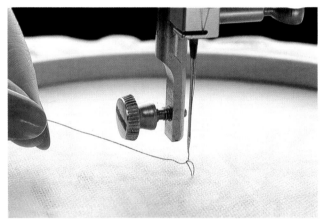

4) Set machine for straight stitching. Rotate the handwheel, while holding needle thread, to bring bobbin thread to the top of the work. Stitch several stitches in one spot to anchor threads. Clip thread tails.

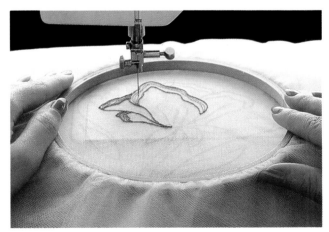

5) Hold hoop flat against bed of the machine with both hands. Run the machine at a steady pace, and trace the outline of design, using the needle as a pencil; keep hoop facing in one direction.

6) Remove lace and stabilizer from hoop. Carefully tear away as much of the stabilizer as possible. Dip lace in cold water to remove any traces of stabilizer and marking pen. Press.

Battenberg Lace

Battenberg lace, which has been made by hand since the seventeenth century, can now be made using machine embroidery techniques on the sewing machine. The lace is made using a decorative tape, called Battenberg tape, that is arranged and pinned to water-soluble stabilizer. The open areas in the design are embellished with fill-in stitches, using a balanced tension on the machine and free-motion stitching techniques (pages 116 to 121).

The two types of Battenberg tape, flat-edge and picot-edge, are available in various widths and colors. The straight edges of Battenberg tape have a heavy cord, or gimp, that is pulled to shape the tape as it curves. Battenberg tape does not have a right or a wrong side, so it can be folded back on itself to shape points or corners.

Patterns for Battenberg designs are available from pattern companies and from some fabric stores and craft stores. Also, patterns are included in some magazines that specialize in lacemaking.

If you are using a pattern designed for Battenberg lace, the yardage requirements for the tape will be listed in the pattern. Or you can determine the yardage by measuring the design, as shown below. Keep the Battenberg tape in workable lengths of one to two yards (0.95 to 1.85 m); tape can be pieced at any point in the design where the tape overlaps.

The stitching is done with machine embroidery thread that matches the Battenberg tape. Use the same thread in both the needle and the bobbin. A 50-weight or 60-weight cotton thread should be used to secure the tape to the stabilizer and a 30-weight cotton or rayon thread for the fill-in stitches. A size 70/9 or 80/11 needle is recommended for use with machine embroidery thread; do not use a needle smaller than a size 80/11 with rayon thread.

Use a 6" to 10" (15 to 25.5 cm) wooden embroidery hoop with a fixing screw, or a spring hoop; the spring hoop may not stretch or distort the tape as much as the wooden hoop. The hoop may be wrapped with twill tape (page 118) to help hold the stabilizer taut. For larger pieces of lace, you may need to move the hoop to stitch the lace in sections.

Types of Battenberg Tape

Battenberg tape is available in two types: straight-edge tape with two straight edges, and picot-edge tape with one picot and one straight edge.

How to Calculate Yardage for Battenberg Tape

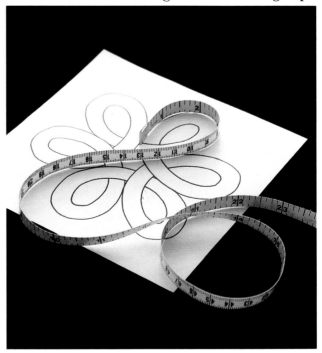

Measure around design, standing tape measure on its edge. Add 3" (7.5 cm) to this measurement for finishing the ends.

How to Make Battenberg Lace

1) Position water-soluble stabilizer in embroidery hoop (page 119). Pin pattern for lace to foam board or Styrofoam®; place hoop over pattern. Trace design on stabilizer, using either a water-soluble or a permanent marking pen. Remove pattern.

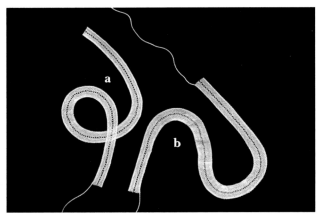

2) Locate gimp cord at edge of tape. Pull out 15" to 20" (38 to 51 cm) of gimp; gather tape, leaving first several inches flat. For designs with inside curves, pull gimp on one edge only **(a)**. For designs with inside and outside curves, pull gimp on both edges, pulling from opposite ends of tape **(b)**.

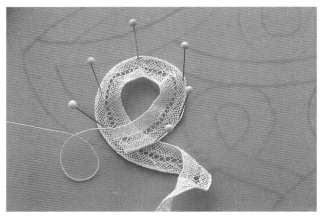

3) Pin outer edge of tape through stabilizer to foam board in shape of design; inner edge will not lay flat. End of the tape should be covered by another layer; place end on top. (Right side of lace faces down.)

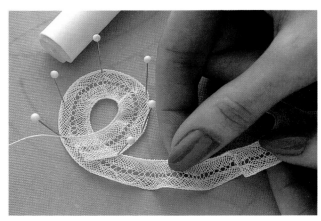

4) Push gathers up toward pinned area, easing and shaping inner curve so it lays flat. When tape is shaped, remove pins and apply glue stick to right side; repin, as necessary.

5) Repeat steps 3 and 4 for each loop or section. It may be helpful to remove pins from previous loops after glue has set.

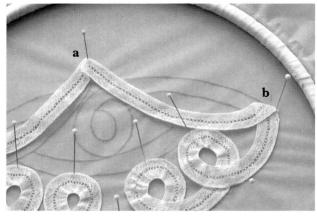

6) Pinch tape to shape corners of design **(a)**. Or fold tape back on itself at corners **(b)**.

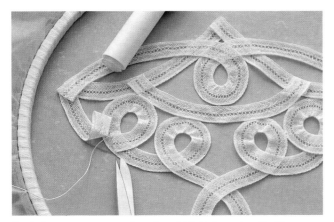

7) Trim excess tape, leaving ½" (1.3 cm) tail. Use additional pieces of tape, if necessary, to complete design. Fold under all ends of tape to secure and hide raw edges. Trim excess gimp. Remove pins.

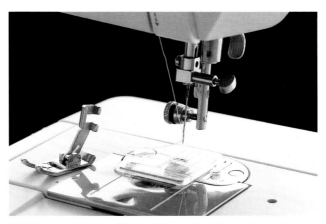

8) Thread the machine with embroidery thread; use same thread for needle and bobbin. Adjust machine for balanced tension (page 52). Cover the feed dogs with cover plate or lower them. Remove presser foot; lower presser foot lifter.

9) Stitch around outer edge of tape, using straight stitch; stitch through all layers where tape overlaps. (Contrasting thread was used to show detail.)

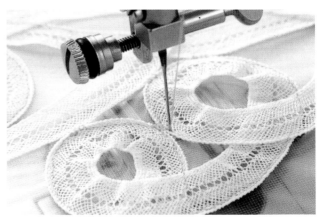

10) Secure edges of tape, where they abut, with three or four stitches, using straight-stitch zigzag. Do this by moving hoop slightly from side to side so needle catches first one side, then the other.

11) Continue stitching until all outer edges of tape are secure. Repeat for inner edges.

12) Sew desired fill-in stitches (pages 130 to 135) in open areas, using free-motion techniques; use machine embroidery thread in needle and bobbin.

Battenberg Fill-in Stitches

There are several kinds of fill-in stitches. Some of the traditional stitch patterns are (clockwise, starting at top) richelieu bars, point duchesse or Y-stitch, bundled bars, grid work, and spider web or windmill. The stitches may be combined in a Battenberg lace design (center).

There are two methods for making Battenberg stitches. One method uses the straight stitch and a technique referred to as *straight-stitch zigzag* to wrap the filler cords. For this method, the water-soluble stabilizer is removed from the centers of the loops before stitching; the stitching is then done without fabric under the needle of the machine.

The alternate method uses the zigzag stitch to wrap the filler cords; the water-soluble stabilizer is not removed until after the filler cords are wrapped. This method is used if the sewing machine skips stitches or jams when there is no fabric under the needle.

How to Sew Richelieu Bars

1) Remove stabilizer from center of loop. Mark dots on opposite sides of loop for each richelieu bar.

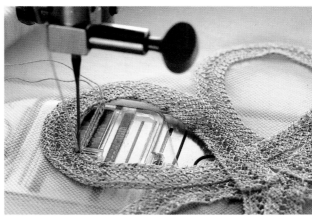

2) Draw up bobbin thread at dot for first richelieu bar; stitch in place a few times to secure stitches. Stitch to opposite dot and back about three times for filler cords, with each row of stitching beside previous row.

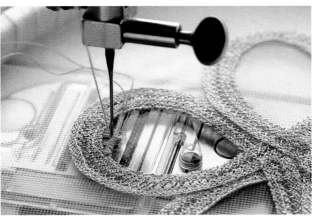

3) Stitch back over filler cords, using straight-stitch zigzag; do this by moving the hoop from side to side so stitches are taken on alternate sides of cords.

4) Stitch on tape to dot for next richelieu bar; repeat fill-in stitches for each bar. Secure the stitches after completing last bar.

Alternate method. 1) Mark dots as in step 1, above, using water-soluble marking pen; do not remove stabilizer. Secure stitches; stitch filler cords for first bar, as in step 2, above.

2) Set machine for narrow zigzag. Stitch over filler cords; move hoop slowly and stitch at moderately fast speed for satin stitches. Straight-stitch on tape to dot for next richelieu bar; repeat fill-in stitches for each bar. Secure stitches after completing last bar.

How to Sew Point Duchesse Stitches or Y-stitches

1) Remove the stabilizer from center of loop. Mark staggered dots on opposite sides of loop; dots should be no more than ¼" (6 mm) apart.

2) Draw up the bobbin thread at dot for first row; stitch in place a few times to secure stitches. Stitch to first dot on opposite side to make filler cord. Secure the stitches.

3) Stitch back over the filler cord for three or four stitches, using straight-stitch zigzag; do this by moving hoop from side to side so stitches are taken on alternate sides of cord.

4) Stitch to next dot on opposite side, stitching back over end of filler cord, as in step 3. Continue stitching in this manner to last dot. Secure stitches.

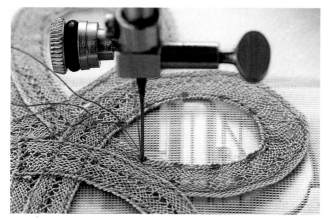

Alternate method. 1) Mark loop as in step 1, above; do not remove stabilizer. Draw up bobbin thread at dot for first row; secure stitches. Raise presser foot lifter and move hoop so threads pull across to first dot on opposite side to make filler cord; secure stitches.

2) Set machine for narrow zigzag; stitch back over thread for three or four stitches. Set machine for straight stitch; raise presser foot lifter and pull threads across to next dot on opposite side. Continue stitching in this manner to last dot; secure stitches.

How to Sew Bundled Bars

1) Remove stabilizer from center of loop. Mark top and bottom of loop; mark each side of loop into quarters. Make additional marks ⅛" (3 mm) on each side of quarter-marks.

2) Draw up bobbin thread at dot for first bar; stitch in place a few times to secure stitches. Stitch to opposite dot to make filler cord. Stitch back over filler cord, as in step 3, opposite.

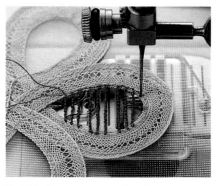

3) Stitch on tape to dot for next bar; repeat fill-in stitches for each bar. Stitch on tape to dot at top of loop. Turn hoop one-quarter turn so bars are horizontal.

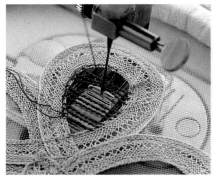

4) Stitch to first bar for center filler cord. Take one stitch over first three bars to pull them together.

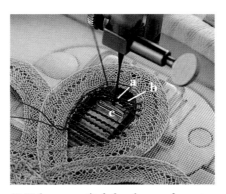

5) Take one stitch back over bars to one side of center cord (**a**). Take one stitch over center cord to other side (**b**). Take one stitch back over all three bars (**c**).

6) Stitch to next group of bars and bundle them; repeat for last group of bars. Stitch to bottom of loop; secure stitches. Stitch over center filler cord, using straight-stitch zigzag. Secure stitches.

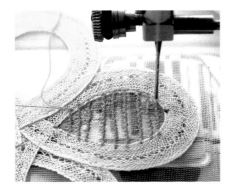

Alternate method. 1) Mark loop as in step 1, above; do not remove stabilizer. Draw up bobbin thread at dot for first bar; secure stitches. Straight-stitch to opposite dot to make filler cord. Stitch back over cord, using narrow zigzag. Stitch remaining bars. Secure stitches.

2) Remove hoop; trim stabilizer from loop, trimming close to bars and tape. Place a new layer of stabilizer under lace. Reposition in hoop.

3) Draw up bobbin thread at dot on top of loop; secure stitches. Straight-stitch to first bar for center filler cord. Push first and third bars toward center bar, using seam ripper; stitch over bars as in steps 4, 5, and 6. Stitch over center filler cord, using narrow zigzag. Secure stitches.

How to Sew Grid Work

1) **Remove** stabilizer from center of loop. Draw up bobbin thread; stitch in place a few times to secure stitches. Stitch across center of loop, using straight stitch; secure stitches. Stitch back over filler cord, using straight-stitch zigzag, as in step 3, page 131.

2) **Stitch** on tape for ¼" (6 mm). Stitch additional rows as in step 1, parallel to first row, keeping rows ¼" (6 mm) apart.

3) **Stitch** parallel rows, in the opposite direction, ¼" (6 mm) apart, as in step 1.

Alternate method. Stitch rows in both directions, as above, stitching across rows, using straight stitch, and back over rows, using narrow zigzag. Do not remove stabilizer before stitching.

How to Sew Spider Webs or Windmills

1) Remove stabilizer from center of loop. Mark top and bottom of loop; mark each side of loop into quarters. Draw up bobbin thread at dot at one end of loop; stitch in place a few times to secure stitches.

2) Stitch to opposite dot to make filler cord. Stitch back over filler cord, using straight-stitch zigzag, as in step 3, page 131. Stitch on tape to dot for next row.

3) Repeat fill-in stitches for two more rows, trying not to catch center of rows with needle. For last row, stitch to opposite dot to make filler cord and stitch back over filler cord, stopping at center.

4) Stitch around center intersection, inserting needle in each space between wrapped bars; stitch about four rows around center to build up web. Continue stitching over filler cord for last row; secure stitches.

Alternate method. 1) Mark loop as in step 1, above; do not remove stabilizer. Secure stitches at dot at one end of loop. Stitch to opposite dot, using straight stitch. Set machine for narrow zigzag; stitch back over filler cords for first row.

2) Stitch on tape to dot for next row. Follow steps 3 and 4, above, for remaining rows, using narrow zigzag to stitch back over filler cords.

Applying Battenberg Lace to a Garment

Remove Battenberg lace from the embroidery hoop immediately after you have finished making it, to prevent any permanent distortion or creasing. To preshrink the lace before it is inserted in the garment, press it with a steam iron on a cotton setting.

For a neat edge finish on a lace insert, attach the outer edge to the garment, using a narrow zigzag stitch, and trim the garment fabric close to the stitching. Edges of necklines, collars, and cuffs may be trimmed with Battenberg tape. The tape is shaped around the garment edge and attached with zigzag stitching.

How to Finish Battenberg Lace

1) Remove lace from hoop as soon as design is completed. Carefully tear away as much of the water-soluble stabilizer as possible.

2) Soak lace in cool, soapy water for about five minutes to remove excess stabilizer, water-soluble pen marks, and glue. Pat the lace dry between layers of bath towel.

3) Place lace face down on padded surface; press with iron on cotton setting to shrink tape and threads.

How to Apply Battenberg Lace to a Garment

How to Finish Garment Edges

1) Pin finished lace to fabric in desired position. Uncover feed dogs or raise them. Attach presser foot. Stitch lace to garment on outer edge of tape, using narrow zigzag stitch.

2) Cut away fabric under the lace carefully, using embroidery scissors.

Place outer edge of tape along hemline or seamline; pin. Apply liquid fray preventer to ends of tape; turn under. Zigzag on inner edge; trim fabric close to stitches. Tack ends of tape by hand.

Creating
Fabrics

Twisted Silk

The look of China silk or silk broadcloth can be changed by twisting the fabric to give it a unique texture. The fabric is first soaked in lukewarm water and then twisted tightly into a ball. The ball of twisted fabric is machine dried; the textural wrinkling that occurs is heat-set by the dryer.

A garment made from this fabric will keep its shape during wearing, but to maintain the original texture, the twisting process should be repeated each time the garment is laundered. After washing the garment, twist it back into a ball and machine or air dry it. Store the garment as a twisted ball, rather than hanging it on a hanger. For traveling, the twisted balls can be packed in the suitcase.

The easiest garments to sew from twisted fabric are straight-cut dresses, tunics, and T-shirts, using the entire 45" (1.15 m) width of the fabric. Instructions for sewing these simple garments are given on pages 142 and 143. Or finish the edges of a length of twisted silk with a narrow hem as on page 143, step 5, to make a scarf or belt.

How to Make Twisted Silk

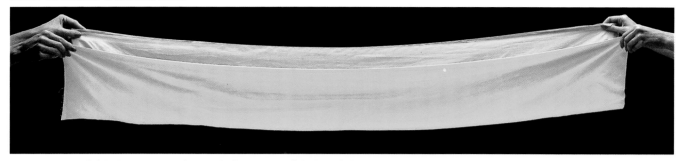

1) **Cut** ends of fabric on crosswise grainline. Soak fabric in lukewarm water until thoroughly wet; squeeze out excess water. Fold fabric in half lengthwise, with one person at each end of fabric; then fold in half again lengthwise.

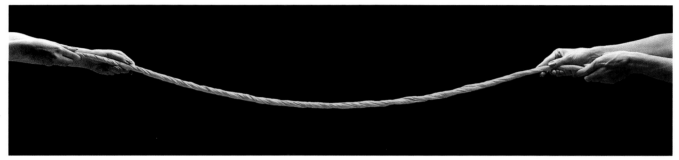

2) **Gather** ends of fabric in hands. Twist fabric in opposite directions, squeezing out any bubbles that form while twisting; continue until fabric is twisted as tightly as possible and begins to curl.

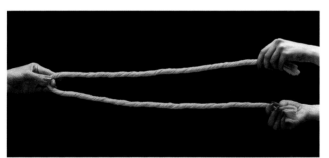

3) **Fold** fabric in half crosswise, with one person holding both ends and other person holding the loop.

4) **Twist** fabric as tightly as possible until it curls into a small, twisted ball.

5) **Wrap** white cotton string around ball of fabric until it is held securely and will not unwind. Take care that twisted ends of fabric are secured under string.

6) **Place** ball in toe of white hosiery, so ball will not unwind. Dry fabric in clothes dryer with towels; towels absorb moisture and help reduce noise. Ball of 2 to 3 yards (1.85 to 2.75 m) of fabric may take more than 3 hours to dry.

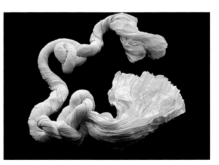

7) **Insert** finger into middle of ball to check for dryness. When ball is thoroughly dry, untwist fabric; if fabric is damp when untwisted, there will be unpleated areas in the finished fabric.

Sewing Garments from Twisted Silk

To sew a simple dress or blouse from twisted silk, the entire width of the 45" (1.15 m) fabric is used. You will need a length of China silk or silk broadcloth, twice the desired length of the garment plus 2" to 3" (5 to 7.5 cm) per yard (0.95 m) for shrinkage. Prepare the twisted silk fabric as on pages 140 and 141.

The neck opening of the garment can be cut to any shape. A bateau, or boat, neckline, 11" (28 cm) wide, or a round neckline, 8½" to 9½" (21.8 to 24.3 cm) wide, works well. Check to see that the neck opening is large enough for the garment to be pulled over the head easily.

How to Sew a Twisted-silk Dress or Blouse

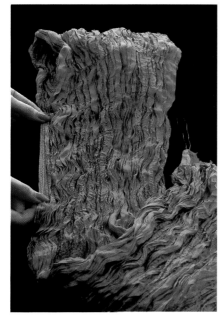

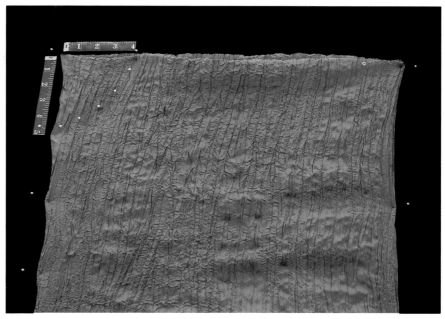

1) Fold fabric in half crosswise, right sides together, with raw edges even and selvages matching. Stitch side seams the width of selvage, stitching from raw edges to about 9" (23 cm) from foldline. Selvages remain unstitched at armholes.

2) Fold in half lengthwise on padded surface, matching side seams and crosswise folds at upper edge. Pin armholes to surface. Pull fabric to smooth out wrinkles; pin. Measure and cut neck opening. For round neckline, cut neck opening 4" (10 cm) from center fold, curving to 4" to 5" (10 to 12.5 cm) below crosswise foldline at center. For bateau neckline, cut opening 5½" (14 cm) from center fold, curving to 1½" (3.8 cm) below foldline at center.

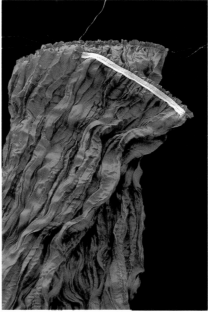

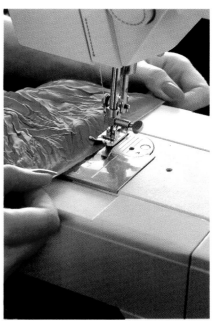

3) Baste ¼" (6 mm) from foldline at shoulders, stitching through both layers. Pull basting thread to gather shoulder seams. For a sleeveless garment, gather seams to 4½" to 5" (11.5 to 12.5 cm) length. For cap sleeves, gather seams to 7½" to 9" (19.3 to 23 cm) length.

4) Cut seam binding ¾" (2 cm) shorter than the shoulder seam; center under seamline. Stitch the shoulder seam on gathering threads, using short stitch length and catching seam binding in stitching. Tack seam allowances to one side at sleeve edge.

5) Stitch narrow hem along the neckline and hemline, using wide zigzag stitch and short stitch length, stitching off the edge of fabric slightly so edge will roll.

Acid-washed Silk

China silk, silk broadcloth, or silk charmeuse can be acid-washed, using white vinegar, to change the appearance and feel, or hand, of the fabric. The vinegar gives the fabric a sueded effect, and also helps to set the color. The silk should be soaked thoroughly in warm water before it is washed with the vinegar so the fabric will absorb the vinegar evenly, resulting in an even color throughout the acid-washed silk.

Acid-washed silk can be washed and dried by machine; little or no pressing is needed if it is removed from the dryer immediately.

Because silks may shrink 2" to 3" (5 to 7.5 cm) per yard (0.95 m), allow extra fabric when calculating yardage for your garment or project.

1) Finish raw edges of fabric. Soak fabric in warm water until thoroughly wet; squeeze out excess water.

2) Fill washing machine with hot water to a low water level. Add 2 cups (0.47 l) white vinegar; agitate a few minutes to distribute vinegar. Place fabric in machine and agitate 12 minutes; follow with the usual rinse and spin cycles.

Before and after. Before silk is acid-washed, it is shiny and smooth (top). Afterward, it has a matte or sueded appearance and a soft, suedelike hand (bottom).

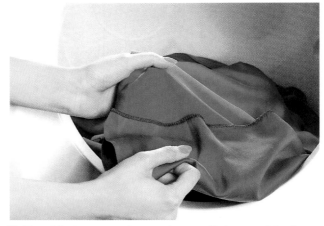

3) Dry fabric at regular setting until thoroughly dry. Repeat washing and drying once or twice, until desired effect is achieved. If pressing is required, press lightly to prevent fabric shine.

Skirt and scarf were made from unfelted fabric. The remaining fabric was felted for the jacket.

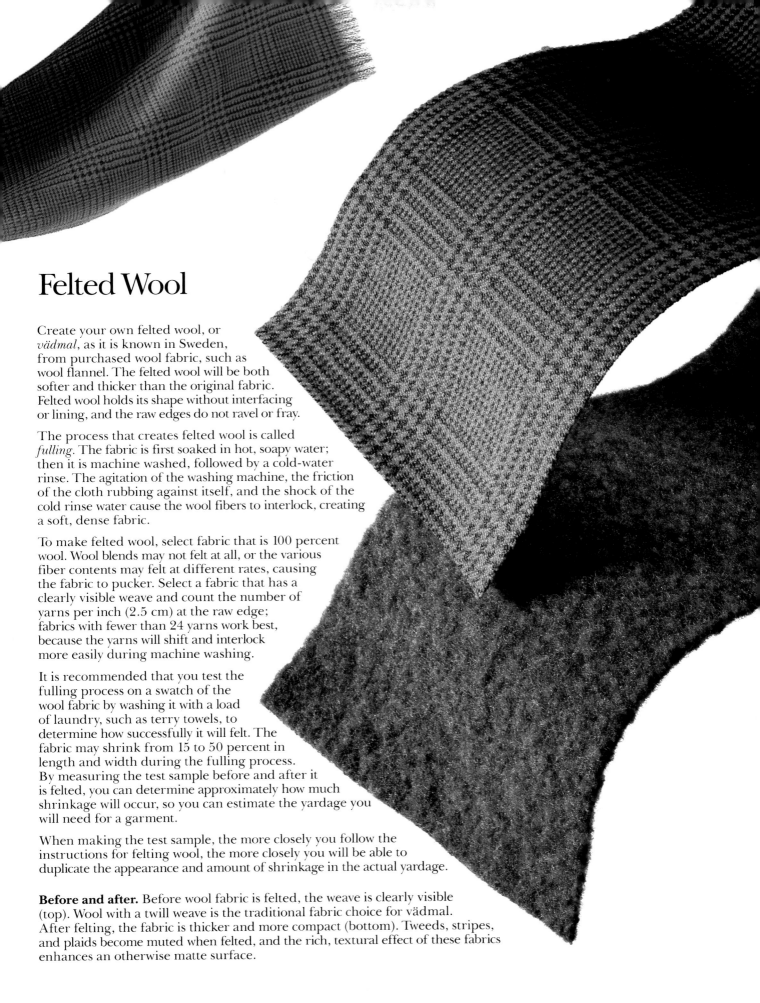

Felted Wool

Create your own felted wool, or *vädmal*, as it is known in Sweden, from purchased wool fabric, such as wool flannel. The felted wool will be both softer and thicker than the original fabric. Felted wool holds its shape without interfacing or lining, and the raw edges do not ravel or fray.

The process that creates felted wool is called *fulling*. The fabric is first soaked in hot, soapy water; then it is machine washed, followed by a cold-water rinse. The agitation of the washing machine, the friction of the cloth rubbing against itself, and the shock of the cold rinse water cause the wool fibers to interlock, creating a soft, dense fabric.

To make felted wool, select fabric that is 100 percent wool. Wool blends may not felt at all, or the various fiber contents may felt at different rates, causing the fabric to pucker. Select a fabric that has a clearly visible weave and count the number of yarns per inch (2.5 cm) at the raw edge; fabrics with fewer than 24 yarns work best, because the yarns will shift and interlock more easily during machine washing.

It is recommended that you test the fulling process on a swatch of the wool fabric by washing it with a load of laundry, such as terry towels, to determine how successfully it will felt. The fabric may shrink from 15 to 50 percent in length and width during the fulling process. By measuring the test sample before and after it is felted, you can determine approximately how much shrinkage will occur, so you can estimate the yardage you will need for a garment.

When making the test sample, the more closely you follow the instructions for felting wool, the more closely you will be able to duplicate the appearance and amount of shrinkage in the actual yardage.

Before and after. Before wool fabric is felted, the weave is clearly visible (top). Wool with a twill weave is the traditional fabric choice for vädmal. After felting, the fabric is thicker and more compact (bottom). Tweeds, stripes, and plaids become muted when felted, and the rich, textural effect of these fabrics enhances an otherwise matte surface.

How to Make a Test Sample of Felted Wool

Cut a piece of 100% wool fabric 12" (30.5 cm) long by width of fabric. Overlap and baste selvages together. Soak test sample in hot, soapy water for 30 minutes. Then wash sample with a load of laundry, such as towels, and dry it, following instructions for making felted wool as closely as possible (pages 149 to 151).

2) Measure length of felted test sample; divide by original length of sample, 12" (30.5 cm).

How to Determine Yardage of Wool Required

1) Remove basting stitches and measure width of felted test sample. Determine length required to lay out pattern on this width of fabric by referring to pattern envelope or by laying out pattern pieces on another fabric folded to this width.

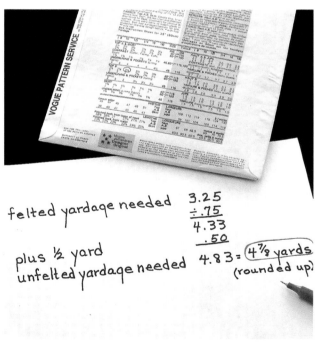

3) Divide length requirement from step 1 by result of step 2. Add ½ yard (0.50 m) to allow for possible ruffling at cut ends. This is the length of wool fabric needed for felting.

How to Make Felted Wool

1) Finish raw edges of wool, if desired. Overlap and baste selvages together to form a tube. This prevents fabric from becoming twisted around the agitator of washing machine and prevents or minimizes ruffled or uneven appearance at edges.

2) Soak fabric for 30 minutes in 100° to 120°F (42° to 49°C) hot, soapy water. This evenly wets the fabric, preventing uneven fulling, and begins to open up the wool fibers. Drain water, and remove fabric.

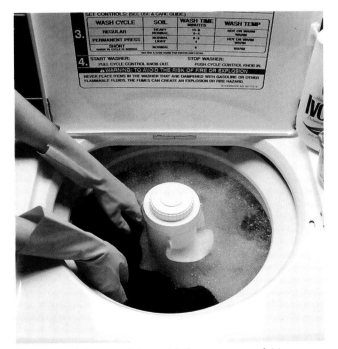

3) Fill washing machine with hot water and ½ cup (119 ml) liquid dishwashing soap. Coil wet fabric loosely around agitator. For small load, it may be necessary to add a terry towel to balance the load. Place lint filter over end of washing machine hose to collect lint.

4) Check fabric about every five minutes during wash cycle, wringing out a section to examine texture. The longer the fabric is washed, the thicker it becomes. Stop washing when desired appearance is reached. Do not felt the fabric too much; process may be repeated if more felting is desired.

(Continued on next page)

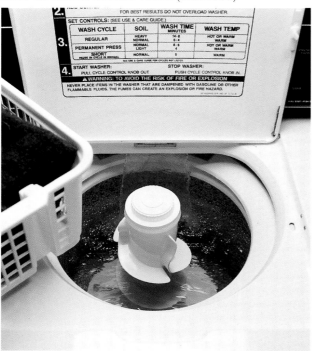

5) Spin dry fabric, using delicate cycle so wrinkles will not be set into fabric. Remove fabric from washing machine while cold rinse water enters machine; impact of rinse water onto fabric may cause uneven felting.

6) Return fabric to washing machine for cold-water rinse cycle. Spin dry, using delicate cycle for one minute or less, to remove most of the water without causing permanent wrinkles.

7) Remove fabric from washing machine immediately. Remove basting stitches.

8) Shake fabric. Remove any creases by pulling fabric sharply several times.

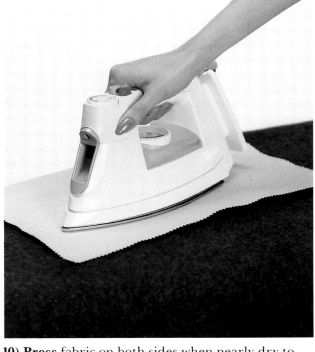

9) Machine dry fabric, using low temperature setting, if more felting is desired; check fabric frequently to prevent too much felting. Or hang fabric over heavily padded clothesline to dry.

10) Press fabric on both sides when nearly dry to the touch, using lots of steam; use press cloth or iron soleplate guard to prevent scorching or a shiny surface. Pressing helps to stabilize the fabric and smooth out the wrinkles.

11) Trim selvages from felted wool if fabric appears ruffled along selvages. If fabric is heavily felted, the selvage may not have shrunk as much as the fabric, causing ruffled appearance. Press fabric along edges after trimming selvages.

12) Hang well-pressed fabric for about 12 hours to dry completely; fabric retains a lot of moisture even after it is pressed.

151

Sewing Garments from Felted Wool

When sewing a garment from felted wool, select a pattern that has simple design lines. Because of the thickness of the fabric, avoid designs that have darts, pleats, or gathers. Felted wool may stretch somewhat, causing an unlined garment to conform to the contours of the body. If you want to prevent this, the felted wool garment may be lined.

For accuracy in cutting, the pattern should be laid out on a single layer of felted wool; make full-size pattern pieces, as necessary.

Use a size 90/14 or a 100/16 needle for sewing felted wools. For decorative seams and edge finishes, use topstitching thread, lightweight yarn, or other decorative thread.

Conventional seams (a) are sewn right sides together and pressed open. They are frequently used for a tailored appearance, although these seams may be too bulky for heavily felted wools. In conventional seams with braid trim (b), the seams are stitched wrong sides together, and the raw edges are covered with a trim, such as slentre braid (pages 228 and 229). Because the seams are enclosed on the inside, this method is especially suitable for unlined garments.

Lapped seams (c) are less bulky than conventional seams and have a sporty appearance.

Topstitched edge finishes (d) are usually used with lapped seams, because they are similar in appearance.

To eliminate bulk, you may want to sew single-layer collars and cuffs. The collar and cuffs may be attached to the garment using a conventional or lapped seam. The outer edges may be finished using the topstitched edge finish.

How to Sew a Conventional Seam

Without braid trim. Stitch seam, right sides together. Using steam, press flat; then press open over seam roll. Protect fabric with an iron soleplate guard or press cloth. Place clapper over seam; press down firmly. Hold in place until fabric is cool and dry.

With braid trim. Stitch seam, *wrong* sides together; press (left). Trim seam allowances, and cover them with braid trim. Attach braid by hand; finish ends (page 229).

How to Sew a Lapped Seam

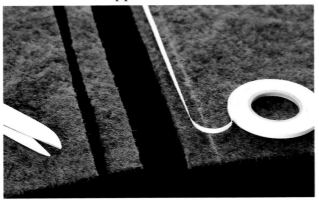

1) Trim off seam allowance from overlapping garment section. Mark seamline on right side of underlapping garment section, using chalk or water-soluble marking pen. Apply basting tape to seam allowance.

2) Align edge of overlapping section to the marked seamline. Stitch close to the edge through all layers. Remove basting tape. Stitch again ¼" (6 mm) from first row of stitching. Trim excess seam allowance on inside of garment.

How to Sew a Topstitched Edge Finish

1) Turn under seam or hem allowance; press. Stitch a scant ⅜" (1 cm) from pressed foldline; stitch again close to edge.

2) Trim excess seam or hem allowance from wrong side of garment.

Creative Lace

A large variety of laces (above) is available in fabric stores or by mail order. You can choose from many already-embellished laces, or add embellishments such as sequins, beads, soutache, and ribbon to plain lace. Color accents for lace include silvers and rainbow-hued iridescents as well as black accents on black lace for evening or white on white for the bride.

Lace fabric may be purchased and then embellished for a bodice or skirt of a garment. Or using appliqués or insets on a wide range of garments is an easy way to add just a touch of lace. Lace appliqués and lace sections of a garment combine well with traditional fabrics, such as velvet, satin, and taffeta; or add lace to a tailored wool garment or a denim jacket to soften the look. Choose the type of lace according to the weight of the fabric with which it will be combined. For example, for a wool or denim jacket, use a heavier crocheted cotton lace.

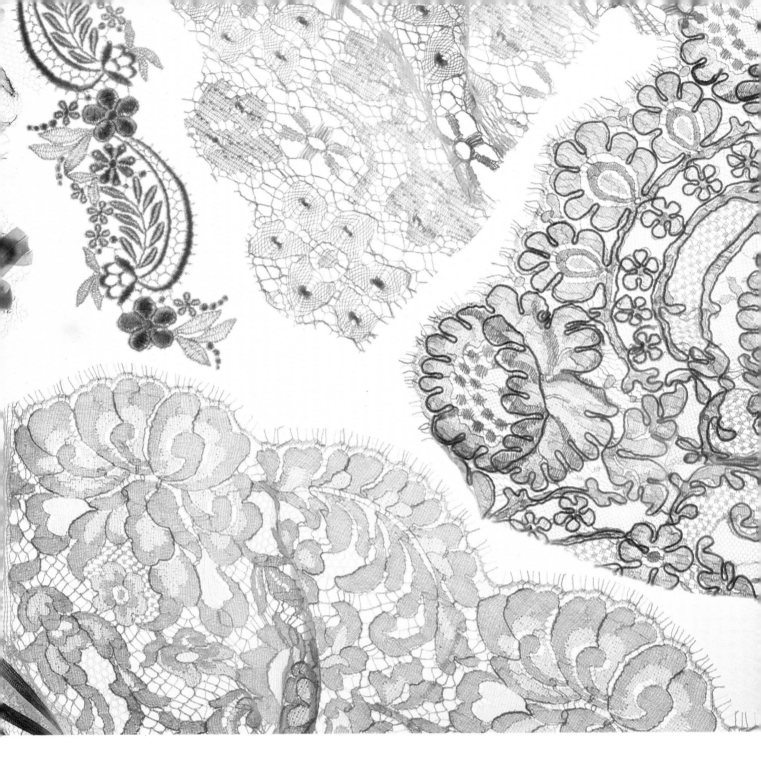

Tips for Sewing Lace

Use as few seams as possible. Choose a pattern with a simple design, and eliminate any unnecessary seams, such as straight center front or center back seams.

Wrap the toes of the presser foot with transparent tape, or cover the lace with tissue paper as you stitch, if the toes get caught in the lace while sewing. If the lace gets pulled down through the hole in the general-purpose or zigzag needle plate, put tissue paper under the fabric.

Study the lace design before you cut, to decide where to place seams and what technique to use to sew them. Because they are see-through, laces require seams that call as little attention to themselves as possible.

Mark pattern symbols that fall in an open space on the lace by placing a small piece of transparent tape on the wrong side of the fabric, and mark the symbol on the tape.

Creative Lace Ideas

In addition to sewing with lace, create your own lace fabric by adding embellishments to the lace, piecing it, or dyeing it.

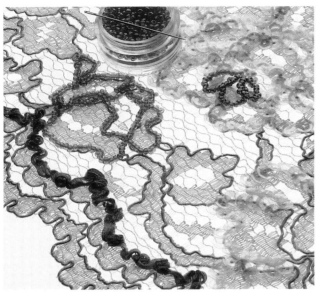

Add gathered ribbon, sequins, and strings of seed beads to lace fabric.

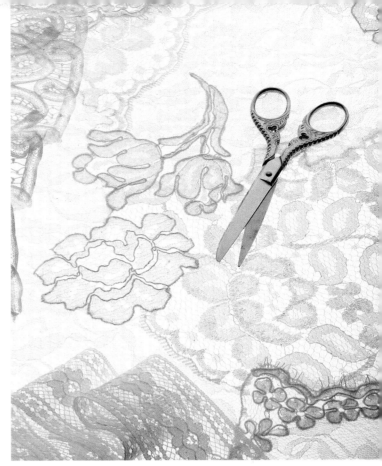

Make your own lace fabric from pieces of lace, either antique or new. Trim the underlap away. Individual motifs may be used to cover gaps between pieces. This process is similar to a crazy-quilt technique.

White lace can be dyed with tea or coffee to achieve an ecru or beige color. Test scraps of lace before dyeing entire piece. Rinse and let dry.

Creating Hand-dyed Fabric

The range of colors possible in hand-dyed fabrics is greater than that available commercially. Hand-dyed fabric gives you a sequence of colors, ranging from light to dark, or makes a smooth transition from one color to another. It also allows you to create a specific color that may not currently be in style.

Using just five colors of dye, the primaries (red, yellow, and blue) plus black and brown, you can dye literally thousands of colors. You can create fabric colors that are intense or subdued, pale or dark. You can dye fabrics in a rainbow of colors and a wide range of neutrals. The possibilities are endless.

For hand dyeing, a Procion® fiber-reactive dye is recommended. These are the dyes the textile and garment industries use. Procion dyes bond with fabric, and are lightfast and washfast. Procion dyes produce a transparent color. This means the dye penetrates the fabric rather than sitting on top. This also means the weave structure of the fabric is visible and there is no change in the feel of the fabric.

Procion dyes can be used on all natural fibers, from cotton to silk to rayon. They do not work on synthetic fabrics or blends containing synthetics. They work in a warm-water dye bath, so no heating or boiling is required, just warm tap water. And, compared to other dyes, fiber-reactive dyes are relatively safe to use.

Although these dyes are some of the safest available for hand dyeing, remember that dyes are chemicals and that dyeing is chemistry. Avoid any direct skin contact with the dyes and the setting chemicals by wearing long pants and a long-sleeved shirt, and by protecting your hands with rubber gloves. Avoid inhaling the dye powders; always use a face mask. A pollen mask is adequate unless you do a lot of dyeing, in which case, a professional respirator is recommended. Liquid Procion dyes are available, but they are somewhat less stable and less colorfast than powdered Procion dyes. However, they do not pose the hazard of breathing airborne dye particles.

Never eat, drink, or smoke while dyeing, so you do not ingest any dye powder or solution. Do not dye in your kitchen or any other eating area. Do not dye if you are pregnant. Keep dyes, as you would any chemicals, out of the reach of children. And use your dyeing equipment only for dyeing. Never use your measuring spoons and cups for cooking, too! If you follow these instructions and use common sense, dyeing can be safe.

The equipment needed for dyeing includes buckets, spoons, cups, rubber gloves, and a face mask, and can be found at your local grocery, hardware, or drugstore.

Two of the chemicals needed for dyeing are available from your grocery store: salt (either iodized or non-iodized) and water softener. Dyes, washing soda (also known as soda ash), and Synthrapol® (a special detergent) are available from weavers' supply stores or by mail order. Do not be tempted to buy washing soda from the grocery store because it contains bleach.

The easiest technique to use with fiber-reactive dyes is immersion dyeing: the fabric is put into the dye pot and comes out one color. You can modify the technique by blocking part of the fabric from dye penetration by folding and tying it.

Guidelines for Dyeing

Two basic aspects to consider when mixing colors are hue and value. Tints are lighter values; shades are darker values. It is possible to dye any color, but the way you achieve each depends on whether it is a hue, a tint, or a shade. Test the hue on a fabric scrap when mixing the dye concentrate.

	Red	**Red-Violet**	**Violet**	**Blue-Violet**	**Blue**
Red Dye	6 tsp. (30 mL)	4½ tsp. (22.5 mL)	3 tsp. (15 mL)	1½ tsp. (7.5 mL)	0
Blue Dye	0	1½ tsp. (7.5 mL)	3 tsp. (15 mL)	4½ tsp. (22.5 mL)	6 tsp. (30 mL)
	Blue	**Blue-Green**	**Green**	**Yellow-Green**	**Yellow**
Blue Dye	6 tsp. (30 mL)	3 tsp. (15 mL)	1 tsp. (5 mL)	¼ tsp. (1.25 mL)	0
Yellow Dye	0	3 tsp. (15 mL)	5 tsp. (25 mL)	5¾ tsp. (28.75 mL)	6 tsp. (30 mL)
	Yellow	**Yellow-Orange**	**Orange**	**Red-Orange**	**Red**
Yellow Dye	6 tsp. (30 mL)	5¾ tsp. (28.75 mL)	5 tsp. (25 mL)	3 tsp. (15 mL)	0
Red Dye	0	¼ tsp. (1.25 mL)	1 tsp. (5 mL)	3 tsp. (15 mL)	6 tsp. (30 mL)

Hues are created by mixing the primary colors red, blue, and yellow in various proportions. The concept is simple: red plus yellow makes orange; red plus blue makes violet; and blue plus yellow makes green. Vary the proportions, and you get greenish blues, reddish oranges, and so on.

For most colors, a total of six teaspoons (30 mL) of dye powder per yard (0.95 m) of fabric gives a strong hue. Because the primary colors have different strengths, the proportion of each color you need to mix to get a specific hue will vary. Yellow, for example, tends to be weaker than blue, so mixing three teaspoons (15 mL) of each will not give a true green; rather, more of a blue-green. The chart at left shows the proportions for mixing secondary colors, such as violet, and tertiary colors, such as red-violet and blue-violet. To create other hues, experiment to find the proper amounts to mix, always maintaining the six-teaspoon (30 mL) total per yard (0.95 m) of fabric.

When mixing two hues to produce a third hue, you can generally tell what the third hue will be by dipping a scrap of fabric into the concentrated dye mixture, as in step 2, page 162.

Tints are achieved by decreasing the amount of dye powder in a dye bath. For a medium tint, use three teaspoons (15 mL) of dye powder per yard (0.95 m) of fabric; for a light tint, try one teaspoon (5 mL) per yard (0.95 m). With few exceptions, the value of dyed fabric is determined by how much dye powder is used, not by how long the fabric sits in the dye bath. Removing fabric from the dye bath early will only result in a fabric that is less lightfast and washfast. To dye a series of tints, use half the amount of dye for each piece of fabric. For example, to make four fabrics from true blue to light blue, mix four dye baths: the first using 6 teaspoons (30 mL) of dye, the second using 3 teaspoons (15 mL) of dye, the third using 1½ teaspoons (7.5 mL), and the fourth using ¾ teaspoon (3.75 mL).

Shades are dyed by adding black or brown to a hue. Blacks and browns are very strong colors; it does not take much of them to darken a hue. Use a total of 6 teaspoons (30 mL) of dye powder per yard (0.95 m) of fabric; for example, ¼ teaspoon (1.25 mL) of brown plus 5¾ teaspoons (28.75 mL) of yellow. Experiment with proportions to achieve a particular shade.

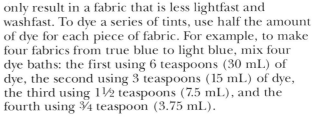

Gray shades are achieved by adding black dye to a hue.

Earth shades are achieved by adding brown dye to a hue.

Fabrics for Dyeing

Fabrics should be of all-natural fibers with no surface finish. Refer to the end of the fabric bolt to see if a fabric has been treated, for example, with a permanent-press finish. It is possible to dye a fabric with a permanent-press finish; however, it will take two to three times the amount of dye to produce a particular color, and it may be more difficult to dye it evenly.

Night-before Preparation

Wash fabric in Synthrapol® to remove sizing and to preshrink.

YOU WILL NEED

1 yd. (0.95 m) 100 percent cotton fabric, with no surface finish.

Synthrapol®, a special detergent (available from weavers' supply stores, and by mail order).

Procion® fiber-reactive dyes in red, blue, yellow, black, and brown for entire spectrum of possible colors (available from weavers' supply stores, and by mail order).

¼ cup (59 mL) washing soda, also called soda ash (available from weavers' supply stores, and by mail order). Do not use grocery store variety.

Plastic or enamel bucket, 3-gallon (11.4 L) capacity or larger.

Set of measuring spoons, set of measuring cups, plastic or wooden mixing spoons.

Rubber gloves.

Face mask (available from hardware, drug, or dime store).

1 cup (237 mL) salt, either iodized or non-iodized.

1 to 2 tablespoons (15 to 30 mL) water softener, if you have hard water.

Rubber bands or nylon cord, if tie-dying.

How to Dye One Yard of Cotton Fabric (immersion method)

1) Mix dye powder with a little hot tap water to make a smooth paste (see chart, page 160, for quantity of powder). Add 1 cup (237 mL) warm water gradually, stirring until dye is dissolved.

2) Test hue by dipping the wet fabric scrap into dye concentrate. Test will be somewhat darker than final color, because fabric is still wet and dye concentrate is darker than the final dye bath. Adjust the hue, if necessary, by adding a little more of one of original dye colors (see pages 160 to 161).

3) Fill dye pot with 2 gallons (7.6 L) hot tap water. Add 1 cup (237 mL) salt and stir until dissolved. Stir in 1 to 2 tablespoons (15 to 30 mL) water softener for hard water. Stir in dissolved dye.

4) Add clean, thoroughly wet fabric to dye bath. Wearing rubber gloves, stir with your hands for 30 minutes; keep fabric submerged. Do not allow fabric to bunch up or to float above surface.

5) Dissolve ¼ cup (59 mL) washing soda in 1 to 2 cups (237 to 473 mL) hot water and add to dye bath. Do not pour washing soda solution directly onto fabric. Stir briefly, making sure all the fabric stays submerged. Dye fabric 1 hour longer, stirring every 10 minutes.

6) Wash fabric in hot water, using Synthrapol. Dry in clothes dryer at hottest temperature for 30 minutes. Press.

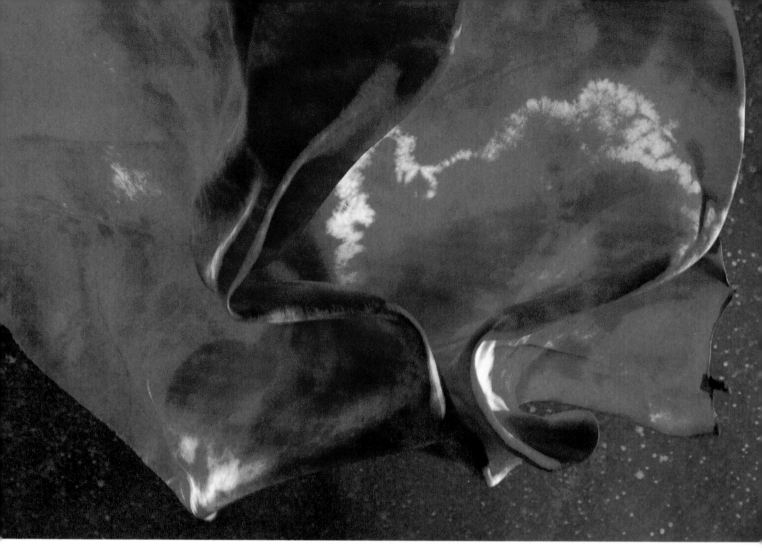

Tie-dyeing

Tie-dyeing involves folding, twisting, or scrunching fabric, then tightly tying off sections so the dye does not color the entire fabric. The tying, a resist technique, blocks part of the fabric from contact with the dye. Tie-dying is the easiest and most familiar resist technique. Rubber bands, cords, and strings are used to hold the fabric in place and block the dye from penetrating the fabric. Dye may be applied by the immersion method or direct application method.

Fabric or garments such as T-shirts, leggings, or items made of 100 percent cotton or silk may be tie-dyed. Other natural fibers including linen or rayon may be used. For silk, use cotton cord for tying. Innumerable combinations of color and patterns are possible, depending on how the fabric is folded and tied, and whether one or more colors are used. With some dyes, the various component colors penetrate fabric at different rates, resulting in a multicolored halo effect called starburst (opposite).

Folding the fabric in preparation for tying works best if the fabric is damp. Experiment with the tying techniques, using small pieces of fabric. For stripes and checks,

use a ¼-yard (0.25 m) square of fabric. For a starburst effect, use a ½-yard (0.50 m) fabric rectangle. Once you have mastered these methods of folding and tying, invent and experiment with other methods. You may want to sew your swatches together to make a unique quilt, or incorporate them into a garment as a decorative panel, a yoke, or a pocket facing.

By applying these tying techniques and color-mixing principles, you can dye fabric in any pattern, color, or range of colors imaginable. Practice using the three primary colors: red, blue, and yellow. Experiment by adding black and brown to create shades. Mix dyes to create a beautiful new color, then develop sequences of tints and shades using that color as your starting point. Or, create two new colors, and dye fabric to make a smooth transition between them. Then introduce pattern.

Immersion Method

After folding and tying, immerse the fabric bundle in a dye bath. See page 162 for a list of supplies and directions for preparing the fabric and the dye. Read the entire section on dyeing (pages 158 to 163), and follow any precautions given. Tie-dyed fabric may be immersed in successive dye baths for a multicolored effect. Fabric may also be retied and immersed to create more patterning.

Direct Application Method

The direct application method uses the same folding and tying techniques as above, but offers more control as to the placement of the dye. It is also easier to utilize more colors. The dye is applied with an applicator such as a squeeze bottle. Use the color guidelines on pages 160 and 161. Follow any precautions given on page 158.

Mix dye solution as follows to make 4 oz. (119 mL) of solution. Add 2 teaspoons (10 mL) dye, 1 tablespoon (15 mL) of urea and ⅛ teaspoon (0.7 mL) of water softener, if necessary, to ½ cup (119 mL) warm water. Mix thoroughly so dye is completely dissolved. This mixture should be used within two days. Tie or bundle as on pages 165 to 167. Apply dye directly to bundle fabric or garment from squeeze bottle. Dye may be applied exactly where desired.

Let fabric sit on newspaper for an hour to soak up excess water. Carefully wrap in plastic wrap and let sit for at least two nights to allow dye to set. Seal the plastic completely. Open and lay the fabric on "clean" newspaper to dry. Allow fabric to sit at least 24 hours before washing to ensure maximum color. Rinse the fabric under running lukewarm water. Transfer immediately to hot water with 1 teaspoon (5 mL) per gallon (3.78 L) of Synthrapol® soap or 2 to 3 tablespoons for a washer load. Wash for ten minutes and rinse. After rinse water runs clear, dry fabric in dryer.

Deep, intense color may require double or triple the amount of dye and more rinsing. Reds require a lot of rinsing.

Night-before Preparation

Wash fabric in Synthrapol to remove sizing.

Soak in bucket of soda ash solution: use one cup (237 mL) of soda ash per gallon (3.78 L) of water, and soak overnight. Do not crowd fabric.

YOU WILL NEED

Fabric or garment.

Synthrapol®, a special detergent, available at weavers' supply stores.

Procion® fiber-reactive dyes, available at weavers' supply stores.

¼ **cup (59 mL) soda ash**, available at weavers' supply stores. (Do not use grocery store washing soda.)

Set of measuring spoons, cups, and wooden mixing spoons.

Rubber gloves; face mask.

Urea, available at weavers' supply stores.

1 to 2 tablespoons (15 to 30 mL) water softener, such as Mataphos®, if you have hard water.

Squeeze bottles.

How to Make a Starburst Pattern

Immersion method. Bunch damp fabric into tight ball. Wrap tightly with nylon cord (you should not be able to get your fingers underneath cord). Tie ends to secure. Dye as on pages 162 and 163. A halo effect occurs when blue dye penetrates fibers farther than red.

Direct application method. Prepare fabric (as above) and bunch into tight ball; wrap tightly with cord. Apply dye from squeeze bottle. Follow directions (above) to complete.

How to Make a Striped Pattern

Immersion method. Fold damp fabric into pleats about 1" (2.5 cm) wide. Wrap rubber bands around pleated fabric, spacing closely for narrow stripes, farther apart for wide stripes. Dye as on pages 162 and 163.

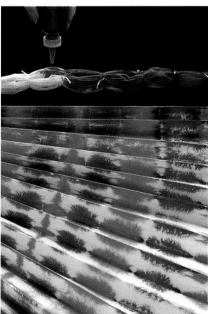

Direct application method. Prepare fabric (page 165). Fold into pleats and wrap as for immersion method (above). Prepare dye (page 165) and apply from squeeze bottle. Follow directions (page 165) to complete.

How to Make a Plaid Pattern

One-color plaid. Fold damp fabric into pleats about 2" (5 cm) wide. Fold pleated strip accordion-style, ending with a square bundle. Wrap nylon cord tightly around bundle, as if tying a package, wrapping several times in each direction. Dye as on pages 162 and 163.

Two-color plaid. Dampen dyed fabric. Refold into pleats; offset fold lines slightly from original ones, or as desired. Fold and wrap as in step 1. Dye with second color, as on pages 162 and 163.

Marbling Fabrics

Marbling is a way of decorating fabric or paper by floating pigments on a thickened water base, manipulating the pigments into a desired pattern, and transferring the pattern to fabric or paper. Probably the most familiar use of marbled paper was as endpapers in old books.

Marbling allows you to "paint" on fabric, even if you cannot draw. You do not need an extensive knowledge of color and design to produce beautiful results. It does not take a lot of space. It can be done using readily available, inexpensive materials. And the result of your efforts is unique.

Marbling is a printing process, and each print is one-of-a-kind. It can be done using paints, inks, dyes, or virtually anything that transfers color to fabric. It can work with almost any fabric, too, but usually the best results are achieved with natural fibers. Either white or colored fabrics can be used. However, the fabric color affects the results, since the coloring agents are very transparent. Texture is important, too; the smoother the surface of the fabric, the sharper the design.

To marble fabric, float drops of color on a thickened liquid base, stir them with a stick or comb to create the marbled pattern, and then lay the pretreated fabric on top to transfer the color. Rinse, dry, and heat-set, and the fabric is ready to be included in your next sewing project.

For simplicity, start with a small project, such as napkins. Use 100 percent cotton fabric and airbrush medium, a liquid paint packaged in squeeze bottles. Once you become proficient using these materials, you may want to experiment with larger pieces of fabric, other fibers, and different coloring agents. Acrylic tube paints and Turkish inks marble well, for example, and smooth silks accept the marbled color beautifully.

YOU WILL NEED

100 percent cotton fabric (must fit into pan without folding).

Ammonium alum (available from drugstores, art and craft supply stores, weavers' supply stores, and by mail order) to prepare fabric prior to marbling.

Basin or bucket for soaking fabric; rubber gloves.

Pan of nonporous material (such as a disposable aluminum pan) about 1½" to 3" (3.8 to 7.5 cm) deep and width and length larger than fabric to be marbled.

Small pan for testing how paints spread.

Carrageenan, a nontoxic emulsifier (available as a powder from art and craft supply stores, weavers' supply stores, and by mail order).

Blender for mixing carrageenan with water.

Airbrush medium in your choice of colors (available from art and craft supply stores, weavers' supply stores, and by mail order).

Orange stick or stylus and a hair pick for drawing through the paint.

Newspaper for cleaning base between prints.

Night-before Preparation

Fabric:

Wear rubber gloves when mixing ammonium alum.

Mix 4 to 6 tablespoons (60 to 90 mL) ammonium alum in 1 gallon (3.78 L) water in bucket.

Soak fabric in ammonium alum for 20 minutes, stirring once; wring fabric.

Dry mediumweight to heavyweight fabric in clothes dryer. Line dry fine cotton or silk; keep fabric wrinkle-free to avoid ammonium alum marks from uneven drying.

Press dry fabric with hot iron. Marble ammonium alum-treated fabric within one week. Wash out ammonium alum if fabric will not be marbled within one week.

Base:

Mix ½ to 1 level tablespoon (7.5 to 15 mL) powdered carrageenan in a blender full of warm water while agitating. Agitate 1 full minute.

Empty into pans. Mix more carregeenan as necessary to fill both large and small pans to depth of 1 inch (2.5 cm). Let stand overnight.

How to Marble Fabric

1) Drop paint on surface of carrageenan in small pan to test how well it floats. Drop carefully, taking care not to break surface of carrageenan. A drop should spread 1" to 3" (2.5 to 7.5 cm). If a color does not float well, add distilled water to paint, one drop at a time. If a color does not spread well, add rubbing alcohol to paint, one drop at a time. Test again.

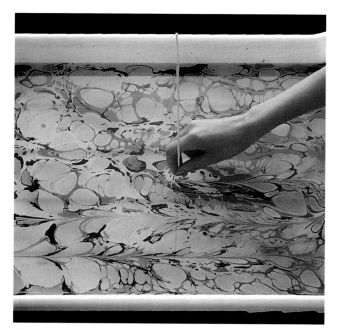

2) Drop paints on carrageenan in large pan. Draw stylus slowly back and forth across surface, at about 1" (2.5 cm) intervals. Take care not to create bubbles by drawing too fast.

3) Draw stylus up and down across surface again at 1" (2.5 cm) intervals, perpendicular to first pattern.

4) **Draw** hair pick across surface. Hair pick may be drawn in any pattern you like, but usually perpendicular to direction of last drawing works best.

5) **Lay** ammonium alum-treated fabric on the base, lowering middle first, then easing ends down so no air gets caught between fabric and pigment. Pattern will adhere almost immediately to natural fiber fabrics. For blends, pat lightly to ensure printing.

6) **Pull** fabric over edge of pan, leaving as much base as possible. Rinse under running water to remove excess paint and base. If colors rinse out significantly, increase the proportion of ammonium alum when preparing fabric. The minerals in water affect this, so judge by trial and error. Wring fabric and line dry.

7) **Clean** base before marbling another piece of fabric, using newspaper folded to width of tray. Scrape paint off surface by pulling newspaper across base. Repeat marbling process for remaining fabric, beginning with step 2. Drop paints in same sequence to color-coordinate fabric. Age marbled fabric two weeks. Set color by drying in hot dryer 30 minutes.

Discharge Dyeing

Discharge dyeing removes dye from fabric. This may result in a lighter shade of the original fabric color, or create an entirely different color. Designs are created on the fabric by removing the dye in certain areas and leaving the original fabric color in the remainder of the fabric. Dyes from some fabrics may not discharge well, causing little or no change in color.

One technique for discharging the dye from a fabric uses a liquid solution of one part household chlorine bleach and five parts water. The fabric is submerged in the solution until the color changes.

Another technique uses a discharge paste, made by mixing chlorine bleach and water with monagum powder, available from dye supply stores. The paste is applied to the surface of the fabric by painting it on or by screen printing.

For either technique, the bleach must be neutralized after the dye is discharged to prevent excessive damage to the fibers. Neutralize the bleach by soaking the fabric in a solution of one part white vinegar and two parts water. Then wash the fabric, using laundry detergent without bleaching agents.

Most fabrics of 100% rayon, cotton, or linen fibers work well for discharge dyeing. Do not discharge the dye from silk and wool fabrics, because they will deteriorate. Avoid using fabric blends, because it is difficult to discharge the dye from blends.

Test the discharge process on swatches of various fabrics to see which fabrics contain dyes that discharge and to see if you like the resulting color. To quickly test a fabric, apply a small amount of undiluted bleach. Within a few minutes, the color of the fabric should change. If not, apply a little more bleach; if the fabric dries before the color changes, it is not suitable.

Although bleach is a common household product, it is a toxic chemical that needs to be used with care. Use utensils and durable plastic or glass containers that are not used for food. Use bleach in a well-ventilated room, drawing the air flow away from you.

Jacket fabric has been discharge dyed using discharge paste.

Skirt fabric has been discharge dyed using liquid discharge solution.

Length of time needed to discharge the dye depends on the type of fabric and the amount of color change desired. Graduated colors can be made by varying the length of time the fabric stays in the discharge solution.

Discharge Dyeing Using a Liquid Discharge Solution

To discharge the dye from fabric, submerge it in a discharge solution of one part chlorine bleach and five parts water at room temperature. Use a sturdy plastic or glass container, large enough so the fabric can move freely when agitated. Mix a quantity of solution sufficient to cover the fabric in the container.

To make a design, the prewashed fabric can be bundled, using rubber bands, before it is submerged. You may want to experiment with different sizes of rubber bands; large, thick rubber bands create a different effect than small, thin ones. Wide latex strips, available from medical supply stores, may also be used.

Another way to make a design is with gathering threads. The fabric is gathered by pulling up rows of hand basting. The design you achieve depends on the placement of the stitches.

The length of time the fabric is left in the discharge solution affects the way the design will look. If the fabric is removed from the solution before the inside folds of the fabric become wet, there will be more color variation in the fabric. Keep in mind that the fabric will appear lighter after it is dried.

After the dye is discharged, the bleach is neutralized to prevent it from causing excessive damage to the fibers. This is done by soaking the fabric in a neutralizing solution of one part white vinegar and two parts water, then washing and rinsing it thoroughly.

How to Discharge Dye Using a Liquid Discharge Solution

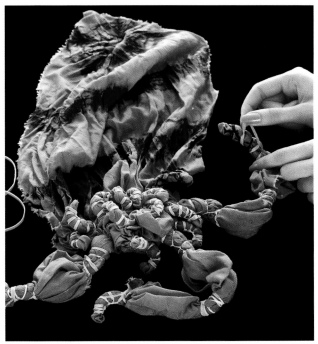

1) **Prewash** the fabric to remove sizing; machine dry. Bundle fabric (pages 176 and 177). Wet fabric thoroughly with clear water; gently squeeze out excess water. Mix discharge solution, opposite. Wearing rubber gloves, submerge fabric in solution, and agitate fabric gently for length of time desired, opposite.

2) **Rinse** the fabric thoroughly with clear, cold water, handling fabric carefully; fabric is weaker when wet. Squeeze out excess water. Remove rubber bands or gathering threads.

3) **Mix** neutralizing solution, opposite. Soak fabric in solution at least ½ hour, agitating it occasionally to ensure that solution penetrates all fibers. Gently squeeze out excess solution. Rinse with cold water.

4) **Wash** fabric thoroughly in warm water, using a mild laundry detergent without bleaching agents; rinse thoroughly. Neutralize and wash fabric again if fabric smells of bleach. If fabric smells of vinegar, wash fabric again. Line dry or machine dry fabric.

How to Bundle Fabric Using Rubber Bands or Latex Strips

Circular design. 1) Bundle fabric at center, wrapping rubber band or latex strip around fabric and twisting it on same side of bundle, as shown.

2) Continue to bundle fabric. Discharge dye, using liquid discharge solution (pages 174 and 175) or discharge paste (pages 178 and 179).

Accordion-pleated design. 1) Fold dry fabric in accordion pleats. Wrap latex strips or rubber bands around pleated fabric. Discharge dye, using liquid discharge solution (pages 174 and 175) or discharge paste (pages 178 and 179).

2) Refold dry fabric in opposite direction in accordion pleats, if windowpane effect is desired. Wrap pleated fabric, as in step 1, left. Discharge dye again, using liquid discharge solution (pages 174 and 175) or discharge paste (pages 178 and 179).

How to Bundle Fabric Using Gathering Threads

Wave design. 1) Stitch planned or random wavy lines, using hand basting.

2) Pull threads to gather fabric; knot threads. Discharge dye, using liquid discharge solution (pages 174 and 175) or discharge paste (pages 178 and 179).

Diamond design. 1) Fold fabric in half lengthwise; lay flat on padded ironing surface. Fold each half evenly in accordion pleats; press folds lightly.

2) Hand-baste evenly spaced triangles at folds, through all layers, with each triangle about half the width of folded fabric; leave thread tails. Pull threads to gather fabric; wrap tails around gathers, and knot threads. Discharge dye, using liquid discharge solution (pages 174 and 175) or discharge paste (pages 178 and 179).

Discharge Dyeing Using a Discharge Paste

To discharge the dye from fabric in specific areas, use a discharge paste, made by mixing monagum powder, water, and chlorine bleach. It is easier to control the placement of discharge paste than of liquid discharge solution, allowing you to have more control over the design.

Three tablespoons (45 mL) of monagum powder are mixed with 1 cup (0.25 L) of warm water, then allowed to set for half an hour until the paste thickens and clarifies. Chlorine bleach is added to the monagum-water paste, one teaspoon at a time, until the desired strength is achieved. Check the strength of the discharge paste on a fabric swatch after each teaspoon of bleach is added, to determine how quickly the dye discharges. The less bleach is added to the paste, the gentler it will be on the fabrics.

The discharge paste may be used at room temperature. However, if the dye tends to discharge too quickly to control the color change, the paste may be chilled in the refrigerator to slow down the reaction time.

When the paste is the desired strength, check the consistency. The paste will have been thinned somewhat by adding the bleach; however, if it is still too thick, it can be thinned by adding a small amount of water. The discharge paste can be applied to fabric that has been bundled (pages 176 and 177).

The bleach is neutralized after the dye is discharged to prevent it from causing excessive damage to the fibers. This is done by soaking the fabric in a neutralizing solution of one part white vinegar and two parts water.

How to Discharge Dye Using a Discharge Paste

Bundling. 1) Mix discharge paste, opposite. Prewash fabric to remove sizing; machine dry. Bundle fabric, using rubber bands or gathering threads (pages 176 and 177). Apply discharge paste to surface of bundled areas, or to fabric between bundles.

2) Allow paste to set until desired color change occurs; keep in mind that color will be lighter after it is dried. Rinse fabric thoroughly with running water, allowing water to flush away paste; do not rub. Squeeze out excess water.

3) Remove rubber bands or gathering threads; handle fabric carefully because it is weaker when wet. Then neutralize, wash, and dry the fabric as on page 175, steps 3 and 4.

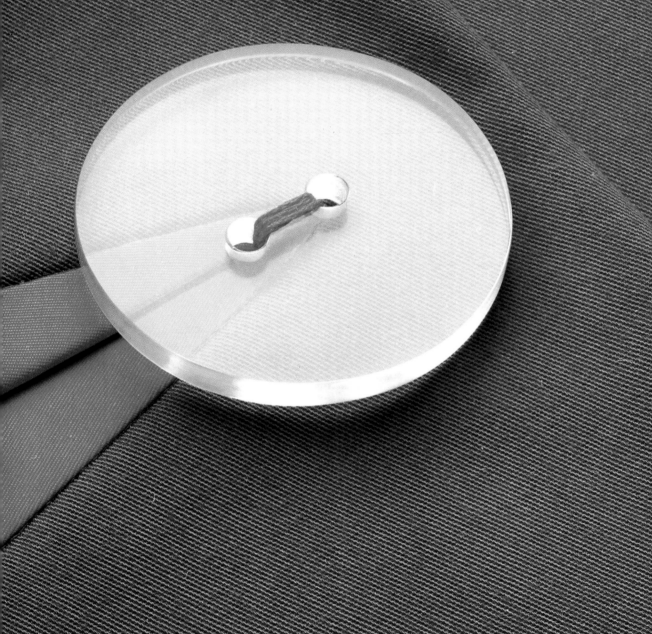

Creative Seams

Seams are a necessity in any garment, but they also provide opportunities for creativity. With unusual seaming techniques, ordinary garments become unique. These creative techniques may be used for the existing seams on a pattern or for seams you have added (page 194).

Stitch seams so the seam allowances are on the outside of the garment, then fringe or fray them for a decorative effect. Or plan the placement of the selvage along a seamline, and overlap the seam so the selvage shows. Or use a contrasting fabric as the binding for bound and lapped seams.

Frayed seams (left) are stitched wrong sides together, and the edges are then frayed by laundering, for a textured effect.

Edgestitched seams allow the inside of a reversible fabric to be seen along the seamlines for an interesting contrast. The seams are stitched wrong sides together; then the seam allowances are turned under and edgestitched.

Fringed seams offer textural interest along the seamlines. Straight-grain seams are stitched wrong sides together; then the fabric is raveled to make the fringe.

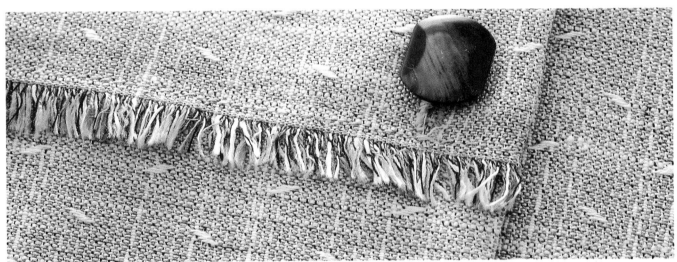

Lapped seams with exposed selvages have the look of a coordinating trim. This technique is used on fabrics that have interesting selvages.

Bound and lapped seams are stitched with contrasting binding fabric for a decorative look.

Frayed Decorative Seams

To achieve the textural effect of frayed decorative seams, the garment is washed and dried several times, until the cut edges curl and fray.

Frayed seams work best on fabrics that are 100 percent cotton or silk, including cotton or silk broadcloth, cotton flannel, and denim, but other machine-washable fabrics may be used.

Before sewing the garment, you may want to make a test sample of a seam and launder the sample to see how the fabric frays.

The same basic technique may be used to make frayed trims from strips of fabric. The trims may be made from several layers of fabric for a fuller texture.

Frayed trim can be applied in rows for a sporty effect.

How to Sew a Frayed Decorative Seam

1) Cut garment sections with desired seam allowances, from ⅜" to 2" (1 to 5 cm) wide. At the end of any seam that will be intersected by another frayed seam, cut out a square the width of the seam allowance to eliminate bulk.

2) Stitch seams, with wrong sides together and raw edges even. Clip the seam allowances to within ⅛" (3 mm) of seamline; space clips ¼" to 1" (6 mm to 2.5 cm) apart.

3) Wash and dry the garment by machine until desired curling and fraying is achieved.

How to Sew Frayed Trims

1) Mark trim placement lines on garment section. Cut one to three fabric strips for each row of trim, with length of each strip equal to length of placement line, and width two times the finished width of trim.

2) Layer strips; baste lengthwise along center, through all layers. Fold strips in half lengthwise; press. Position strip on garment section, aligning fold to placement line; pin strip in place.

3) Stitch through all layers, close to fold. Remove basting. Clip all layers of trim to within ⅛" (3 mm) of stitching line; space clips ¼" to 1" (6 mm to 2.5 cm) apart. Wash and dry garment, as in step 3, above.

Edgestitched Seams

Edgestitched seams are effective on reversible fabrics, because the inside of the fabric is exposed at the seams. Used on French terry, the seams add a subtle contrast in texture; on double-faced fabrics, the second color at the seams can be even more of a contrast. Edgestitched seams are easiest to sew on straight seams, but may be used on seams with slight curves. For garments with sleeves, select a pattern that has a raglan or dropped set-in sleeve.

Casings, seam allowances, or hem allowances can be turned to the outside of the garment and edgestitched for a coordinated edge finish.

How to Sew an Edgestitched Seam

1) Cut ⅝" (1.5 cm) seams. Mark notches and construction symbols with water-soluble marking pen or chalk, instead of clipping. Stitch seams, with wrong sides together and raw edges even.

2) Press seams open. Turn seam allowances under, half the width of seam allowance. Press; pin in place. On curves, stitch ¼" (6 mm) from raw edges and clip to stitching for easier turning. Stitch close to folded edges through all layers.

How to Sew a Coordinated Edge Finish

Press casing, seam allowance, or hem allowance to right side. Turn under raw edge; press. Stitch as in step 2, left.

Fringed Seams

Fringed seams add an interesting texture at the seamlines. They can only be used for seams that are on the straight of grain, such as yokes and plackets, or at the center front or center back of a garment.

For a coordinated look on collars, faced edges, or enclosed seams, a self-fabric fringed trim can be sewn into a curved or straight seam.

Fringe a small piece of fabric as a test before making the garment, because the lengthwise and crosswise yarns in the fabric are frequently of different weights or colors, causing the fringe to look different in each direction. You may find that the varied looks of the fringe are appealing, or you may decide to fringe only those seams that run in the same direction.

Fringed trim, made from fabric strips, can be inserted in enclosed seams for a decorative effect. For a fuller effect, layer two fabric strips.

How to Sew a Fringed Seam

1) Cut out the garment, allowing ¾" (2 cm) seam allowances. Stitch seam, *wrong* sides together and raw edges even. Press seam flat.

2) Trim the seam allowance that will not be fringed, to ⅛" (3 mm).

3) Press ¾" (2 cm) seam allowance over trimmed seam allowance. Topstitch ¼" (6 mm) from seamline, using short stitch length.

4) Ravel threads from raw edge to topstitching; clip seam allowance to stitching about every 6" (15 cm), to make fringing easier.

How to Sew a Fringed Trim in an Enclosed Seam

1) Cut a fabric strip on straight of grain, with length of strip equal to length of seamline, and width equal to finished width of fringe plus ⅝" (1.5 cm) seam allowance.

2) Insert strip between garment section and facing, aligning raw edges. Stitch seam, using short stitch length; grade and clip the seam allowances.

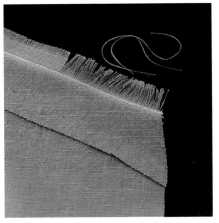

3) Press seam. Understitch facing seam, taking care not to catch strip in stitching. Clip seam allowance to stitching about every 6" (15 cm). Ravel threads to seamline.

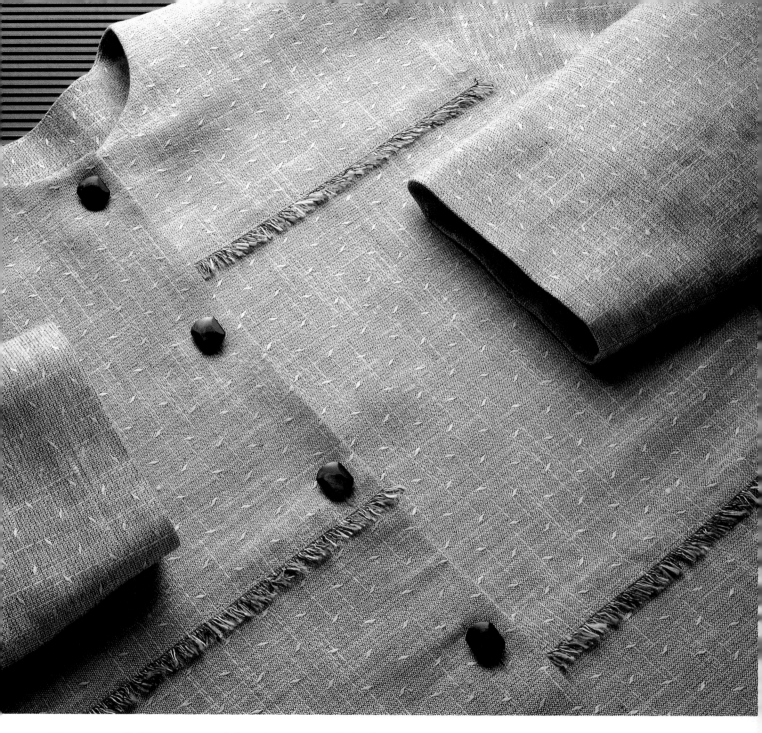

Lapped Seams with Exposed Selvages

Some fabrics have attractive selvages that you may want to feature as a trim. The exposed selvages can be used to accent existing seamlines or seamlines you have added to the pattern (page 194).

This method is limited to straight seams or edges that are cut on the lengthwise grain. Changing the grainline allows this technique to be used for vertical, horizontal, or diagonal seams.

For a selvage finish at a straight hemline, center front opening, or pocket edge, eliminate the seam or hem

allowance, and place the seamline or hemline on the selvage when cutting out the pattern.

Before using this method, preshrink the fabric to see whether the selvage shrinks more than the fabric, causing it to draw up and pucker. Preshrink washable fabric as recommended in the fabric care instructions; preshrink fabric that requires dry cleaning by steaming it evenly with a steam iron and allowing it to dry thoroughly on a flat surface.

Selvages may have a decorative fringed appearance and matching or contrasting tightly woven yarns.

How to Sew a Seam with an Exposed Selvage

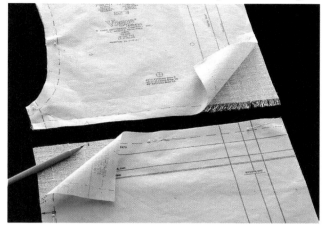

1) Cut one garment section on the selvage, eliminating seam allowance; for fringed selvages, fringe may extend beyond seamline. Cut other garment section with ⅝" (1.5 cm) seam allowance; this seam allowance will underlap the selvage. Mark notches, using water-soluble marking pen or chalk.

2) Mark seamline of underlap section ⅝" (1.5 cm) from raw edge. Finish seam allowance of underlap.

3) Align selvage with marked seamline; pin in place. Topstitch through selvage and underlap.

Bound & Lapped Seams

Bindings can be used to trim some or all of the seams in a garment. The lapped method for bound seams distributes the bulk of the seam allowances. The width of the finished binding may vary, with a maximum width of ⅝" (1.5 cm).

For best results, the binding strips are usually cut on the bias, but they may be cut on the straight of grain if the seams are straight.

Determine in which direction each bound seam will lap, and stitch the binding to the overlapping seam allowance. As a general rule, princess or side front seams are lapped toward the sides of a garment, side seams are lapped toward the garment back, and horizontal seams are lapped downward. When bindings are used for set-in sleeves, bind the armhole of the bodice and lap it over the sleeve cap.

On some garments, you may also want to bind the edges with a coordinating binding.

How to Sew a Bound and Lapped Seam

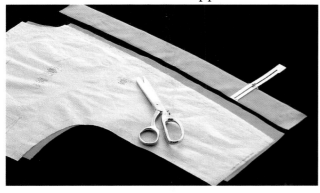

1) Cut regular ⅝" (1.5 cm) seam allowances on seams to be bound. Cut binding strips the length of edge plus 2" (5 cm). Cut width of strips two times finished width of binding plus 1¼" (3.2 cm); for example, for ½" (1.3 cm) binding, cut strips 2¼" (6 cm) wide.

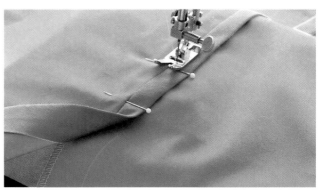

2) Stitch binding strip to overlapping garment section, right sides together, with strip against the feed dogs; ease binding at outside curves, and stretch it slightly at inside curves.

3) Trim seam allowances to width of binding. Press binding over seam allowances and around raw edge to wrong side. Mark placement line on underlapping garment section, finished width of binding plus ⅝" (1.5 cm) from raw edge, using water-soluble marking pen or chalk.

4) Finish raw edge. Place bound garment section over underlapping garment section, aligning outer edge of binding to marked placement line; pin through all layers. Stitch in the ditch. At end of seam, trim excess binding even with edge of garment section.

How to Sew a Coordinating Bound Edge

1) Trim seam or hem allowance from garment. Cut binding strips, the length of edge plus 2" (5 cm), and width six times finished width plus ¼" (6 mm). Press binding in half lengthwise; place on the right side of garment, raw edges even. Stitch seam, with seam allowance the finished width of binding.

2) Fold binding around edge; press and pin. Stitch in the ditch from right side of garment, catching the folded edge on wrong side.

Adding Seams for Interest

A basic garment design can become more interesting with the addition of one or more seams. When several seams are added, the new garment sections that are created can be cut from several different fabrics. A patchwork effect can be achieved with a variety of fabrics in different prints or textures. Or try color blocking by using a different color of fabric for each garment section.

Make a copy of the pattern that you can mark and cut apart when adding the new seams. Draw the seamlines on the new pattern, and check the seam placement by pin-fitting the pattern. Then cut the pattern apart and add seam allowances.

How to Add Seams to a Pattern

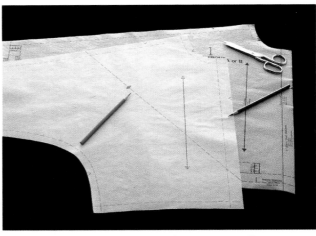

1) Trace pattern piece onto tissue paper. Draw desired new seamlines on new pattern. Mark notches to indicate where garment sections are to be matched during stitching.

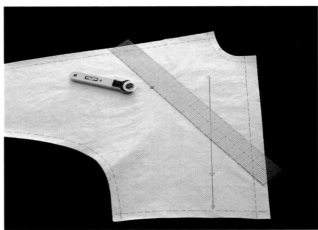

2) Extend the grainline on each new pattern section, or mark a new grainline parallel to the original. Cut pattern apart on the new seamlines.

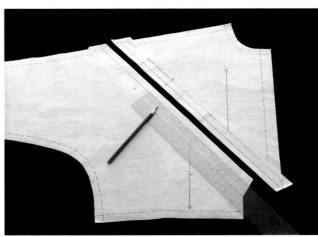

3) Add tissue paper at new seamlines; mark width of desired seam allowances. Extend notches to cutting lines of pattern.

Double & Triple Piping

Double and triple piping can be an effective way to enhance a simple garment, by accenting the design lines. The piping can be used as an edge finish or sewn into a seamline.

Bias fabric strips, cut 1½" (3.8 cm) wide, are used to cover the cording. The length of each strip should equal the combined lengths of the seams or edges to be piped plus extra for seam allowances; piece strips together, as necessary.

Rattail cord is recommended for the cording, because it provides a firm edge and is less likely to be caught by the zipper foot when the piping is stitched.

For best results, use an adjustable zipper foot so you can control how close you stitch to the piping. Tighten the fixing screw of the zipper foot firmly so the foot does not shift and break a needle. Or, if your machine has an adjustable needle position, align the needle with the zipper foot.

To make the piping, thread the machine with thread to match the color of the piping that will be on the outer edge; use this color for stitching all rows of piping.

How to Make Double and Triple Piping

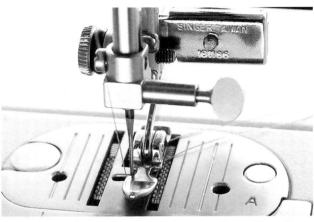

1) Cut bias fabric strips, opposite; piece the strips together, as necessary. Press seams open.

2) Position zipper foot on right side of needle; adjust foot or needle position so needle is close to inside curve of opening on foot. Tighten fixing screw firmly.

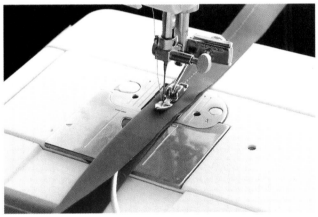

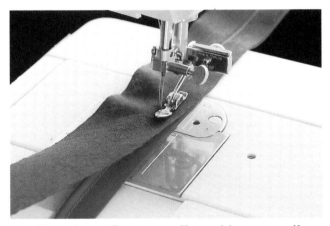

3) Fold strip that will be on outer edge around cording, with wrong sides together and raw edges even. Secure cording to end of strip, using a pin. Stitch, guiding cording along edge of foot.

4) Adjust zipper foot or needle position so needle is aligned to *edge* of foot; tighten fixing screw firmly. Place second strip over piping, right sides together, aligning raw edges. Stitch as close as possible to cording.

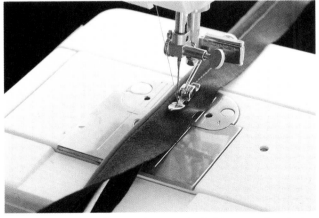

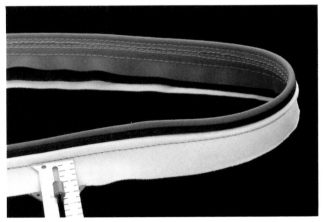

5) Adjust zipper foot as in step 2. Fold second strip around cording, and secure end with a pin; raw edges will not match. Stitch, guiding cording along edge of zipper foot.

6) Repeat steps 4 and 5, using third fabric color, if triple piping is desired. Trim seam allowances of piping, if necessary, to match those of garment.

Applying Double & Triple Piping

Double and triple piping can be used at seamlines or garment edges. They should not be used around sharp corners, but may be used for rounded corners.

When used at a seamline, the piping is applied to one garment section; then the seam is stitched, and the piping laps over the other section. Determine the direction in which you want the piping to lap, so it is applied to the correct garment section. As a general rule, princess or side front seams are lapped toward the sides of a garment, side seams are lapped toward the garment back, and horizontal seams are lapped downward.

If the piping is being used at garment edges, collars, and cuffs, the facing or lining is attached by hand, concealing the rows of stitching on the underside of the piping for a neater edge finish.

How to Insert Double or Triple Piping into a Seam

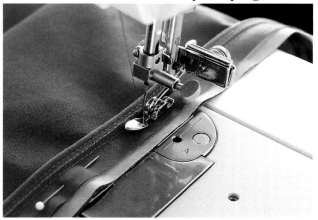

1) **Pin** piping to garment, with right sides together and raw edges even. Adjust zipper foot as on page 197, step 2. Stitch, guiding cording along edge of foot.

2) **Adjust** zipper foot as on page 197, step 4. Place garment sections right sides together, with raw edges even. Stitch seam as close as possible to cording. (Presser foot has been raised to show detail.)

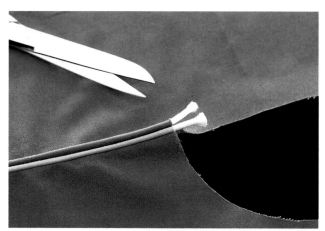

3) **Pull** out cords slightly, if the piped seam will be intersected by another seam or turned back at a hemline; clip ends the width of seam allowance.

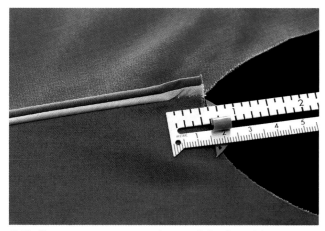

4) **Pull** seam to return cords to original position. Stitch intersecting seam, using zipper foot.

How to Apply Double or Triple Piping at an Edge

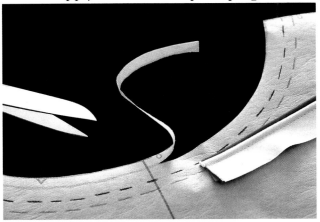

1) Cut facings and lining pieces, following pattern. Decrease size of pattern for garment section at seamline by width of piping; add seam allowance. Cut the garment section from adjusted pattern.

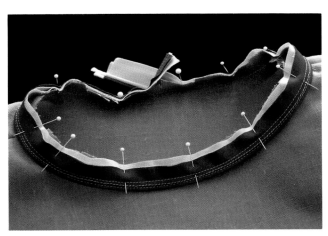

2) Pin piping to garment, with right sides together and raw edges even.

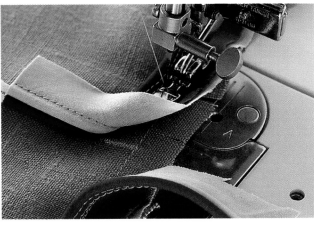

3) Adjust zipper foot as on page 197, step 4. Stitch seam, stitching as close as possible to cording; on circular edge, leave 1" (2.5 cm) unstitched at each end. Grade seam allowances and clip curves.

4) Pull up cords slightly, if necessary, for smooth inside curve. For circular edge, overlap piping and curve ends into seam allowance, so ends taper to raw edge; stitch.

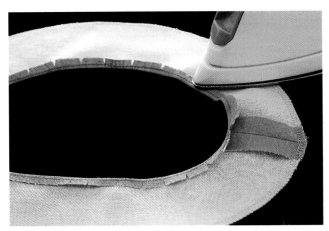

5) Stitch facing or lining piece on seamline. Trim seam allowance and clip curves. Press under facing or lining ⅛" (3 mm) beyond stitching.

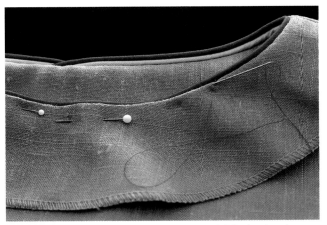

6) Pin facing to garment section so folded edge is aligned to stitching line at outer row of piping; slipstitch along folded edge.

Pockets

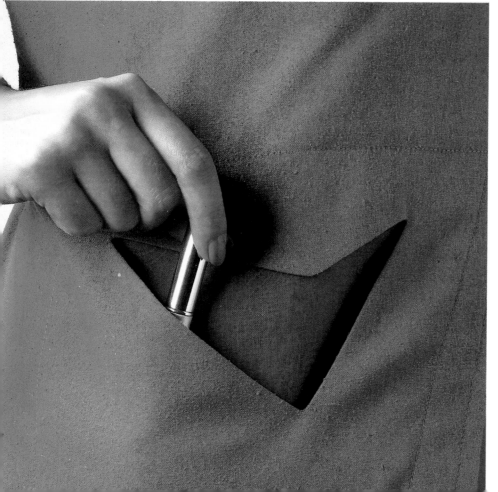

Design your own creative pockets to enhance the style of a garment, making the pockets any shape or size desired. To add even more interest, sew the pockets from contrasting fabric.

Window Pockets

Window pockets (above and left) are inventive and easy to sew, and can be used for either lined or unlined garments. The pockets can be varied by changing the size or shape. Contrasting fabric may be used for the pocket piece, to emphasize the pocket opening.

Foldover Pockets

On lined foldover pockets, the top of the pocket folds back to make a contrasting flap. Plan the shape of the pocket to complement the fabric or garment design. The pocket shapes on the garments above mimic the designs in the print fabric and the shape of the neckline. Or the pocket can repeat the shape of other garment details; for example, the notched pocket at right may be used for a garment with notched lapels.

How to Sew a Window Pocket

1) Draw desired size and shape of pocket on paper, drawing pocket opening and placement lines for topstitching.

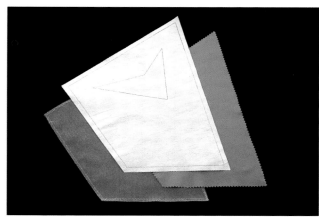

2) Make a tissue pattern, drawing cutting lines ⅜" (1 cm) outside topstitching lines. Cut one piece from lining, wrong side up. Cut another piece from matching or contrasting fabric, right side up; this piece will show at pocket opening. Finish edges.

3) Mark mirror image of pocket opening on right side of fusible interfacing. Cut fusible interfacing ½" (1.3 cm) larger than pocket opening, using pinking shears. Fuse interfacing to wrong side of garment section at desired position.

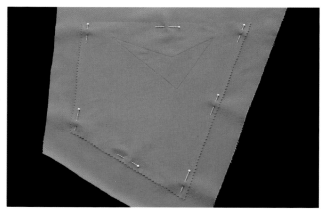

4) Position pocket lining on garment, right sides together; pin in place. Stitch through all layers, from wrong side, following marked lines for pocket opening.

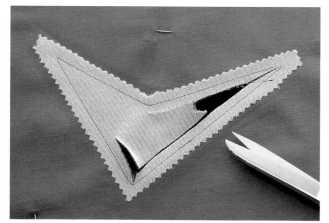

5) Trim fabric layers ¼" (6 mm) inside stitching lines; clip as necessary.

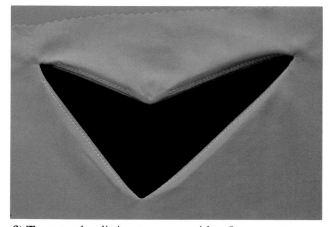

6) Turn pocket lining to wrong side of garment; press. Understitch edge of opening to prevent lining from showing on right side.

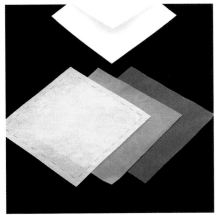

7) Position pocket piece, right side down, over pocket lining; baste from wrong side ⅜" (1 cm) from edges of pocket piece.

8) Topstitch around pocket from right side, along basting stitches. Remove basting.

How to Sew a Foldover Pocket

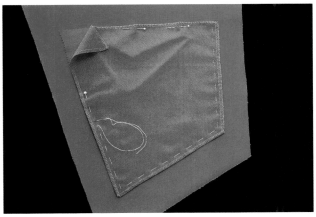

1) Design pocket, and cut the shape from paper in actual size; fold flap to check design. Make pattern from tissue, adding seam allowances. Cut one piece from each of two fabrics.

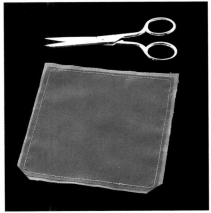

2) Place pieces right sides together, and pin. Stitch around edges; do not leave an opening. Trim corners and seam allowances; clip curves.

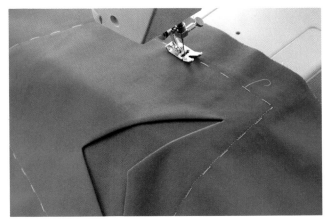

3) Cut small slash in lining close to lower edge. Turn pocket right side out, through slash.

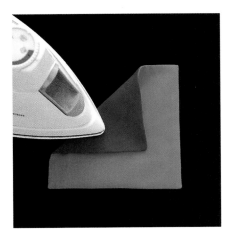

4) Press seam so lining does not show on lower pocket and outer fabric does not show on flap. Press flap.

5) Fuse slashed opening closed, using piece of fusible interfacing.

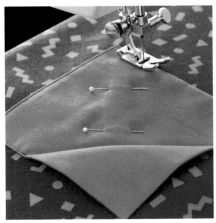

6) Pin pocket to garment; topstitch in place, backstitching at each end of pocket opening.

Triangular Pockets & Buttonholes

Triangular buttonholes are a variation of the couture bound buttonhole. These novelty buttonholes can be the main focal point of a garment when sewn in contrasting fabric, or can add a subtle finishing touch when sewn in matching fabric. The fabric piece for the buttonhole is cut on the straight of grain, resulting in chevroned stripes when a striped fabric is used.

To determine the length of the buttonhole opening, add the diameter of the button plus the thickness and an extra ⅛" to ¼" (3 to 6 mm) for ease. Make test samples of the buttonhole to check the fit of the button and to master the technique before sewing buttonholes on the actual garment.

The triangular pocket is a variation of the traditional welt pocket. The basic sewing technique is the same as for sewing triangular buttonholes.

The triangular pocket may be used alone, or on the same garment as triangular buttonholes.

This pocket may be used instead of a welt pocket or added to a pattern that does not include a pocket. The pocket opening may be any size, but a 5" to 6" (12.5 to 15 cm) opening works well.

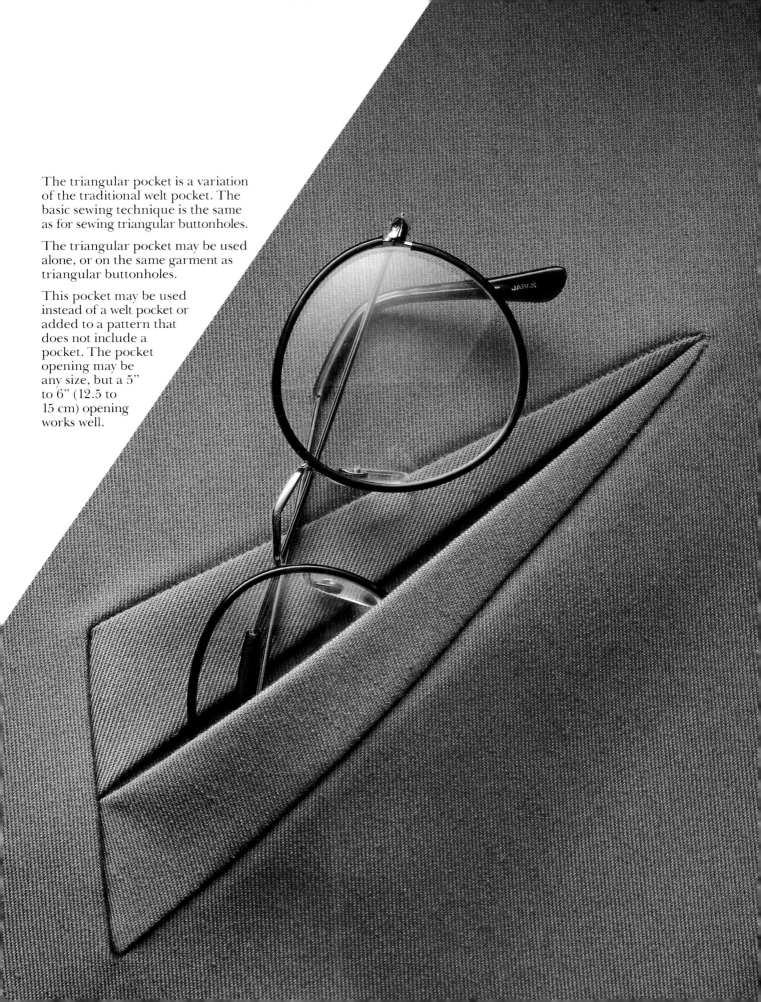

How to Sew a Triangular Bound Buttonhole

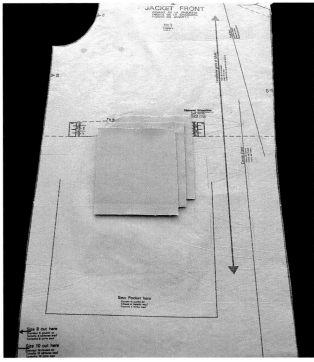

1) Plan shape and size of buttonholes. Cut a straight-grain fabric patch for each buttonhole, with length 2" (5 cm) longer than buttonhole opening and width four times finished width of buttonhole at wide end.

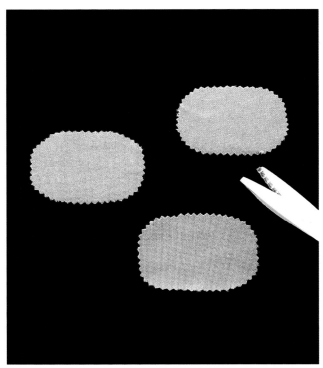

2) Cut a piece of fusible interfacing for each buttonhole, 1" (2.5 cm) longer and wider than finished triangle, using pinking shears.

3) Mark points of triangular buttonhole on garment, using tailor's tacks. Remove all but one strand of each tailor's tack. On wrong side of garment section, center interfacing over buttonhole; fuse interfacing in place.

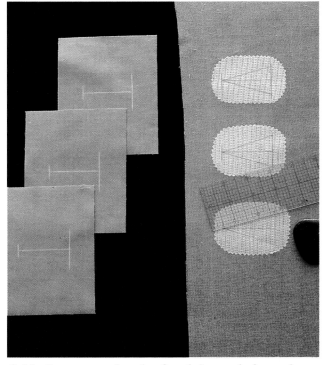

4) Mark center and ends of each buttonhole on the interfacing and wrong side of patch, using chalk. Mark lines of triangles on interfacing.

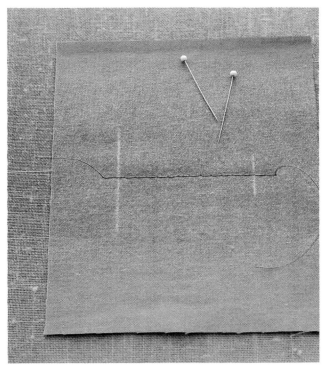

5) Place patch on garment section, right sides together, using pins to align markings. Machine-baste through center marking.

6) Stitch around marked triangle, using 20 stitches per inch (2.5 cm); begin on one side of triangle, and take one or two stitches across each point. Remove basting.

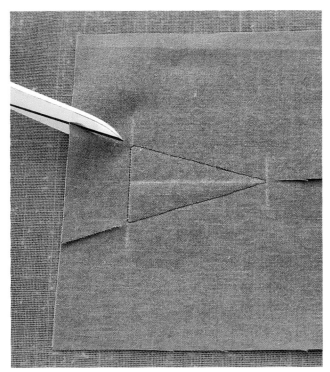

7) Cut three slashes through patch only, cutting from outer edge of patch to within ⅛" (3 mm) of corners of triangle, as shown.

8) Cut patch and garment section through center of buttonhole, stopping ¼" (6 mm) from widest end. Clip to, but not through, corners.

(Continued on next page)

9) Turn patch at wide end of buttonhole to wrong side; press seam at wide end.

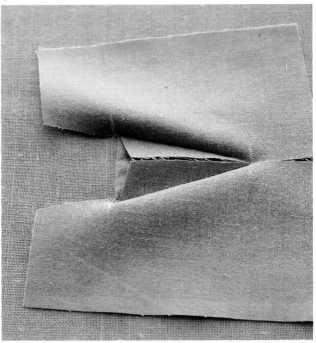

10) Press patch toward buttonhole opening on two remaining seamlines.

11) Turn sides of patch to wrong side; wrap around center opening to form lips of buttonhole. Press from right side, taking care that lips are even.

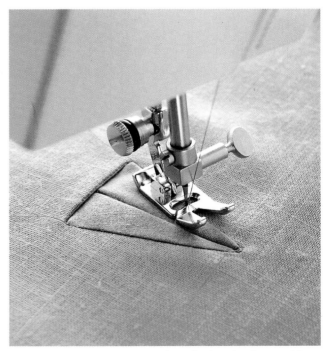

12) Stitch in the ditch on sides of triangle, from wide end to point, using matching thread and short stitch length; stitch in place at ends to secure stitches.

13) Turn garment back on itself; stitch across wide end of buttonhole over previous stitching, through all thicknesses. Trim excess fabric.

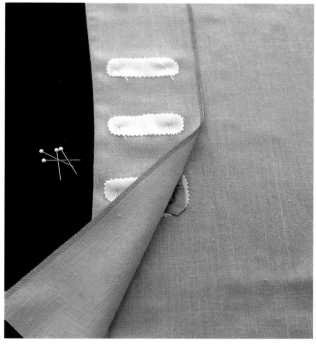

14) Attach the garment facing; press. Mark ends of buttonhole openings on facing, using pins. Cut a piece of fusible interfacing for each buttonhole, 1" (2.5 cm) longer than opening and 1" (2.5 cm) wide. Center interfacing, fusible side up, over pin-marked openings on right side of facing.

15) Mark opening on interfacing, using pencil. Mark oval shape, tapering from ends of buttonhole to ⅛" (3 mm) from marked line at center of buttonhole. Stitch around oval through interfacing and facing, taking two stitches across each end.

16) Slash on center line. Turn interfacing to wrong side of facing. Press seamlines with tip of iron; fuse interfacing in place. Slipstitch facing to garment section around oval opening.

How to Sew a Triangular Welt Pocket

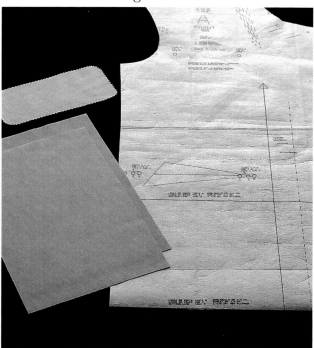

1) Cut two pieces of straight-grain fabric for pocket, with width of piece 2" (5 cm) longer than pocket opening, and length four times finished width of triangle at wide end plus 3" (7.5 cm). Cut a piece of fusible interfacing 1" (2.5 cm) longer and wider than finished triangle, using pinking shears.

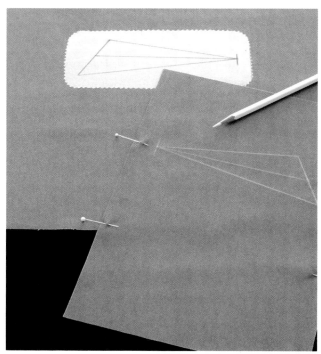

2) Mark points of triangle on garment and apply interfacing as in step 3, page 207. Mark pocket opening on interfacing; mark lines of triangle. Divide the length of one pocket piece into thirds, and pin-mark. Mark pocket opening on wrong side of pocket piece, one-third down from top; mark lines of triangle.

3) Follow steps 5 to 11, pages 207 and 208. Stitch in the ditch on lower side of triangle, from wide end to point, using matching thread and short stitch length; stitch in place at ends to secure stitches.

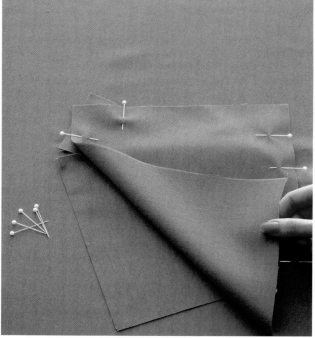

4) Center second pocket piece over first piece, on wrong side. Pin pocket pieces together.

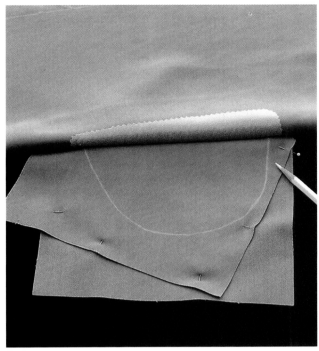

5) Place garment right side up. Lift garment section to expose lower ends of pocket pieces. Mark curved stitching line for pocket bag, starting and ending at ends of pocket opening.

6) Stitch across pointed end of triangle to reinforce point. Continue stitching on marked line around pocket bag.

7) Continue stitching across wide end of pocket opening over previous stitching, through all thicknesses.

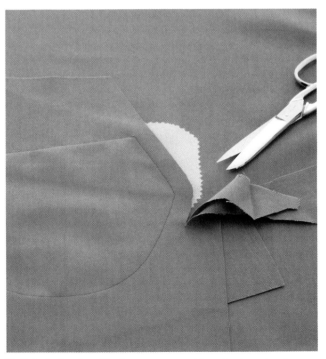

8) Stitch in the ditch on upper side of triangle, from wide end to point, using matching thread and short stitch length; stitch in place at ends to secure stitches. Trim excess fabric around pocket bag; finish edge.

Couture Sleeve Detail

Careful shaping and attention to detail in constructing sleeves makes them professional-looking. Once you have mastered the basics of sleeve construction, you may want to move beyond the instructions in your pattern envelope and add one or more of the following couture details to your sewing repertoire.

Shaped Center Seams

A popular design detail is the two-piece sleeve, with a center seam running from cap point to wrist. In this variation on a traditional tailored sleeve, all of the ease has been incorporated into the seam. The result is a sleeve that sets into a garment beautifully, requiring only a minimum of shaping.

In order to retain the shape of this type of sleeve, first sew the seam and press it open over a curved edge, such as a pressing ham or sleeve board, clipping where necessary. Then, apply interfacing. For a sleeve that will be lined, use a wool interfacing for a soft, cushioned seam; a stiff interfacing such as Sta-Form™ for a sharp, rigid seam; or hair canvas for a tailored seam, depending on the fabric of the garment. For an unlined sleeve, choose a bias strip cut from the fashion fabric or from silk organza.

Topstitching the center seam gives this two-piece construction more body and adds decorative detail. If topstitching is not used, the interfacing should be attached by hand to the seam allowances only.

Covered Shoulder Pads

Use covered shoulder pads in dresses, blouses, sweaters, and unlined jackets for a professional finish. Save money by covering pads with lining fabric or flesh-colored nylon tricot. A covered shoulder pad completes the look of couture sleeves.

How to Interface a Sleeve with Shaped Center Seam

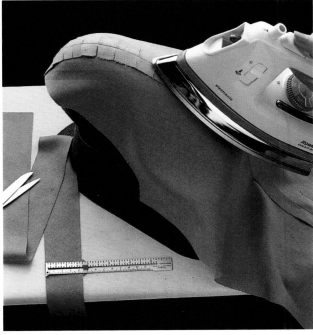

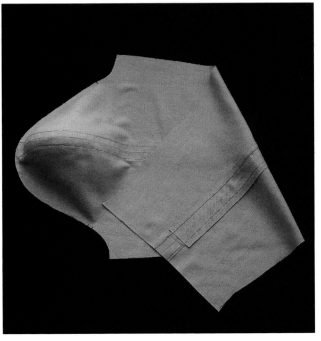

1) Cut interfacing on the bias 1¾" (4.5 cm) wide by finished length of sleeve. Stitch sleeve center seam. Press over a curved edge, clipping curves where necessary. Pin interfacing to sleeve, working from right side of sleeve.

2) Baste stitching lines through all thicknesses, with sleeve cap positioned on ham. Topstitch from hem edge on right side, ½" (3.8 cm) on each side of seam. If topstitching is eliminated, attach interfacing by hand to seam allowances only.

How to Cover Shoulder Pads

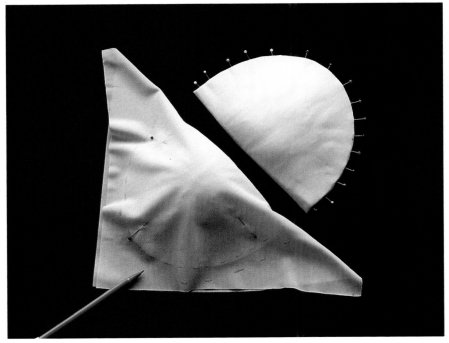

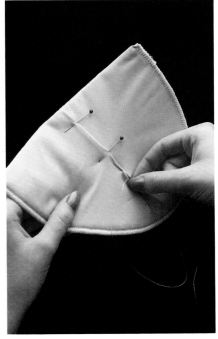

1) Cut a 12" (30.5 cm) square of fabric. Place shoulder pad on fabric with armhole edge along the diagonal. Fold fabric over pad. All-bias fabric shapes easily to pad. Draw outline of pad, add ⅝" (1.5 cm) seam allowance, and cut. Serge around edges. Or fold seam allowances in on underside of pad, and slipstitch around cut edges.

2) Slipstitch a dart in underside to hold in contoured shape. Tack pointed ends to armhole seam allowances and rounded portion to shoulder seam.

Bias-cut Sleeves

A beautiful effect can be achieved by cutting sleeves on the bias. Bias-cut sleeves also provide an easy solution to the problem of matching plaids from garment body to sleeve.

Cutting sleeves on the bias changes how a sleeve will drape and is especially effective with softer fabrics. With a solid-colored fabric there is a subtle change. When a stripe is used to create a chevron pattern, this detail becomes the focal point of the garment.

Due to the nature of the grain, bias sleeves will hang thinner and longer than the same sleeve cut on the straight grain. Therefore, as with any bias garment, let sleeves hang after setting them into the garment for at least 24 hours before hemming or applying cuffs. Be sure to hang the garment with shoulder pads inserted, preferably on a padded hanger, so the sleeves will hang naturally.

Tips for Cutting and Sewing on the Bias

Cut seam allowances 1½" (3.8 cm) wide. When fabric is cut on the bias, an explosion of fibers occurs along the cut, making the edge significantly longer than the original and intended length. If you stitch too close to the edge, your stitching line will be too long, resulting in a buckled, puckered seam. Pressing cannot correct this problem. The solution is to stitch bias seams 1½" (3.8 cm) from the cut edges, where the fibers are still intact.

Mark stitching line to ensure stitching a straight seam when sewing on the bias.

Use the smallest needle size possible and a stitch length of 12 to 15 stitches per inch (2.5 cm).

Stretch seam slightly as you sew, to prevent stitches from breaking when you wear garment.

Trim the seam allowances after sewing seams, if required. It is not always necessary to trim bias seam allowances. On a skirt, for example, the extra fabric in the seam allowance provides additional support along the seamline.

Leave bias seam allowances unfinished; bias does not ravel.

How to Cut Sleeves on the Bias

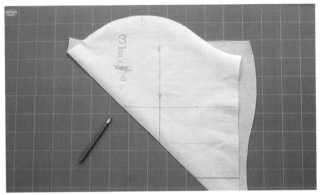

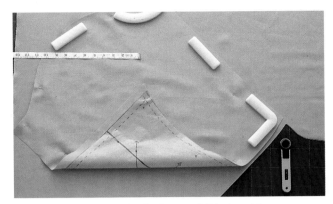

1) Fold pattern to form right angle at grainline marking. Mark new grainline along folded edge.

2) Place sleeve on single layer of fabric with new grainline on lengthwise grain of fabric; cap will point toward selvage. Cut, allowing 1½" (3.8 cm) seam allowances. Turn over pattern. Cut second sleeve with cap pointing toward opposite selvage.

How to Cut a Chevroned Bias Sleeve

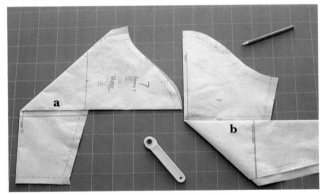

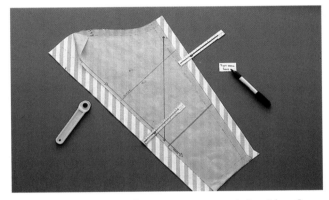

1) Fold pattern at center from shoulder dot to lower edge. For down-pointing chevron, fold pattern again from top to form right angle (**a**); diagonal crease is new grainline. Or, for up-pointing chevron, fold pattern from bottom to create new grainline (**b**). Cut pattern apart at center line.

2) Place right sleeve front pattern on right side of single layer of striped fabric, with new grainline following stripe; cut with 1½" (3.8 cm) lengthwise seam allowances. Mark lengthwise stitching lines on wrong side of fabric. Mark each sleeve section on wrong side as it is cut.

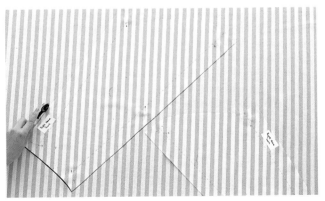

3) Place right sleeve front, right side up, on fabric; position next to right sleeve back pattern, matching stripes at a right angle to create a chevron at center *seamline.* Cut right sleeve back.

4) Cut the front and back for left sleeve using right sleeve pieces as a pattern. Place right sides of fabric together, matching stripes.

215

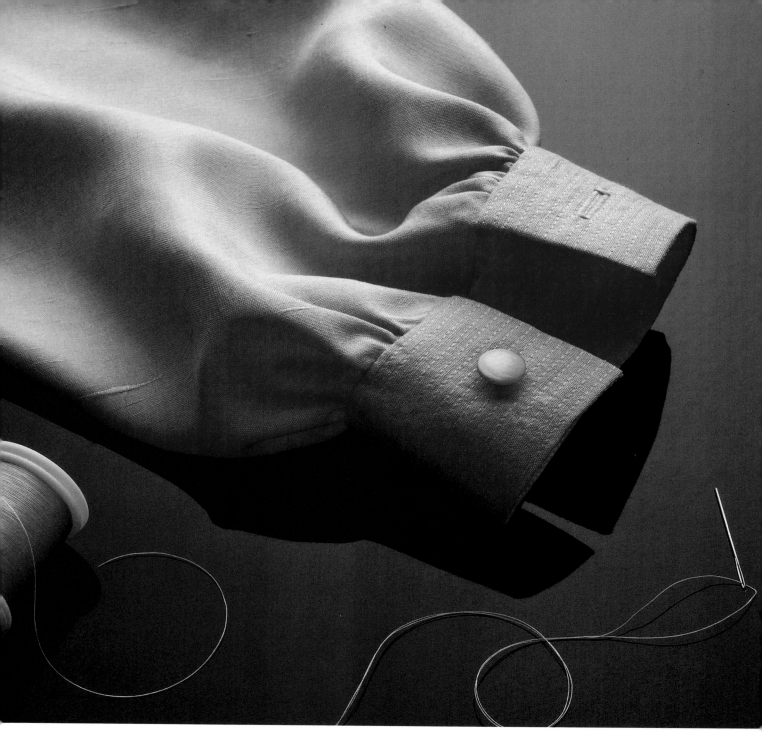

Channel-stitched Cuffs

Channel-stitching, a popular design detail, appears on cuffs, yokes, collars, and plackets. These closely spaced, parallel rows of stitches may look as if they were added to a completed garment as an afterthought, but for a couture look, they must be part of the construction process.

Shaping techniques, such as applying steam, heat, and pressure to add curve to flat fabric, are also crucial to achieving a couture finish for a garment. A cuff, for example, needs to wrap naturally around the wrist

for a polished look. Shaping techniques ensure that it will, by eliminating the excess facing and interfacing fabric that results when the three layers of a cuff are curved.

Couture sewing is an art. Practicing couture techniques requires a commitment to sharpen sewing skills beyond the basics. That commitment is amply rewarded in professional-looking garments and personal satisfaction.

How to Channel-stitch and Shape a Cuff

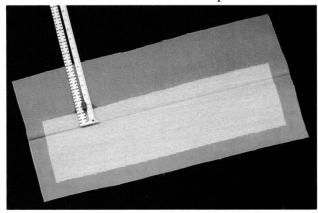

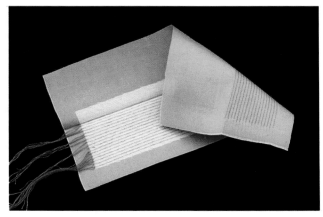

1) Cut interfacing for cuffs, extending ⅝" (1.5 cm) over center fold. Baste or fuse to the wrong side of fabric, on the side that will face outward on garment.

2) Stitch along fold line on right side of fabric using 15 to 20 stitches per inch (2.5 cm); begin and end at seamlines. Stitch parallel lines ⅛" (3 mm) apart; do not stitch in seam allowances. Tie off threads on wrong side.

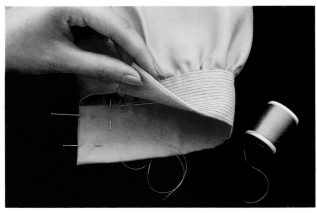

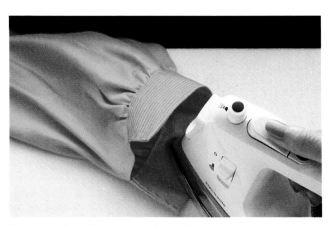

3) Stitch cuff to sleeve, right sides together. Press seam allowances toward cuff; grade. Fold cuff under at fold line, working from right side of cuff. Turn seam allowances under on long edge and ends, so cuff curves as it will when it is worn. Baste, using silk thread.

4) Steam inside cuff gently on ironing board, so it shrinks slightly.

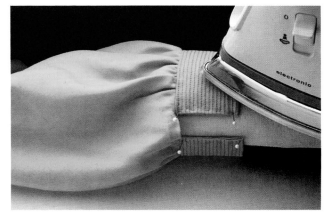

5) Wrap cuff around seam roll. Pin, and gently steam and press from right side. Repeat as necessary to shape cuff. Allow to dry completely.

6) Slipstitch long edge and ends of cuff by hand. Cuff will retain shape without excess fabric on inside.

Discovering Design Details

Feel free to incorporate design details from other patterns, fashion magazines, ready-to-wear, or your imagination.

Some design details can be added without making a pattern; they need not be complicated to attract attention, and may simplify the construction of a garment and save time. One of the easiest is to eliminate facings whenever possible by substituting contrasting trim. This accomplishes two things: it eliminates bulk, and it provides design interest.

Try trimming wool with suede or leather, summerweight wovens like silk tweed or noile with linen, or cotton knits and wool jersey with a contrasting knit or ribbing. To ensure a smooth fit around curves, cut woven trim on the bias and cut knit trim on the crosswise grain. Suede and leather trim should be cut in the direction of greatest stretch. Synthetic suedes such as Ultrasuede® lack grain and may therefore be cut in any direction, since little stretch can be expected. Experiment on scrap fabric to get the desired effect.

Another simple design idea copied from ready-to-wear is the substitution of one large button for a series of buttons on a jacket (left). Choose the button carefully and it will become an accessory. Because a large buttonhole is seldom attractive, substitute a fabric loop sewn into the seam for the buttonhole closing.

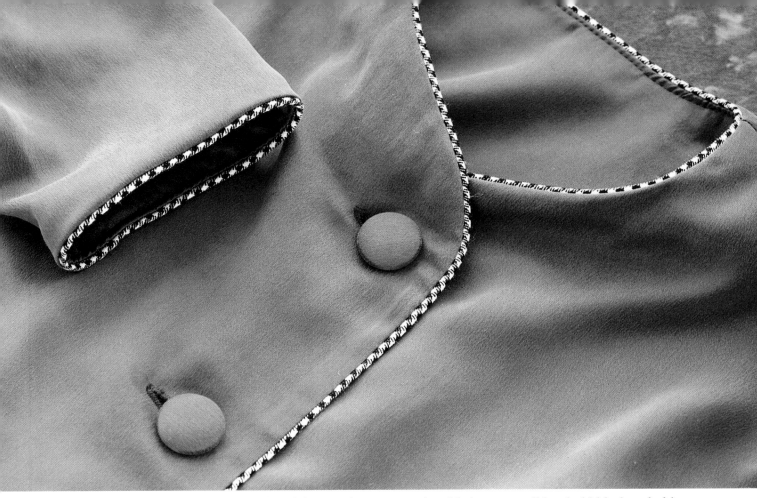

Add piping to the edges of a blouse. The piping can be a contrasting fabric or a small but bold black-and-white print. The facings need to be cut separately.

Trim a wool jacket by substituting suede or leather for a section of the garment, such as the front band, pocket flap, or cuff.

Roll-up sleeves on a jacket can become a fashion accent by facing the sleeves in a contrasting or coordinating fabric.

Copying Design Details

Garments and accessories with creative and interesting styling details command high prices, which cover not only originality, but construction time as well. This is where the home sewer has an advantage. High-fashion details rarely require additional fabric; it is simply a matter of investing a little extra time and knowing how to copy and add the detail. The end result is a unique garment with an expensive look.

Design details may be found anywhere from the "designer section" of the best department store to the trendiest boutiques in town. Or, turn to fashion magazines for inspiration. When shopping, keep an eye out for anything that seems well made or unique. Look closely at pockets, collars, lapels, topstitching, plackets, waistbands, and hem finishes. To a salesclerk, you are admiring the workmanship. As a sewer, you are subconsciously measuring and planning the steps to incorporate this detail into your next garment.

Since rulers and measuring tapes do not create goodwill in a ready-to-wear store, body parts must act as your measuring devices. Pocket width may be the distance of five outstretched fingers. Flap detailing may be the depth of one thumb. Back hem length may be longer than the front by one forefinger. Note carefully the placement of the design detail on the garment itself. How far is the detail above or below the armhole? Is it centered or closer to the side or

front? How large are buttons — the size of a thumbnail or of the nail on your little finger?

Success in duplicating a design depends upon detailed observation. Record your observations the minute you leave the store. Do not rely on your memory. Always carry a notebook and pen in your purse to write down ideas for your next sewing project. Sometimes a design seen two years ago may be the perfect solution for customizing and creating additional interest for a current sewing project.

Another place to look for design detail inspiration might be right in your own closet. Look for a garment with a favorite pocket, waistband, yoke, cuff, or collar. Making a pattern of a design detail (opposite) is a simple process. The fastest way to make a pattern of the detail is to trace it with wax paper and a tracing wheel. This gives you a pattern minus the seam allowances.

Normally, when copying a finished garment, 5/8" (1.5 cm) seam allowances are added. Sometimes, adding and sewing a seam of 5/8" (1.5 cm) can result in a design detail that is slightly smaller than the original. For a more accurate copy, add up to 7/8" (2.2 cm) to cut edges, but stitch 5/8" (1.5 cm) seams. The amount to add to the cut edges will vary, depending on your tracing and cutting techniques, the size of the design detail, and the weight of the fabric. Now is the perfect time to change the design detail slightly, if desired.

How to Make a Pattern to Duplicate a Design Detail

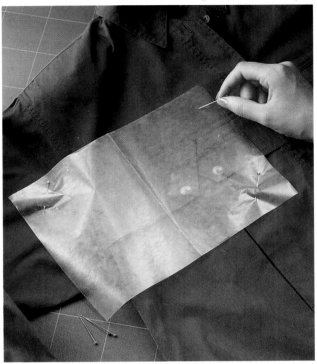

1) **Fold** or draw grainline on wax paper. Place paper over design detail, aligning grainlines. Pin to secure.

2) **Trace** around the finished edges of the design detail, using a tracing wheel.

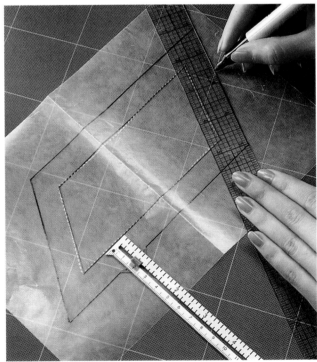

3) **Remove** paper from garment. If detail is symmetrical, fold along center line, and true edges. Add ⅝" to ⅞" (1.5 to 2.2 cm) to all cut edges. Depending on your tracing and cutting techniques, the size of the design detail, and the weight of the fabric, the amount to add to the cut edges will vary slightly.

4) **Cut** design detail according to pattern. Stitch, using a ⅝" (1.5 cm) seam allowance.

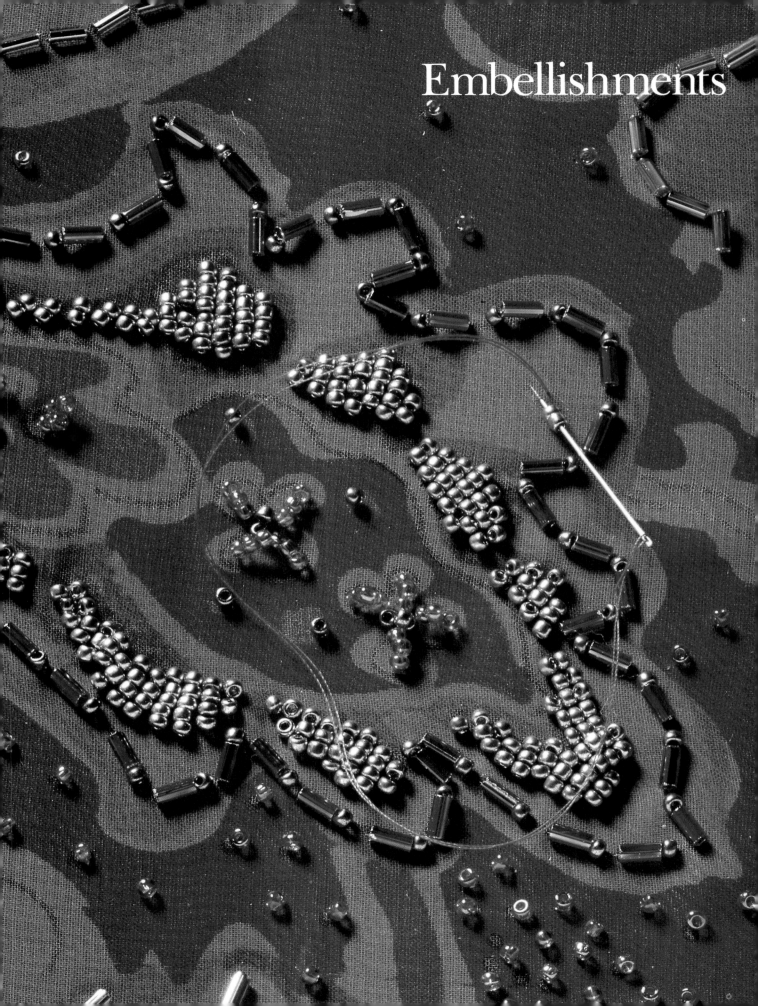

Ribbonwork

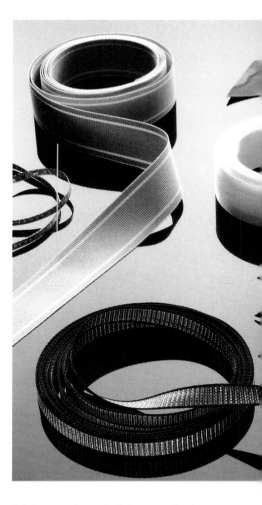

Ribbonwork, an heirloom technique, can be used creatively on today's sewing projects. Many different effects can be achieved, depending on the type of ribbon used, its width, and placement.

Grosgrain, double-faced satin, and other reversible ribbons can be used for ribbonwork. Ribbons found at estate sales or in old sewing baskets can add a special heirloom effect. If you plan to wash the project, use ribbons that are washable. Check ribbons for colorfastness and shrinkage, especially old ribbons or those of unknown fiber content. The width of the ribbon may vary, depending on the effect you want.

Diagonal ribbonwork can be used to accent a jacket lapel.

224

Ribbons ³⁄₈" or ½" (1 or 1.3 cm) wide work well, but narrower or wider ribbons can also create interesting designs. Plan the design, keeping in mind where the ribbon will start and end. The ends of the ribbon can be turned under and stitched, covered by another piece of ribbon, or stitched into a seam.

For the diagonal design, the length of ribbon required depends on the width of the ribbon and how closely spaced the diagonal lines are, but usually you will need a length of ribbon about twice the depth of the design times the number of "V's" in the design. Double this amount of ribbon for the diamond design.

Diamond ribbonwork can be used to decorate a hidden placket on a blouse.

How to Sew a Diagonal Ribbonwork Design

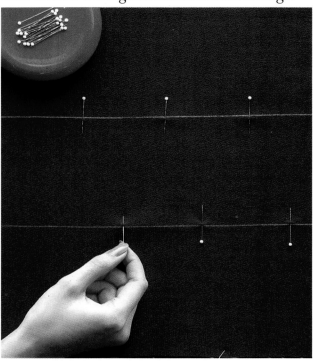

1) Mark lines for outer edges of design on fabric, using chalk or water-soluble marking pen. Plan placement of diagonal lines; mark points of diagonal lines an equal distance apart, using pins.

2) Attach reversible ribbon to fabric, using pins, folding ribbon *under* at each pin mark; align folds to outer edges, with centers of folds at pin marks. Glue-baste ribbon, if desired, to prevent shifting.

3) Stitch along overlapping edge of ribbon to fold, as shown, using matching thread or fine monofilament nylon thread. Pivot at fold, and stitch to opposite fold. Continue stitching in this manner to end of ribbon. (Contrasting thread was used to show detail.)

4) Stitch along other edge of ribbon to fold; stitch in place a few times to secure stitches. Raise presser foot and needle; pull thread past overlapping ribbon, as shown. Secure stitches, and stitch to opposite fold.

5) Continue stitching in this manner to end of ribbon.

6) Clip threads on right side of fabric; clip threads on wrong side, if desired.

How to Sew a Diamond Ribbonwork Design

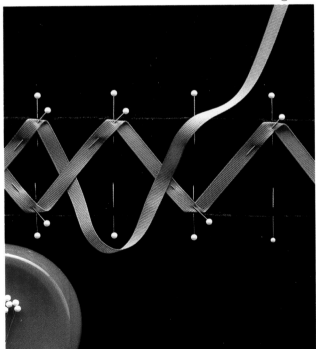

1) Mark lines and placement points, as in step 1, opposite. Pin first ribbon in place, as in step 2, opposite. Weave second ribbon alternately over and under first ribbon; pin.

2) Stitch as in steps 3 and 4, opposite, except stop stitching at intersecting ribbon; raise presser foot and needle, pull threads past intersecting ribbon, and continue stitching. Clip threads.

Slentre Braid

Slentre braid is fast and easy to make. This flexible braid has a distinctive appearance, with a half-round shape on one side and a flat, plaited look on the other. It can be made from one or several types of cord, ribbon, yarn, or narrow trim. A multicolored trim can be customized to coordinate with a specific fabric.

You may want to make a short length of slentre braid as a test sample, using one-yard (0.95 m) lengths of each of the cords or trims you are planning to use in the final project. This helps you to become familiar with the braiding technique and to check how the braid looks, before making a long piece.

To make a long, continuous braid, have an assistant help shape the braid as you interlace it.

Slentre braid may be used at seamlines or as an edge finish. When it is used at seamlines, the seams may be stitched as shown on pages 152 and 153.

How to Make Slentre Braid

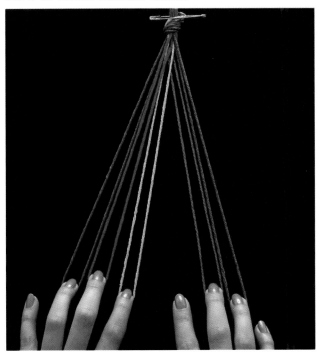

1) Cut five strands of cord; fold each in half. Tie all cut ends together; pin to padded, stationary surface, using safety pin. Hold three loops on fingers of left hand and two loops on fingers of right hand.

2) Insert index finger of right hand through middle loop on left hand, then into ring-finger loop.

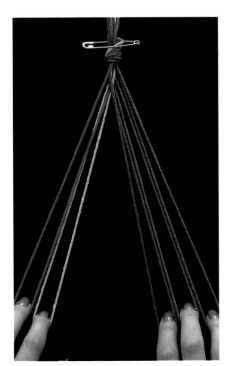

3) Draw ring-finger loop through middle loop, dropping ring-finger loop from left hand; there are now three loops on right hand and two loops on left. Pull hands apart to snug the braid in place at tied ends.

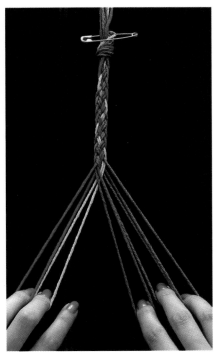

4) Shift loops on fingers of left hand by walking loops over so index finger is free. Repeat process, alternating hands until length of cord is braided.

5) Secure braid at ends by stitching across braid. Attach braid to garment by hand. To finish ends, enclose end in a seam **(a)** or fold end under just beyond stitches **(b)**; stitch.

Beadwork

Glamorous beaded garments and accessories can be created, using machine sewing or handstitching techniques. Machine sewing is used to apply beading-by-the-yard, and handstitching is used to apply individual beads. A few well-placed beads can add an exquisite look to an otherwise basic item. You may want to sew a more elaborate beaded design, or make a beaded appliqué that can be attached to a garment.

Beading by Machine

Beading-by-the-yard may be applied by machine by couching over the beads with a zigzag stitch. Various types, sizes, and colors of beading-by-the-yard are available, including a few types of beaded piping.

One of the most common types of beading-by-the-yard is molded plastic pearl beading. Pearl beading should not be confused with strung pearls, which are sold on a string and applied individually by hand.

Cross-Locked™ glass beads are braided onto cotton thread; the threads form a cross on the back of each bead, resulting in evenly spaced beads. Cross-Locked glass beads are flexible, strong, and easy to handle.

Large beads are more difficult to work with, because they are less flexible. Therefore you may want to avoid using them when sewing curved designs or when attaching beads to edges.

It is recommended that you use a specialty presser foot, such as a beading or piping foot, if one is available for your sewing machine. The groove in the bottom of the presser foot must be large enough to allow the beads to ride in the groove as you sew.

An adjustable zipper foot, or any zipper foot that can be used with the zigzag stitch, can also be used for applying beading-by-the-yard. The beads are then guided along the edge of the foot. Be careful not to hit them with the needle; this can break the needle and the beads.

Fine monofilament nylon thread is excellent for applying beads by machine. It blends in with the color of the beads and fabric so it is virtually invisible. Fine machine embroidery thread may also be used.

Adjust the zigzag stitch length so a complete zigzag is equal to the distance between the beads. Adjust the stitch width so the needle will stitch over the beads without hitting them. Always test-sew, stitching slowly and turning the flywheel by hand, to be sure the needle clears the beads. You may want to practice sewing with the zigzag stitch set to the widest stitch width until you feel confident stitching over the beads; then narrow the stitch width so it is closer to the beads.

Leave a tail of beading at the beginning of the stitching line, and hold the beading and thread tails when you start to sew. To prevent puckering, hold both the fabric and the beading taut as you stitch, and loosen the needle thread tension, if necessary.

When beading is applied to smaller areas, the fabric can be held taut in an embroidery hoop. This is especially helpful when you are sewing curves.

Types of beads available by the yard include nailheads **(a)**, rhinestones **(b)**, molded plastic pearls **(c)**, and Cross-Locked glass beads **(d)**.

How to Sew Beading by Machine

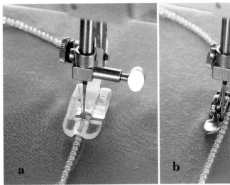

Beaded designs. 1) Mark design line on fabric to use as guide for stitching. Position beading in the groove under beading foot (**a**) or to the right of adjustable zipper foot (**b**). Adjust zigzag stitch length and stitch width, opposite. Stitch over beads, holding fabric and beading taut as you sew.

2) Prevent puckered fabric when sewing large beads by stitching so the right swing of needle is between the beads (**a**) and the left swing of needle is next to the center of each bead (**b**).

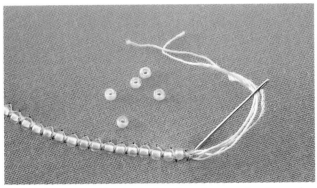

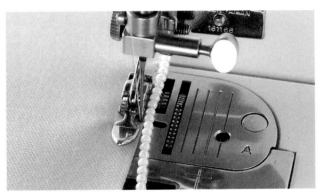

3) Secure Cross-Locked glass beads at ends of row by removing several beads and knotting the threads close to last remaining bead; thread the tails through a needle and pull to wrong side. Most other types of beading may be cut at ends without raveling.

Beaded edges. Place beading next to fabric edge. Use zipper or beading foot, and adjust stitches, opposite. Stitch over beads, so right swing of needle extends over edge of fabric between beads; left swing of needle catches fabric edge next to center of each bead. Secure ends as in step 3.

How to Insert Beaded Piping

1) Place beaded piping on garment section, right sides together and raw edges even. Using zipper foot, straight-stitch close to beads. If seam allowances of garment and piping are not the same width, trim the wider seam allowance.

2) Pin facing and garment section, right sides together, with beaded piping between layers. Straight-stitch over previous stitching, using zipper foot. Trim and clip seam allowances; press.

Beading by Hand

Hand beadwork is used to apply individual beads to a garment or project. Several types of beads are available for beading by hand. A wide variety of effects can be achieved, depending on the beads that are used and how they are combined.

All beads shown here are actual size.

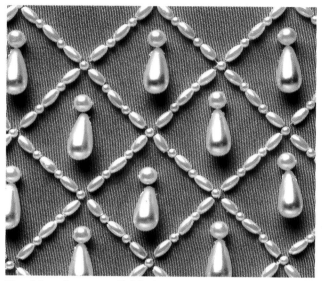

Pearl beads are available in many shapes and sizes.

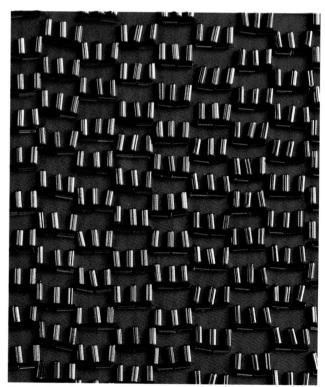

Bugle beads are tubular in shape, ranging in length from 2 to 40 mm. They may be smooth or six-sided.

Seed beads are small and round, with a center hole.

Faceted beads have flat surfaces that are cut or molded.

Drops are pear-shaped beads with a hole at the narrow end or lengthwise through the bead.

Fancy beads include any beads that do not fit into a specific category.

Roundels are doughnut-shaped beads, smooth or faceted. They are often used with seed beads.

Hand Beadwork

Hand beadwork is done using a beading needle, a long, fine needle with a small, round eye. The needles are available in sizes ranging from 10 to 14; the larger the number, the smaller the needle. Needles in sizes 12 and 13 are fine enough to fit through most beads, yet the eyes are large enough to be relatively easy to thread. Several beads can be threaded on a beading needle at one time. Because a beading needle is fine, it can be backed out of the fabric when it is necessary to remove a stitch.

Cotton-wrapped polyester thread is recommended for most beadwork projects. The cotton fibers make the thread easy to handle, and the polyester core provides added strength. The thread can be waxed by drawing it over a cake of beeswax to reduce tangling and knotting and to help the thread slide more smoothly through the fabric. Fine monofilament nylon thread can be used for beading on net.

For beading, it is necessary to have the fabric stretched tightly in either an embroidery hoop or a scroll frame, available at craft stores. This minimizes the amount of shrinkage that occurs when the fabric is beaded and prevents the fabric from becoming puckered or wavy. An embroidery hoop is used for small projects; for larger projects, such as beaded dresses, a scroll frame is used.

If an embroidery hoop is used, select a wooden hoop with a fixing screw so it can be tightened firmly. The hoop should be large enough to accommodate the entire beading design, to prevent damaging any beads. If a scroll frame is used, it should be large enough for either the length or the width of the fabric.

For each garment section to be beaded, cut a piece of fabric that is large enough to allow for any shrinkage that will occur when the fabric is beaded. When positioning the fabric in the hoop or frame, it is important that the grainlines of the fabric are squared, especially on beaded garments; if not, the garment will not hang correctly.

The pattern seamlines and cutting lines and the beadwork design are marked on the right side of the fabric. If a scroll frame is used, the fabric is marked before it is positioned in the frame; if an embroidery hoop is used, the fabric is marked after it is in the hoop. Simple beadwork designs can be marked freehand, but it is easier and more accurate to mark detailed designs using a marking tool called a *pounce pad*. The pounce pad, filled with cornstarch or charcoal, is rubbed over a perforated pattern to transfer marking dots to the fabric. A pounce pad is available from sign-painter suppliers or can be made inexpensively by filling a tennis sock with cornstarch.

An alternate method is to mark the design on a tissue paper pattern. This method is used for beading on chiffon, lace, or other sheer fabrics in a scroll frame; the tissue paper helps to stabilize the fabric during beading. The design is marked on the tissue instead of on the fabric, and the two layers are placed in the scroll frame together. The design is then beaded through both layers, and the tissue is torn away after the beading is completed.

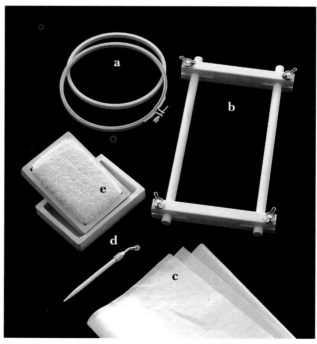

Beading supplies include wooden embroidery hoop **(a)** or scroll frame **(b),** used to stretch the fabric tightly, and tissue paper **(c),** or a needle wheel **(d)** and pounce pad **(e),** used to mark the beading design.

How to Design and Mark the Beading Design

Pounce pad method. 1) Photocopy design, or draw on paper; if beading a garment section, draw pattern seamlines, cutting lines, and grainline. Plan placement of various sizes, colors, and types of beads; plan types of stitches for sewing on beads (pages 240 and 241).

2) Pin pattern on thick layer of corrugated cardboard or cork board. Perforate paper pattern on design lines, seamlines, and cutting lines, using needle wheel.

3) Place beadwork pattern, right side up, on right side of fabric; pin or baste in place, aligning grainlines. Rub pounce pad over needle holes until powder from pad sifts through holes. Remove pattern, and spray fabric with hair spray to prevent smudging.

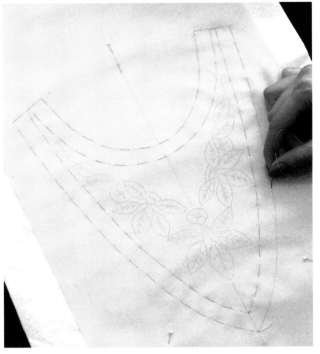

Tissue paper method. Plan beading design, as in step 1; trace on tissue paper. Place tissue under sheer fabric, right sides up, aligning grainlines; pin. Baste fabric to tissue on seamlines and cutting lines; place in scroll frame (pages 238 and 239).

How to Position the Fabric in an Embroidery Hoop

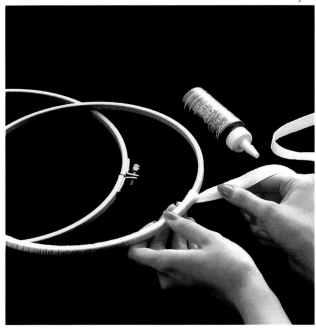

1) Secure one end of cotton twill tape to inner ring of wooden embroidery hoop, using fabric glue. Wrap ring with tape in diagonal direction, overlapping tape by half its width; pull tape firmly while wrapping. Secure other end of tape with glue. Allow glue to dry before using hoop.

2) Place fabric, right side up, over inner ring. Push outer ring over inner ring, making sure fabric is taut. Partially tighten screw and gently pull fabric until it is very taut; keep grainlines straight. Tighten fixing screw with screwdriver. Mark seamlines, cutting lines, and beadwork design on fabric (page 237).

How to Position the Fabric in a Scroll Frame

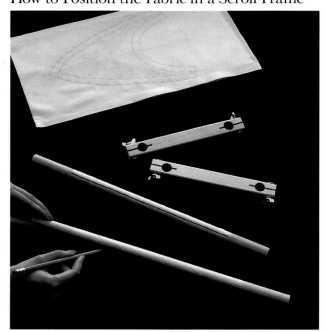

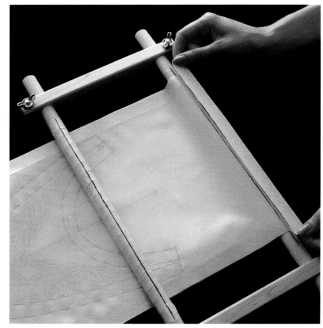

1) Mark seamlines, cutting lines, and beadwork design on fabric (page 237). Apply masking tape to lengthwise edges of fabric. Wrap tape around cross braces of frame. Hold cross brace firmly against table and, using pencil, draw line on cross brace where it touches table; repeat for other cross brace.

2) Assemble scroll frame. Tape one edge of fabric to cross brace, aligning the crosswise grainline of fabric to the marked line on the cross brace.

3) Roll fabric evenly around cross brace, keeping the grainline straight. If using tissue paper for marking design, roll tissue and fabric together.

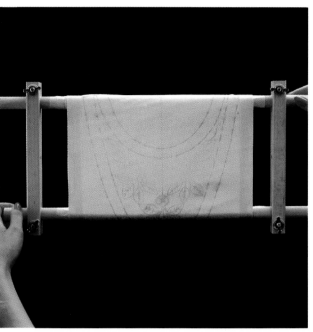

4) Tape opposite end of fabric to other cross brace, aligning crosswise grainline of fabric to marked line. Roll fabric onto cross brace to tighten fabric lengthwise, keeping grainline straight.

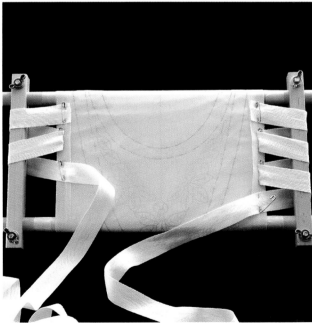

5) Pin end of 1" (2.5 cm) twill tape to edge of fabric, and loop tape over vertical brace. Pull tape slightly and pin again to edge of fabric. Repeat on opposite side of fabric, keeping grainline straight. Work back and forth across and down fabric until fabric is stretched taut.

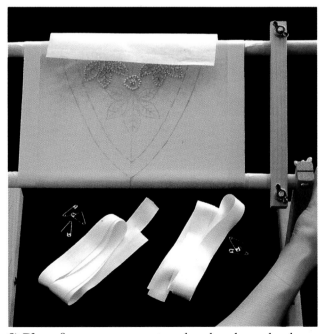

6) Place frame on supports so beadwork can be done without holding frame. After exposed fabric is beaded, unpin twill tape and place tissue paper or quilt batting over beads. Roll fabric to expose remaining unstitched area, keeping grainline straight; tissue or batting allows you to roll beaded fabric evenly, and cushions beads.

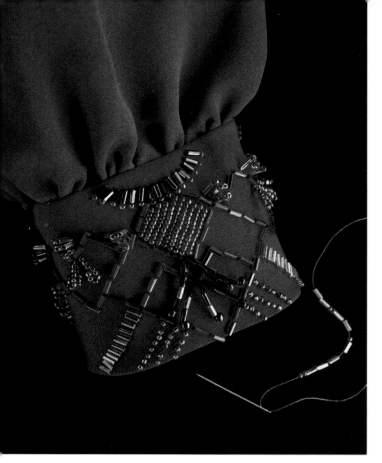

Handstitching the Beadwork

Based on two basic stitch types, the stop stitch and the running stitch, there are several variations of stitches used for beadwork. A beading needle and a double strand of waxed thread is used for beading. The eye of the needle can be backed through the fabric when it is necessary to remove a stitch. Secure the threads after every 1" to 1½" (2.5 to 3.8 cm) of stitches by knotting or backstitching.

Work from the center out toward the edges of the design. When using a scroll frame for beadwork, pass the needle from one hand above the fabric to the other hand below the fabric. To prevent distortion, do not press down on the fabric.

To make garment construction easier, stop stitching the beadwork ¼" (6 mm) from the seamlines. Compare the size of each beaded section to the pattern; if there has been shrinkage from the beadwork, adjust the cutting lines before cutting the garment section. Stitch the seams, using a zipper foot. Then complete the beadwork along the seamlines without using a hoop or frame.

How to Sew Beadwork Using the Stop Stitch

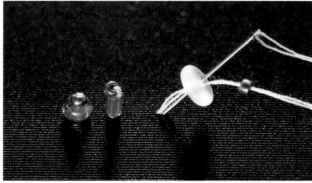

Basic stop stitch. Bring needle up through two beads on right side of fabric; the last bead threaded is called the *stop.* Bring needle back through first bead, then down through fabric to wrong side. This stitch is frequently used for attaching one large and one small seed bead, or a bugle bead and a seed bead.

Dangle stitch. Bring needle up through several beads on right side of fabric; the last bead, or the stop, is usually a small seed bead. Bring needle back through all beads except stop bead, then down through fabric to wrong side. Knot the threads on wrong side after each dangle stitch.

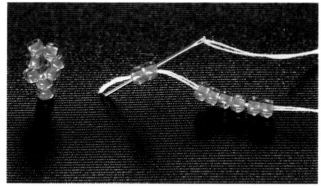

Dangle loop stitch. Bring needle up through several beads on right side of fabric; use several of these beads as the stop, forming a loop. Bring needle back through remaining bead or beads, then down through fabric.

How to Sew Beadwork Using the Running Stitch

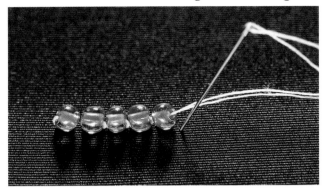

Basic running stitch. Bring needle up through a bead on right side of fabric; bring needle down to wrong side next to bead. Continue weaving needle up and down through fabric, catching a bead in each stitch. This stitch can be used for all types of beads.

Fence stitch. Weave needle up and down through fabric, as for basic running stitch, threading needle through a bugle bead, a seed bead, and a second bugle bead in each stitch. Take a short stitch so bugle beads stand on end.

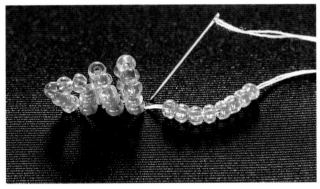

Bouclé stitch. Weave needle up and down through fabric, as for basic running stitch, threading several beads in each stitch; work stitches as close together as possible to use as filling stitches. This stitch can be used for all types of beads, but works best for round beads.

Satin stitch. Thread several beads on each running stitch, working closely spaced rows to fill in a large area. For napped fabrics, place a piece of felt, cut to shape, in the design area; this prevents beads from sinking into nap.

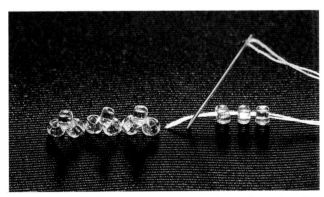

Edging stitch. Bring needle up through three beads on right side of fabric. With second bead raised away from fabric, take short stitch so third bead lies next to first bead. Take next stitch close to previous stitch. This stitch works best for round beads and is often used at edges of appliqués.

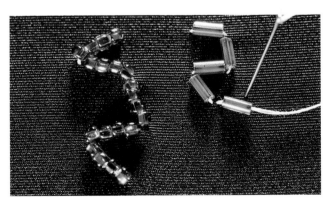

Vermicelli stitch. Weave needle up and down through fabric as for basic running stitch, threading one or more beads in each stitch; take each stitch in a different direction to form zigzag pattern.

Beaded Appliqués

For elaborate designs on large projects, such as garments, it is easier to make a beaded appliqué and attach the appliqué by hand than it is to sew the beading directly to the project. The appliqués can be easily removed before the project is dry-cleaned, to ensure that the beading will not be damaged during cleaning.

For appliqués, the beading is done through two layers of lightweight fabric, such as organza, in a color that matches the project as closely as possible.

How to Make a Beaded Appliqué

1) Position two layers of organza in embroidery hoop, and mark beading design (pages 237 and 238). Use beading design that has relatively smooth edges, avoiding jagged lines at edge of appliqué. Apply beads, using stitches on pages 240 and 241.

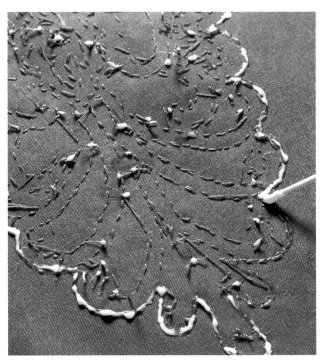

2) Turn hoop over; apply fabric glue to outer row of stitches on wrong side of fabric, using wooden pick. Also apply dot of glue to knotted thread ends. Allow glue to dry.

3) Remove fabric from hoop. Cut on outer edges of design, as close as possible to stitches without cutting them, using sharp embroidery or appliqué scissors.

4) Stitch appliqué to project next to outer row of beads, using basting stitches; take care that stitches are hidden between beads on right side. Baste around center area of appliqué to support the weight of the appliqué and to keep it from shifting.

Suede Lace

For a luxurious effect, synthetic or natural suede can be embellished with cutwork designs resembling the look of lace. Suede lace can be used to accent a collar or pocket, to border a suede skirt, or to embellish home decorating accessories.

The openings are cut into the suede, using an artist's knife and a few simple leather punch tools. Unlike the openings in traditional cutwork, openings in suede are not stitched, because they will will not ravel.

Select a lace to use as a guide for making the cutwork pattern. The lace design can be simplified to adapt it for cutwork openings. For accuracy in cutting, the pattern should not be reused.

YOU WILL NEED

Lace, used as guide for cutwork pattern.

Plastic tracing film with matte finish, available from leather craft stores, used for durable pattern that cuts easily.

Spray adhesive, used as temporary bond to keep pattern from shifting; spray adhesive will not harm fabric.

Cutting mat or tooling board.

Artist's knife with curved and straight blades; replacement blades.

Leather punch tools, available from leather craft supply stores.

Mallet, either wooden, rubber, or rawhide.

Cutting and punch tools include single-blade punch tools **(a)**, round-hole punch tools **(b)**, straight-blade artist's knife **(c)**, and curved-blade artist's knife **(d).**

How to Make Suede Lace

1) **Mark** cutting lines of pattern on plastic tracing film. Press lace to shape of pattern piece, using steam; use seamline of pattern as guide for placement of outer edge of lace. Secure lace to pattern with removable tape.

2) **Place** tracing film over lace, matching cutting lines. Trace lace design on tracing film to mark the cutwork openings, adapting design lines as desired. Remove tracing film.

3) **Spray** reverse side of plastic tracing film with spray adhesive; keep work area covered with paper when adhesive is being sprayed and while it is wet. Place tracing film, adhesive side down, on right side of suede.

4) **Cut** suede and film on cutting lines. Punch out the design areas over cutting mat by pounding punch tool with mallet. Or cut on design lines, using artist's knife. Remove film from suede.

246

Tips for Cutting Cutwork Openings

Use curved-blade artist's knife to cut curved edges, following design traced from lace.

Use straight-blade artist's knife to cut straight edges, following design traced from lace.

Use single-blade punch tool to cut straight ends of an opening; select a blade equal in width to opening. Cut long edges of opening, using straight-blade artist's knife or single-blade punch tool.

Use round-hole punch tool to cut rounded ends of an opening. Cut long edges of opening, using straight-blade or curved-blade artist's knife.

Fiber Art

Piecing

Piecing is sewing small sections of fabric together to create larger ones. It may be done by hand or machine. Scraps can be combined to create geometric shapes or pictorial scenes, or they may be assembled randomly. Several fabrics may be stacked and cut at the same time, using a rotary cutter and mat. This makes preparing the fabric for many traditional piecework patterns an easy job. Ethnic piecing traditions such as Seminole patchwork (page 252) also provide shortcut methods for creating pieced fabrics. A small pieced strip inserted diagonally into a belt or jacket front band, a miniature pieced "quilt" inserted into a man's tie, a randomly pieced jacket or vest are just a few ways piecing may be used to make a garment unique.

A "prairie point" is another form of piecing. It is a triangularly folded piece of fabric sewn into a seam. Prairie points seem to float on the surface of the fabric. They can add interesting textural and color punctuation to a pieced garment, accessory, or quilt.

How to Make a Prairie Point

Fold a strip of fabric in half lengthwise. Bring folded edges together at center. Press and trim the ends to form a triangle. Stitch into seam. Folded edges may face either up or down.

Necktie with a pieced insert can be made using a commercial pattern and choosing the piecing design and location.

Vest features a variety of piecing designs and prairie points for surface interest.

Pieced belt or waistband can tie an outfit together by coordinating colors from the garment or accessories.

Seminole Patchwork

The quick and easy strip-piecing techniques of the Florida Indians have traditionally been done on the sewing machine. Two of the Seminole patchwork patterns, checkerboard and diagonal, are shown below and can be made using a quick piecing technique. Seminole patchwork can be incorporated into vests, belts, and ties, or combined with other patchwork designs.

How to Sew a Seminole Patchwork Strip (checkerboard)

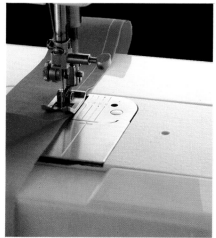

1) Cut equal strips of two different fabrics on the straight grain. Stitch the strips together, using a 1/4" (6 mm) seam allowance. Press the seam to one side.

2) Cut pieced fabric perpendicular to seam, into strips the same width as the original. A see-through ruler and rotary cutter are helpful for this.

3) Arrange strips in a checkerboard pattern. Stitch together, using a 1/4" (6 mm) seam allowance; match center seams carefully. Press seams to one side.

How to Sew a Seminole Patchwork Strip (diagonal)

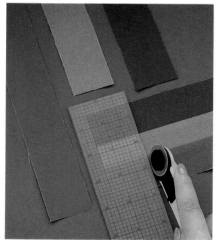

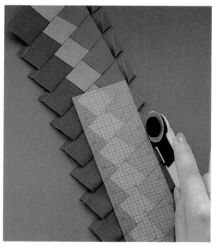

1) Cut equal strips of three different fabrics on the straight grain. Stitch together, press, and cut into strips as in steps 1 and 2, above.

2) Arrange strips so top of center stripe aligns with middle of center stripe on adjoining strip. Stitch, using 1/4" (6 mm) seam allowances. Press seams to one side.

3) Trim off points on raw edges to make the strip even.

Pleating

Pleats are formed by folding and pressing fabric. Some very interesting effects may be achieved with pleating on striped fabrics. An interesting striped fabric can be created by piecing fabric in gradations of color alternately with black as shown. Then the colored stripes are concealed within the pressed pleats. Where the pleats are released at hip level, the colors show with the slightest movement.

For any striped fabric, whether you buy it or piece it yourself, the width of the stripes determines the width of the pleats. Experiment to decide which colors to show and which to hide within the pleats. Pleats may be released from a seam or held in position at one end with edgestitching.

Lightweight wools, cottons, silks, and linens will pleat sharply. Select crisp, firm fabrics for garments with pressed pleats. Also, check to see if stripes are on the straight grain before buying a fabric; pleats will not hang properly if stripes are off grain.

Creating Patchwork Fabrics

Cut a striped fabric apart and stitch it together in a new way to create a coordinating fabric. Creating a new design requires planning, careful fabric and pattern selection, and accurate sewing.

A variety of effects can be achieved, depending on the width of the stripe, the number of colors, and whether the fabric has even or uneven stripes. The design can also be changed by varying the width of the cut strips. This pieced fabric works best as a border on a shirt or top, or for small areas of a blouse or dress, such as pockets, yokes, or cuffs.

Create a fabric with a new look by stitching strips of striped fabric together in a staggered pattern.

Stitch strips of striped fabric together to create a checkerboard effect. Vary the width of the cut strips, or cut all strips the same width.

Add soutache braid along seamlines of pieced striped fabric to embellish the new fabric.

How to Make Patchwork Fabrics

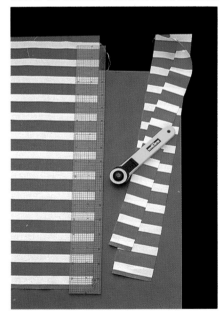

1) Cut crosswise strips from striped fabric the desired finished width plus ½" (1.3 cm) for seam allowances.

2) Realign strips, with color blocks staggered as desired. Pin, with right sides together and raw edges even; stitch ¼" (6 mm) seams. Finish edges, and press open.

Alternative. Cut soutache braid the length of seams. Center braid over seam, and apply as shown.

Slashing

Slashing is a process of sandwiching and stitching together several layers of fabric, and then cutting through some of them in spots to expose successive layers. When washed, dried, and brushed, the cut edges curl and fray to create a richly textured surface. This technique can create colorful, textural effects, and is sometimes called "blooming."

Slashing may be done within a grid of rectangles or triangles, or between a series of lines. The fabrics may be layered as full-size pattern pieces, or as an insert for a yoke or other section of a garment. For inserts, bits and pieces may be sandwiched for interesting color variations and textural effects to pull an outfit together. Use tightly woven natural fiber fabrics, such as cotton.

Slashed panel of blouse is a good beginning project. Use colors in print fabric for inner layers.

How to Make Fabric "Bloom"

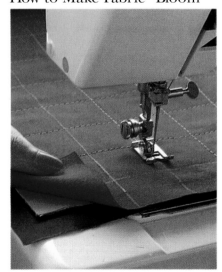

1) Cut six pieces of tightly woven 100 percent cotton according to pattern. Trim seam allowances off the four inner layers. Mark a grid of 1⅜" (3.5 cm) squares on top layer. Stack layers, matching seamlines; stitch together on marked lines.

2) Cut a ¼" (6 mm) slit in center of selected squares along diagonal, using seam ripper. Cut through any or all of the top five layers of fabric; do not cut through the backing layer. Clip from center to corners, using sharp scissors.

3) Wash and dry by machine to make the fabric "bloom." The more times you wash and dry it, the more fabric will bloom. If desired, brush surface with stiff brush to fray cut edges.

Appliqué, Embroidery & Beading

Appliqué, embroidery, and beading are three surface design techniques in which something is applied on top of a base fabric. Often, these techniques are combined to produce striking visual and textural effects on the surface of a garment.

Traditionally, appliqué, embroidery, and beading have been done by hand. Stunning results may also be achieved using the sewing machine. Special presser feet are available for most sewing machines for satin stitching, free-motion embroidery, and for applying braid, beading, and cording. Many threads, such as ribbon threads and embroidery threads, are designed for decorative stitching. The decorative stitches built into your sewing machine, used creatively with interesting threads, cording, and fabric combinations, can yield attractive results.

When planning a sewing project that includes appliqué, embroidery, or beading, be sure to consider the compatibility of your materials. For example, don't use invisible nylon thread to sew an appliqué to linen; the high heat necessary to press the linen will melt the nylon thread. Make sure your ribbon or yarn is colorfast if used on a washable garment. Thinking ahead about compatibility of all materials used and practicing these techniques on scraps will save time and trouble in the long run.

Another surface treatment for a finished garment, which can be used on its own or with other techniques, is painting the surface with fabric or puff paints. Paints can be spattered, sponged, or stamped, and some, such as puff paints, may be used directly out of the tube. A variety of fabrics, including leather, can be painted, but test the paint on scraps of the fabric or leather that you are using. Leather scraps, painted or unpainted, are great for appliqués or accessories.

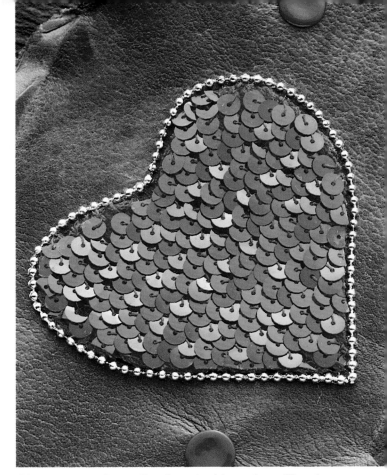

Glue on a sequin appliqué, and add a string of beads to the appliqué.

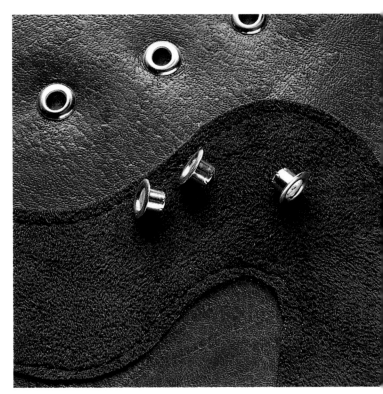

Thread strips of leather through slits in leather or suede, and add upholstery trim by hand. Apply decorative snaps for more interest.

Sew leather appliqués, using the straight stitch on your sewing machine, and add eyelets or snaps.

Color & Design for Quilting

Quilts keep us warm and give us beautiful visual images. It is a satisfying experience to plan, cut, piece, and quilt, but it is even more satisfying to design your own quilt from scratch and choose the best possible colors to interact on the surface of your quilt. We need to rely on our own design sense and experience plus training in design and color to give a feeling of confidence. We all have an inner sense of balance and placement, but for some it may take more time to make a decision. Have confidence in yourself; take time for the design process to work. At each step of the process, stop and look at your design. Display it where you will walk by it and look at it. You will make your decision after a bit of time.

A knowledge of basic color terms makes the process more understandable. The process of designing first a block and then a quilt can be simple. Start with one block design as shown opposite. When the block design has been chosen, as well as the values, the block placement needs to be decided (pages 262 to 263).

Both of these steps are very systematic, making the whole process nonthreatening.

Definition of Color Terms

Value is the degree of lightness or darkness of a color. Light values are tints, and dark values are shades.

Hue is the name of a color.

Tint is a hue with white added, yielding a color lighter than a pure hue.

Shade is a hue with black added, yielding a color darker than a pure hue.

Tone is a hue with gray added, yielding a color with a gray quality.

Intensity or saturation is the purity or grayness of a color, the relative brightness or dullness. Colors with strong intensity are nearer the pure hue, and colors of weak intensity are approaching a gray.

Complementary colors are colors directly opposite each other on the color wheel. Complementary colors give a strong contrast; when mixed together or placed side by side, they tend to gray each other.

How to Design a Quilt

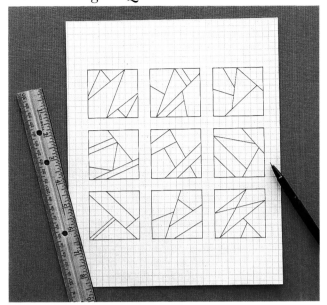

1) Draw a number of 2" or 3" (5 or 7.5 cm) squares on graph paper, with space between each square. Divide each square into six or eight areas.

2) Choose one or two of these designs to do a value study. It is too early to add color, as this introduces another element, so do your value studies using a black pen. You will have black and white as the strongest values, and by drawing lines (fine or heavy, close together or farther apart, and cross-hatching), you will get values of black, white, and gray.

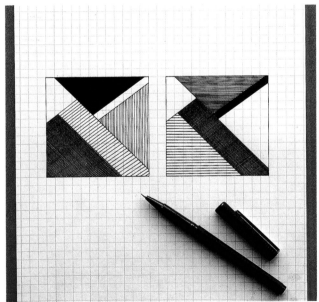

3) Do two or three value studies of the same design. The proportions of black, white, and gray change when the positions are rotated. The designs will look very different if black is placed in the largest shape and, on the next design, in the smallest shape. If the largest shape is solid black, it may overpower the design, especially at the next step in the designing process when the blocks are put together. From these value studies, choose one to work with.

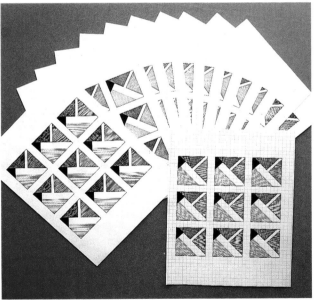

4) Draw a page of the value study you chose, and photocopy it several times. Cut the designs apart, and work with these copies for the next step of the design process. This will save a lot of drawing time. The reproduction process distorts the image; therefore, use the copy as a designing tool, but go back to the original drawing when making templates.

Block Rotations

Until now the quilt block has been a single unit; now work in four-block units. Start by labeling one module as follows: A is the upper left corner, B is the upper right corner, C is the lower right corner, and D is the lower left corner.

After you have gone through the following steps, decide which block you like best and what size you want to make the block. Both the mirror image and the counterclockwise rotations work best with more divisions to the block.

1) Put the first four modules together the same way. The quilt top would then be formed with the units always in the same direction, with AB at the top.

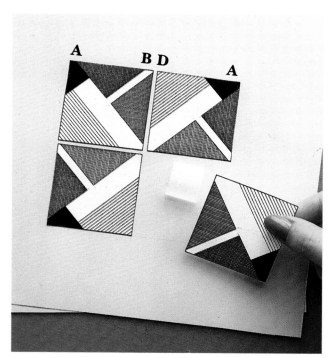

2) Start with AB at the top of the upper left module, and rotate the next module a quarter turn clockwise. DA is now at the top of the upper right module. Continue by rotating each module a quarter turn.

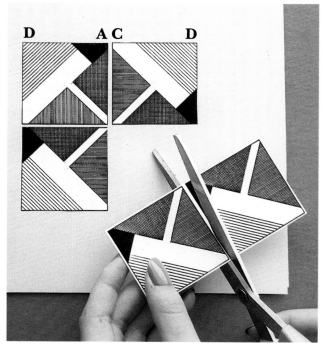

3) Start the block with DA at the top, and continue quarter rotations as in step 2.

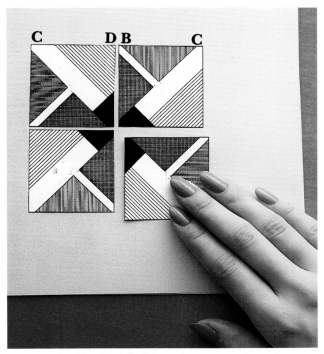

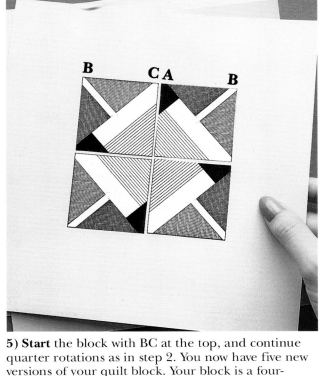

4) Start the block with CD at the top, and continue quarter rotations as in step 2.

5) Start the block with BC at the top, and continue quarter rotations as in step 2. You now have five new versions of your quilt block. Your block is a four-block unit instead of a single unit. It also looks very different from the single module.

Reverse image. Put a mirror on the edge of your design. To draw this reversal, turn your original drawing face down, and take it to a light table or window. With the light coming through the paper, trace the design.

Counterclockwise rotation. To create another design variation, follow instructions for clockwise rotations, except rotate the modules counterclockwise.

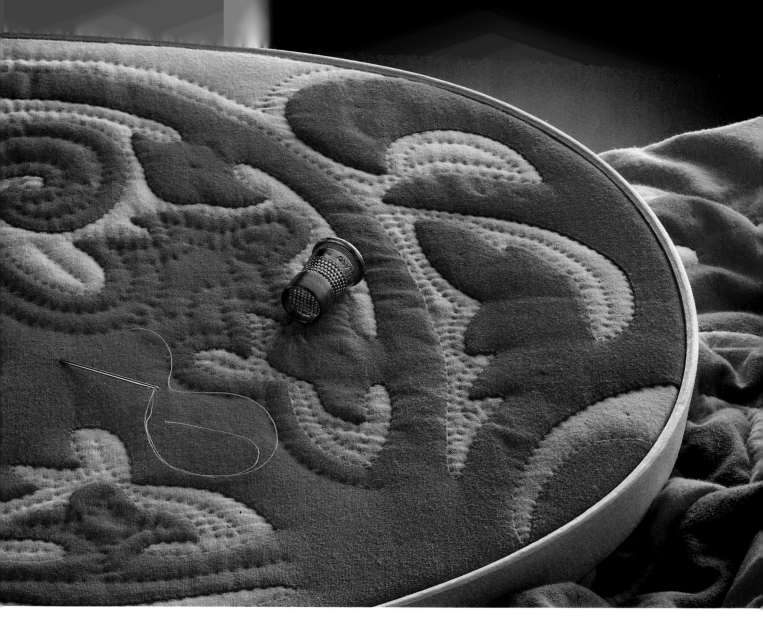

Hand Appliqué for Quilting

Appliqué is often perceived to be a tedious, time-consuming task. It takes time, but you can create any shape or form you desire within the limits of the technique. It can be realistic or abstract; the lines can be curved or straight. In a pieced quilt, most designs are based on straight lines, but in appliqué, most are based on curved lines. There is more freedom in hand appliqué. There are several different appliqué methods. In regular appliqué, several pieces are arranged to create a design; each piece lies directly on the background fabric, except for small areas where an edge of one piece might lie under another. In multilayered appliqué, several pieces lie one on top of the other, giving the design a three-dimensional look.

To make an appliqué quilt top, you will need a needle and thread, pins, scissors, markers, a well-padded ironing board, and a steam iron. Beeswax and a thimble are optional, but helpful. For Hawaiian and other large-motif quilts, you will also need shears. For quilts with motifs that are repeated, you will need to prepare templates for cutting pattern shapes.

Use a good-quality regular sewing thread. Match the thread to the color of the piece you are appliquéing. Work with a length of thread about 18" (46 cm) long. Longer lengths just get in the way and take too long to pull through the fabric, often creating small knots in the thread. And the more a thread is pulled through the fabric, the more it becomes worn, causing it to break. If the thread tends to tangle and break, try pulling it through beeswax.

Sew with the thinnest needle you can use comfortably. This may be a sharp or a between (a quilting needle), size 10 or 12.

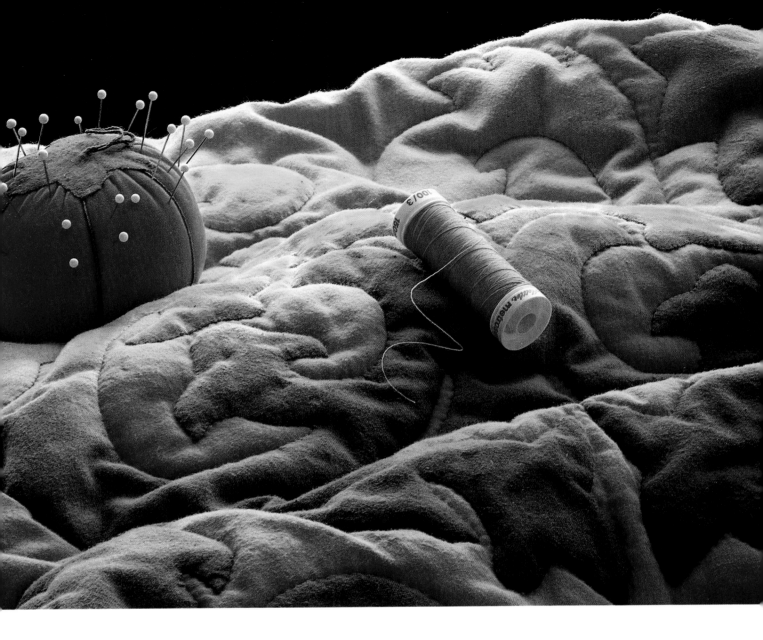

Templates may be cut from plastic or other materials. Cut templates without seam allowances. Add a scant ¼" (6 mm) seam allowance to each piece of fabric when cutting it out. At first, you may want to mark seam allowances before you cut; with practice, you will be able to judge the correct seam allowance by eye and eliminate the marking step.

When marking around templates onto the appliqué fabric, use a sandpaper board under the fabric to keep the fabric and template from slipping, and to make a darker impression with the marker. Make a sandpaper board by gluing a piece of very fine wet/dry sandpaper to a stiff piece of cardboard, plastic, or ¼" (6 mm) plywood.

The best stitch to use for appliqué is the blindstitch. It virtually disappears into the fabric. If you can learn to work the blindstitch both toward and away

from yourself, it can be a big help. Some pieces are easier to sew in one direction than the other. Take very small stitches when blindstitching. The smaller the stitch, the more control. Stitches ⅟16" (1.5 mm) apart or less are recommended.

The heart is a classic design for learning appliqué, because it includes techniques for stitching straight edges, curves, and both inside and outside corners. Careful placement of pins, minimum seam allowances, and the needle-rolling technique, combined with the blindstitch, allow you to sew smooth edges with invisible stitches without basting.

How to Blindstitch a Heart Appliqué Using the Needle-rolling Technique

1) **Trace** outline of design lightly on background fabric. Trace design on right side of appliqué fabric, with straight of grain running through center. Cut out appliqué with scant ¼" (6 mm) seam allowance.

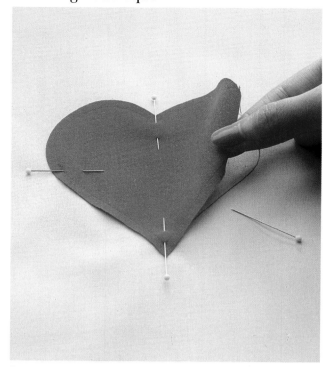

2) **Match** stitching line of appliqué to line drawn on background fabric; pin at top, bottom, and each side. Remove pin on straight edge; turn under seam allowance and repin through fold.

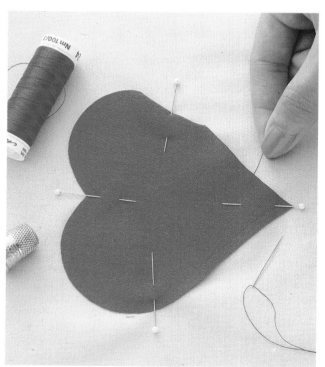

3) **Tie** knot at one end of thread. Bring threaded needle up through fabric from wrong side of appliqué slightly away from point at marked line. Knot will be hidden in fold.

4) **Place** heel of hand on background fabric and hold pinned fold with other hand. Holding fabric taut, use tip of needle to roll under seam allowance to make a smooth line.

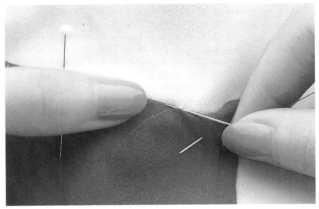

5) Put needle down through background fabric at edge of appliqué. Bring needle up into fold. Keep stitches small and needle parallel to edge of appliqué; pull thread snug. Blindstitch to pin.

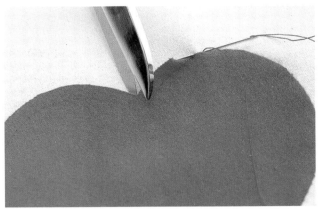

6) Pin fold on curve ½" (1.3 cm) from last stitch. Roll under seam allowance and blindstitch, as in steps 4 and 5. Continue stitching to top of curve. Clip to point. Stitch to ½" (1.3 cm) of inside point.

7) Pin folded edge just beyond clip. Roll under on marked line from pin to stitches, using a little tension from the needle; pull fabric taut so seam allowance will turn under smoothly.

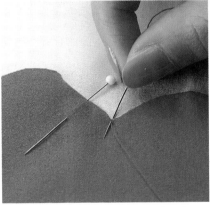

8) Stitch to point, rolling edge just beyond marked line at point; take two small overcast stitches. Stitch remaining curve in small segments.

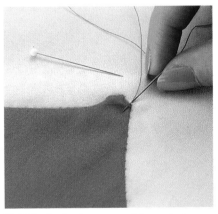

9) Blindstitch to outside point. Remove pin and take a small stitch. Fold seam allowance flat (90° angle) at the point. Take another stitch to secure point.

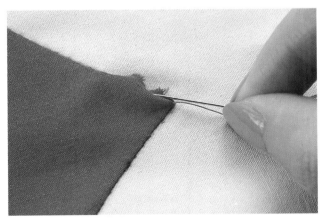

10) Use needle to pleat in seam allowance; this allows you to make a point half the width of the seam allowance. Tuck under remaining seam allowance; blindstitch.

11) End blindstitching by going over the same stitch three times on wrong side of background fabric under edge of appliqué. Run the thread under the appliqué; clip near surface.

Rag Baskets

Rag baskets can be made by machine or by hand. Making rag baskets is a good way to use your stockpile of lightweight cotton or blended fabrics.

Try a basket in just one favorite fabric, or use a variety of fabrics. When choosing several fabrics, look for a mix of large and small florals, geometrics, stripes, checks, plaids, or tone-on-tone prints.

Cut fabric in 1" (2.5 cm) strips on the crosswise grain with rotary cutter or scissors, and ruler. When making a basket by machine, use a size 100/16 needle and a zigzag stitch. For making baskets by hand, use a size 85/13 tapestry needle. Use matching thread on either basket. The cording diameter can be varied on the hand-constructed basket (see You Will Need box).

Use your imagination in embellishing the baskets. Try large wooden or ceramic beads for handles. Wooden handles can be purchased and painted in coordinating colors. You can decorate your basket with woodland figures or silk flowers. Try a sprig of artificial holly for a Christmas basket. Heart-shaped or rectangular wooden bases, available in craft stores, will give your basket a different shape.

Use rag baskets as containers for mail, magazines, craft projects, jewelry, plants, fruit, guest towels, or nursery items. Construct flat coils for coasters, trivets, placemats, and rugs.

YOU WILL NEED

For machine-constructed basket:

Basket cording or clothesline, ¼" (6 mm) diameter or less.

Lightweight cottons or blends.

For hand-constructed basket:

Basket cording, in ¼", ½", or ¾" (6 mm, 1.3 mm, or 2 cm) diameter.

Lightweight cotton or blended fabric; 1" (2.5 cm) strips for either narrow cording, or 1½" (3.8 cm) strips for wider cording.

How to Make Machine-constructed Baskets

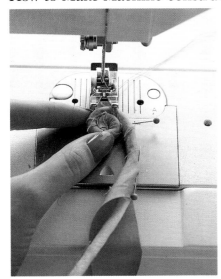

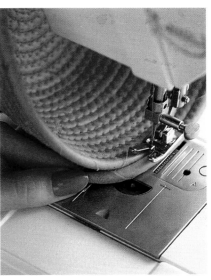

1) **Cover** end of cord with fabric strip, and wrap 5" to 6" (12.5 to 15 cm). Pin to hold in place. Bend into spiral shape, and zigzag together. For an oval basket or placemats, make your first turn 3" to 4" (7.5 to 10 cm) from the beginning.

2) **Continue** to turn and zigzag together until base is desired size. Turn work on edge, pressing base against machine to form sides. At the end of a fabric strip, start another; overlap previous strip. Splice cord, page 270, step 3.

3) **Continue** sewing until basket is the desired height. End by cutting cord and wrapping fabric slightly past end of cord. Stitch end to previous coil.

How to Make Hand-constructed Baskets

1) Taper end of cording with scissors. Thread tapestry needle onto a fabric strip. Take end of strip opposite from needle, and begin wrapping it tightly around cording about 5" (12.5 cm) from end. Wrap almost to end of cording. Bend end of cording to make a loop. Leave a hole in the loop. Wrap over both cords.

2) Start spiraling cord to form a circle. To fasten, insert the needle into the hole that was left and pull fabric firmly. Repeat. Construction now consists of wrapping the cording independently 2 or 3 times and then fastening to previous coil 2 or 3 times. Needle cannot pierce fabric, so find a spot where needle can go through.

3) Overlap new strip over end of previous strip. To splice cording, taper ends of old and new cords for about 4" (10 cm). Overlap the ends; wrap masking tape around the splice. Continue until bottom is desired diameter. Build up sides to desired height by laying cording on top of previous coil.

4) Add handles to last course of basket. Secure cord 3 or 4 times; wrap cord independently 5" to 6" (12.5 to 15 cm). Bend into handle shape. Secure to previous coil 3 or 4 times. Continue halfway around basket, and make second handle.

5) Finish basket by cutting cord at an angle and wrapping with fabric. Weave end of fabric in and out, and cut off.

Rug Braiding

A handmade braided rug is a decorative addition to a room. The manufactured braided rug will never equal the handmade rug in durability and beauty. It can be made in any size desired, from a small mat to a room-size rug. A variety of shapes can be braided: oval, round, square, rectangular, and heart. Patterns are often braided into a rug, and color schemes are planned in detail.

Select two or three colors from your room as the colors for your rug. Don't make the center a solid dark color; your rug will look like a target or a hole in the floor. Color changes should be made one strip at a time at the eleven o'clock position. A complete color change will take three rounds.

Braiding accessories greatly reduce the time spent creating these beautiful rugs. For example, Braid-Aid™ is a tool used for folding fabric strips.

Start with an oval rug as a beginner, because this shape is the easiest. Although the rug is reversible, it will have two distinct sides. Braid on the top side, and lace on the bottom side. The top side will be more colorful and will have a sculptured look. Keep the tension tight and even as you braid, and the rug will be durable enough to last for years.

The most durable rugs are made from 100 percent wool. Collect all your fabric before you start your project. Start by finding things in your own home; old woolen blankets, coats, suits, and scraps from sewing projects can be used. Also, a woolen mill that manufactures blankets or a company that makes coats may sell scraps.

Wash fabrics with warm water in a mild soap solution. They may be machine washed on gentle cycle and dried at low temperatures to preshrink and soften the fabric for easier braiding.

Cut the strips on the straight grain of the fabric to the desired width. The width is determined by the weight of the wool. The length of the center braid is determined by the planned size of your finished rug. It will be the width subtracted from the length of the rug; for example, a 2' by 3' (61 by 91.5 cm) rug will have a center braid of 1' (30.5 cm). When the center braid is the desired length, work a modified square corner; this puts a sharp turn in the braid.

The weakest part of your rug is the lacing. Never shake a braided rug. Don't hang the rug; hanging weakens the lacing. To vacuum, use the attachments and follow around, not across, the braids. To clean, use the same method you use for the rest of your carpeting. Very little water is needed; only the top surface needs to be washed. Professional cleaners who have experience cleaning braided rugs do an excellent job. If storing your rug, roll it up and wrap it in a sheet.

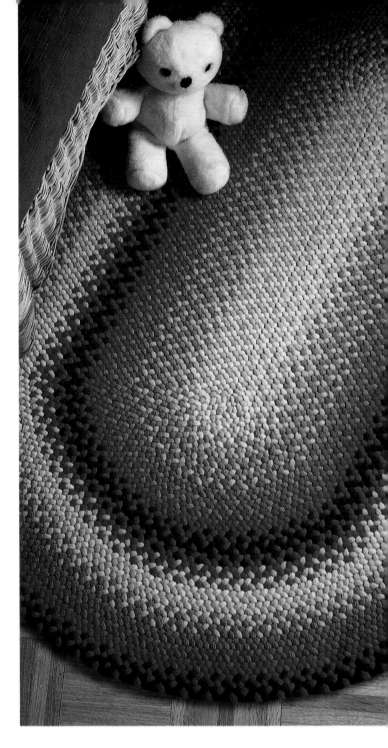

YOU WILL NEED

Strips of 100 percent wool fabric. A rug, 1' × 1' (30.5 × 30.5 cm) requires 1 yd. (0.95 m) or 1 lb. (0.45 kg) of fabric.

Braid-Aid™, a tool for folding strips into tubes (kit of 3).

Braidkin™, a curved bodkin needle used for lacing.

Linen thread, 3-ply for small projects and 6-ply for rugs over 6' × 6' (183 × 183 cm).

Rotary cutter or scissors; ruler.

How to Make an Oval Braided Rug

1) Begin by threading the strips into the Braid-Aids™. Join two of the strips with a bias seam. Trim and press open. (Use a bias seam for adding future strips.)

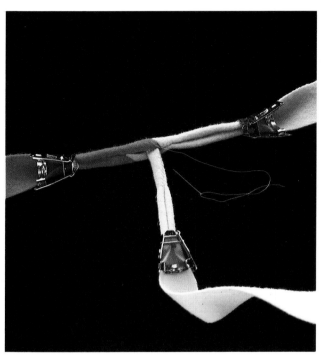

2) Attach the third strip to one side of the seam (T-start), with the opening to the right. For the first few inches (centimeters), hand stitching may be necessary to hold folds in place.

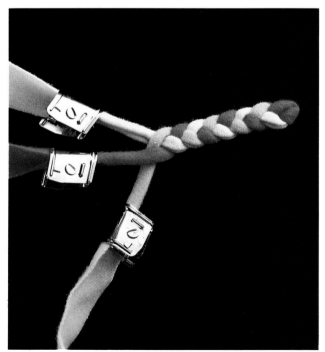

3) Braid right strip over center, left strip over center, and continue alternating strips in this order. Keep the opening to the right. Develop an even tension that is tight enough so you cannot separate the braids with your fingers. Work to desired length.

4) Make modified squared corner by numbering the strips from left to right: 1, 2, and 3. Work 1 over 2, 2 over 1, 3 over 2 tightly. Renumber strips from left to right, and repeat once.

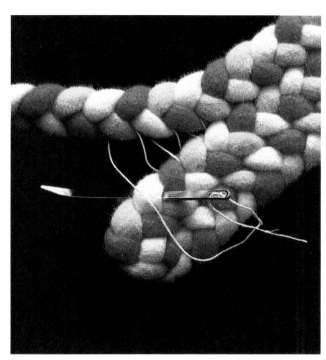

5) Sew two center braids together, starting at first bend and working around T-start; use a sharp needle and linen thread. Switch to bodkin needle. On the straight sides, lace every loop of rug and braid. On the curved ends, skip loops of braid only.

6) Relace if rug cups, skipping more loops of braid. Rippled edge indicates too many skipped loops. On the next round, skip fewer loops, and the problem will correct itself.

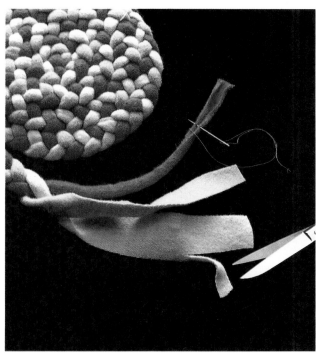

7) Finish rug by tapering each strip 5" to 7" (12.5 to 18 cm) on curve. Turn under the edge of each strip, and blindstitch together with matching thread.

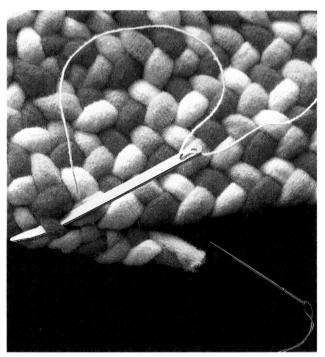

8) Braid to the end. Lace as far as you can, then back-lace several inches (centimeters), and cut the thread. Tuck end into loop, and blindstitch in place.

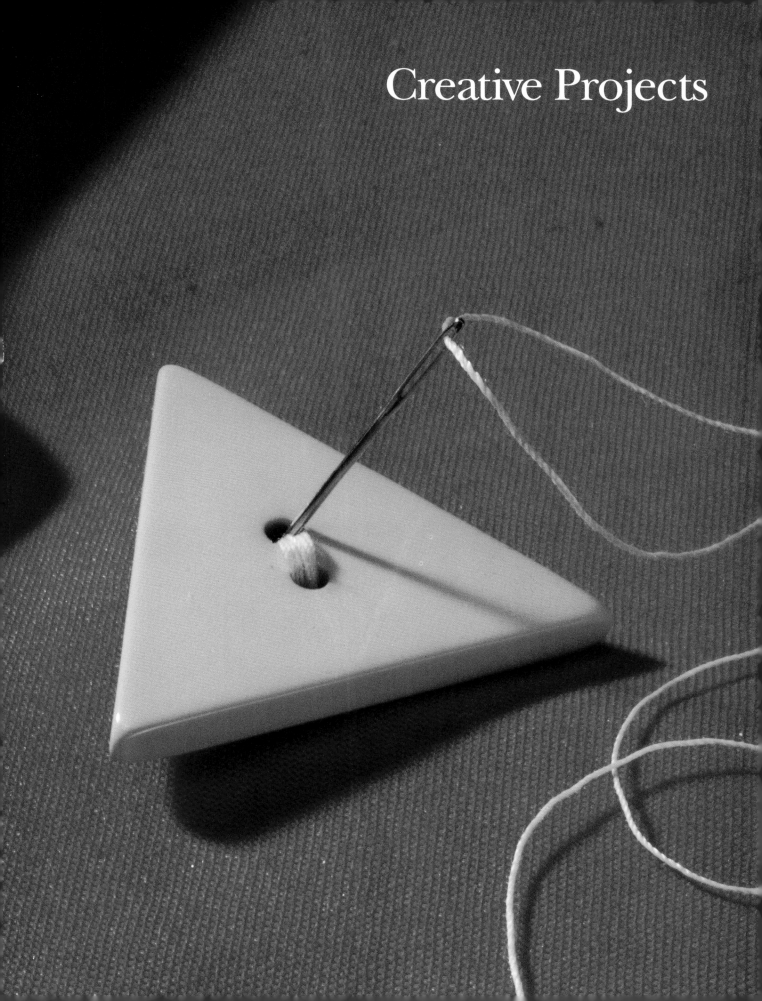

Creative Projects

Portfolios

Portfolios are especially useful for business or school. A basic portfolio can be varied by adding a decorative closure, changing the shape of the flap, or making a contrasting flap.

For the body of a basic portfolio, cut one 29" × 15½" (73.5 × 39.3 cm) piece from outer fabric, interfacing, and lining. For the side panels, cut two 10½" × 2¾" (26.8 × 7 cm) pieces from outer fabric. For the inside divider, cut one 15½" × 10½" (39.3 × 26.8 cm) piece from outer fabric. For ⅜" (1 cm) binding, cut 2½" (6.5 cm) bias strips and piece them together, as necessary, for a combined length of 2¾ yd. (2.55 m).

If a contrasting flap is desired, cut the body and flap as follows. For the body, cut one 23" × 15½" (58.5 × 39.3 cm) piece from outer fabric and interfacing. For the flap, cut one 7" × 15½" (18 × 39.3 cm) piece from flap fabric and interfacing. Cut the lining, side panels, inside divider, and binding strips the same as for the basic portfolio. Apply the interfacing, and seam the body and the flap together in a ½" (1.3 cm) seam; then follow the instructions for the basic portfolio.

To make a more rigid portfolio, cover a piece of plastic canvas with fabric and insert it in the completed portfolio to use as an additional divider. Cut one 21½" × 15" (54.8 × 38 cm) piece of outer fabric and one 10¼" × 14¼" (26.2 × 36.2 cm) piece of plastic canvas.

YOU WILL NEED

Outer fabric, heavyweight and durable.

Lining fabric.

Fusible interfacing.

Button, snap, or hook and loop tape, for closure.

Plastic canvas, 10¼" × 14¼" (26.2 × 36.2 cm), for optional rigid divider.

How to Sew a Basic Portfolio

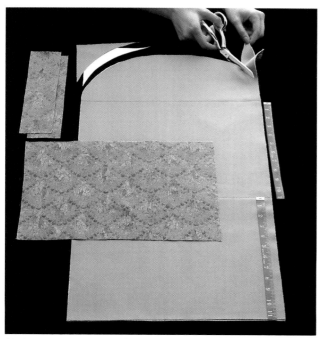

1) Cut fabric (page 276). Apply interfacing to wrong side of outer fabric for body of portfolio. Pin lining over interfacing. Mark two foldlines, with one foldline 11½" (29.3 cm) from one short end and the second foldline 11" (28 cm) from first foldline; machine-baste on marked lines. Cut flap to desired shape.

2) Finish upper edges of portfolio and side panels; finish lower edges of side panels if fabric ravels. At upper edges, turn under ½" (1.3 cm); stitch in place.

3) Stitch binding to upper long edge of inside divider, enclosing edge (page 193). Finish lower edge if fabric ravels. Place divider, right side up, over center portion of body of portfolio, with lower edge extending ¼" (6 mm) beyond bottom foldline. Stitch ¼" (6 mm) from lower edge of divider.

4) Place side panels over divider, with right sides up and raw edges even, aligning upper edge of each side panel to foldline. Baste on outer edge through all layers.

5) Apply binding, starting 12" (30.5 cm) from end of binding strip, to outer edge of portfolio, from bottom foldline on one side, around flap, to bottom foldline on other side. Stitch as for bound edge on page 193, step 1.

6) Fold portfolio on bottom foldline; press. Pin the remaining long edges of side panels to front of bag, aligning upper edges. Continue stitching binding to outer edges on front of portfolio. Cut excess binding ½" (1.3 cm) from upper edge.

7) Fold ends of binding to inside; fold binding around edges. Stitch in the ditch, as on page 193, step 2; for easier handling, stitching may stop 2" (5 cm) from bottom foldline on both sides of portfolio.

8) Stitch front and back of portfolio together for 2" (5 cm) at lower end of each side. Lightly press flap in place. Remove basting stitches at foldlines. Apply closure.

Rigid divider. Fold fabric in half crosswise, right sides together; stitch ¼" (6 mm) seams on sides. Turn right side out; press. Insert plastic canvas. Fold under ¼" (6 mm) on raw edges; slipstitch closed. Place divider in portfolio.

Jewelry bag, above, is made from screen-printed fabric.

Evening bag, below, made from twisted silk, is embellished with machine-stitched beadwork.

Zippered Bags

Zippered bags can be made in several sizes. These lightly padded bags can be used as cosmetic bags, jewelry pouches, or evening bags, depending on the fabrics and embellishments used.

For each bag, you need one rectangle each of outer fabric, polyester fleece, and lining. Cut the rectangles twice the length of the bag plus ½" (1.3 cm) by the width of the bag plus ½" (1.3 cm); this includes ¼" (6 mm) seam allowances. For example, for a finished size of 5" wide × 4" long (12.5 × 10 cm), cut 5½" × 8½" (14 × 21.8 cm) rectangles.

YOU WILL NEED

Outer fabric, polyester fleece, and lining fabric.

One zipper, at least ½" (1.3 cm) longer than cut measurement for upper side of bag.

Travel bags in various sizes and shapes are trimmed with slentre braids.

How to Sew a Basic Zippered Bag

1) **Cut** one rectangle each from outer fabric, polyester fleece, and lining (page 280). Place outer fabric, right side up, on fleece; pin.

2) **Pin** a closed zipper to one upper edge of outer fabric, right sides together, aligning raw edge of fabric to edge of zipper tape; ends of zipper may extend beyond fabric. Stitch ¼" (6 mm) seam, using zipper foot.

3) **Align** opposite side of bag to zipper, right sides together, and stitch, as in step 2.

4) **Open** zipper. Place lining and outer bag right sides together, matching along one upper edge, with zipper sandwiched between layers. With fleece facing up, stitch over previous stitches. Repeat for opposite side of the lining.

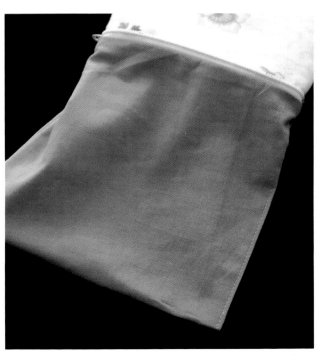

5) Close zipper partially. Pin side seams, right sides together, with lining to lining and outer bag to outer bag; match the zipper seamlines, and turn zipper teeth toward the outer bag. Stitch ¼" (6 mm) seams, leaving 3" (7.5 cm) opening in lining on one side; stitch over zipper teeth. Cut off ends of zipper.

6) Turn bag right side out through opening. Turn in seam allowances at opening; topstitch closed. Fold lining inside bag.

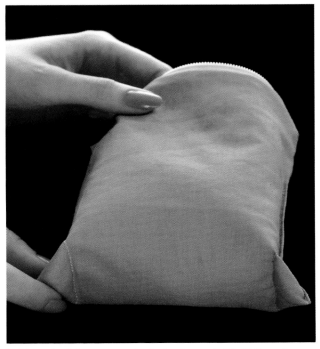

7) Push in lower corners, from right side, to shape the box corners.

8) Turn inside out, and stitch about 1½" (3.8 cm) across corners, through both lining and outer bag. Turn bag right side out.

Handbags with Inset

A creative accessory, such as a clutch, can be the final touch to make a special garment complete. Even the most expensive garment will improve with the addition of accessories. It is easy to coordinate accessories, especially if you have made the garment; you can use scraps of the same fabric or use a design or color from a print fabric.

The cost of ready-made accessories can quickly go over any wardrobe budget. Yet the cost of materials to make accessories is minimal, and you need not be an expert sewer. Find just the right color and fabric for making accessories. You may want to shop for accessory materials when you shop for the fabric and notions for your garment.

This elegant synthetic suede handbag may sell in a boutique for $100, but can be created for far less and can be made in the exact color and style you want. The bag shown, with finished dimensions of about 12¼" × 8¼" (31.2 × 21.2 cm), is only a beginning. Have fun piecing together synthetic suede scraps, stitching a monogram, or combining synthetic suede with snakeskin. Any fabric or design you wish can be used as the inset. Create the bag with an original design, making your own pattern (opposite).

✂ Cutting Directions

From fleece and fusible web, cut two rectangles each, 13½" × 9" (34.3 × 23 cm).

From synthetic suede, cut one rectangle 13½" × 9" (34.3 × 23 cm), three pieces using the pattern (opposite), two facing strips 13½" × 2" (34.3 × 5 cm), and two casing strips 11" × 1" (28 × 2.5 cm).

From lining fabric and interfacing, cut two rectangles each, 13½" × 7½" (34.3 × 19.3 cm).

YOU WILL NEED

12" (30.5 cm) metal snap-close frame, available at fabric stores or by mail.

¼ **yd. (0.25 m) synthetic suede.**

Snakeskin or scraps of synthetic suede, or any fabrics desired, for inset.

¼ **yd. (0.25 m) each of lining,** fleece, fusible web such as Wonder-Under™, and interfacing.

Glue stick or basting glue; thread.

How to Make a Pattern for Handbag Inset

1) **Draw** and cut rectangle, 13½" × 9" (34.3 × 23 cm), from paper. Draw design lines for inset, as shown. Finished inset piece is about 2½" (6.5 cm) wide. This design may be any shape or size desired.

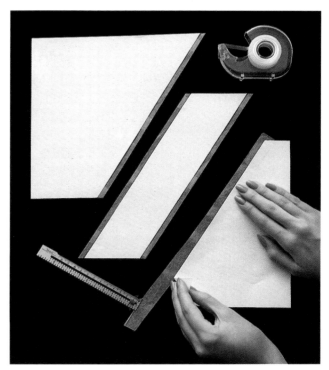

2) **Cut** pattern apart on drawn design lines. Add ¼" (6 mm) seam allowances to by adding strips of tissue paper extending ¼" (6 mm) design lines.

3) **Cut** inset pattern piece from snakeskin or desired inset fabric, and the two larger pattern pieces from synthetic suede.

4) **Place** synthetic suede and inset fabric right sides together; stitch, using ¼" (6 mm) seam allowances. Finger-press seam allowances to suede side. Topstitch suede, close to edge.

How to Make a Handbag

1) Fuse fleece to wrong side of the bag pieces by sandwiching fusible web between fleece and bag. Fuse only the suede, since snakeskin may melt with too much heat. Fuse interfacing to wrong side of lining. (Test any handbag materials to make sure they can tolerate heat needed for fusing.)

2) Center casing strips on suede facing strips, and secure with glue stick along long edges only. Topstitch each long edge, backstitching at each end. Stitch a facing strip to each bag piece, right sides together, with ¼" (6 mm) seam allowance. Trim away fleece at top of bag front and back. Stitch long edges of lining pieces to each free edge of suede facing strip.

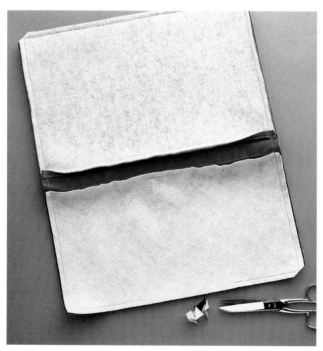

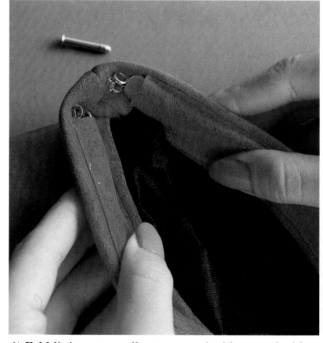

3) Align the two rectangles, right sides together, matching seams. Stitch, leaving a 5" (12.5 cm) centered opening at base of lining; clip corners. Turn right side out; slipstitch opening.

4) Fold lining seam allowances to inside; match side seams, and topstitch top edge ¼" (6 mm) from edge. Smooth lining to inside. Remove metal pins from ends of frame, and insert frame in casing. Replace pins.

Handbag Ideas

Strip-pieced inset (above) adds color to a synthetic suede bag. Thread a strip of fabric through chain for a coordinated look. Ribbon inset (right) gives texture and shine to this evening clutch. Twin-needle topstitched inset (below) gives a tailored look.

Designer Belts

Many ready-to-wear belts can be copied in synthetic suede, which can be purchased by the inch (centimeter), making it very economical. A small amount of 45" (115 cm) synthetic suede is adequate for waist sizes up to 40" (102 cm), depending on the style of belt. A snakeskin-covered buckle or purchased buckle added to a strip of synthetic suede makes a unique and easy belt to complete an outfit. Snakeskin scraps and a buckle kit transform synthetic suede into a luxurious belt; or cover the buckle with matching synthetic suede.

YOU WILL NEED

Synthetic suede, 3" (7.5 cm), depending on the width of the belt and for waists up to 40" (102 cm).

Buckle kit or purchased buckle.

Snakeskin scraps for buckle kit, optional.

Tips for Covering Buckles

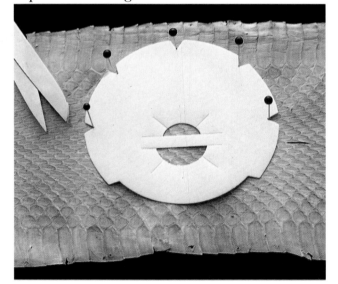

Snakeskin. Avoid any blemishes on skin. Snakeskin has a nap, so position skin so buckle feels smooth when worn. Insert pins at notches to mark position on wrong side. Follow manufacturer's instructions to affix snakeskin.

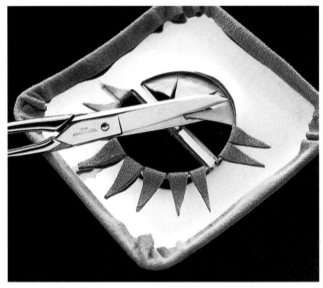

Smooth inner edges. Carefully cut additional slits on inner edges of buckle opening before affixing suede or snakeskin to buckle shape.

How to Make a Crushed Synthetic Suede Belt

1) Measure length of center bar of buckle. Double this measurement and add ¾" (2 cm) to determine cut width of belt. Cut synthetic suede to determined width, with length equal to waist measurement plus 14" (35.5 cm).

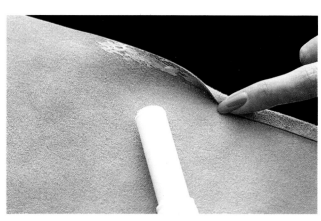

2) Apply glue stick along underside of one long edge. Fold over ⅜" (1 cm) and finger-press in place. Repeat for other long edge.

3a) Angled end. Position belt horizontally, wrong side up. Trim seam allowance diagonally at upper right corner. Apply glue stick along end. Fold end to meet long edge at top, forming 45° angle. Finger-press in place.

3b) Pointed end. Fold one end of belt lengthwise, right sides together. Stitch ¼" (6 mm) seam on short end. Apply glue stick to hold, and turn end right side out.

4) Topstitch ½" (1.3 cm) from folded edges, pivoting at corners.

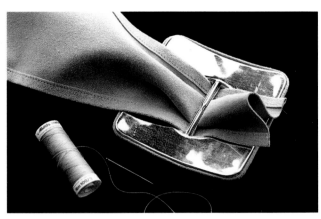

5) Wrap remaining end around center bar of buckle (do not use prong), with end extending about 2" (5 cm). Try belt on to determine the exact finished length. Secure loose end by hand or machine.

Shaped Belts

A basic shaped belt can be a one-of-a-kind accessory when a creative fabric or trim is used. Change the appearance of the fabric by screen printing a design, or embellish the fabric with beading or ribbonwork.

Mediumweight fabrics can be used, because the belt is stiffened by fusing a heavyweight interfacing to the fabric with fusible web. Select a fabric that will not be damaged by the fusing process, which requires steam and heat. Some lightweight synthetic leathers and suedes may be used, depending on the fabric care instructions. For the belt facing, use a durable fabric that will resist abrasion from the hook and loop tape closure.

The instructions included are for a belt with a 35" (89 cm) finished length from end to end. This size is adjustable to fit waistlines from 22" to 30" (56 to 76 cm) and includes 2" (5 cm) ease, to allow for comfort over clothing, and 3" (7.5 cm) overlap at the back. For larger sizes, additional length may be added at the ends of the belt.

This belt is designed for ⅛" (3 mm) piping. If wider piping or multiple rows of piping are used, decrease the size of the belt as on page 199, step 1.

YOU WILL NEED

⅜ yd. (0.35 m) fabric, at least 36" (91.5 cm) wide, if same fabric is used for both the belt and the belt facing; or ¼ yd. (0.25 m) fabric for belt and ¼ yd. (0.25 m) fabric for belt facing.

2⅛ yd. (1.95 m) piping to match or contrast fabric; double piping or triple piping (pages 196 to 199) may be used.

1 yd. (0.95 m) crisp nonwoven interfacing, used for crafts.

1 yd. (0.95 m) paper-backed fusible web.

7½" (19.3 cm) hook and loop tape, ¾" (2 cm) wide, for closure.

Glue stick.

Partial Pattern for Shaped Belt

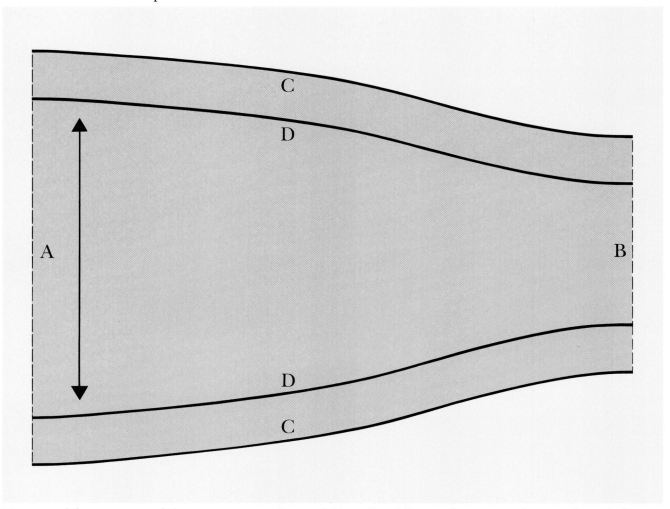

Trace partial pattern actual size onto paper, and extend Lines C and D to make pattern pieces as shown below.

How to Make the Pattern Pieces for a Shaped Belt

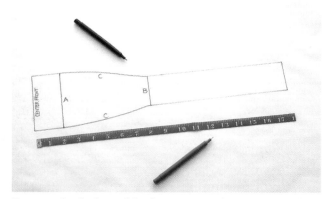

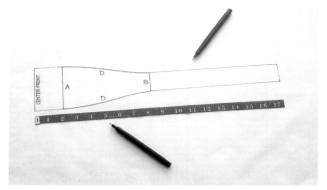

Pattern for belt and facing. Trace Lines A, B, and C from partial pattern, above, onto tracing paper. Extend Cutting Lines C, perpendicular to Line A; draw center front foldline 2" (5 cm) from, and parallel to, Line A. Extend Cutting Lines C, perpendicular to Line B; draw end of belt 18" (46 cm) from, and parallel to, center front line.

Pattern for interfacing and fusible web. Trace Lines A, B, and D from partial pattern, above, onto tracing paper. Extend Cutting Lines D, perpendicular to Line A; draw center front foldline 2" (5 cm) from, and parallel to, Line A. Extend Cutting Lines D, perpendicular to Line B; draw end of belt 17½" (44.3 cm) from, and parallel to, center front line.

How to Sew a Shaped Belt

1) Cut one belt and one facing, using pattern, opposite. Cut two pieces each of interfacing and fusible web, using pattern, opposite. Cut one belt carrier, 1⅜" × 5" (3.5 × 12.5 cm).

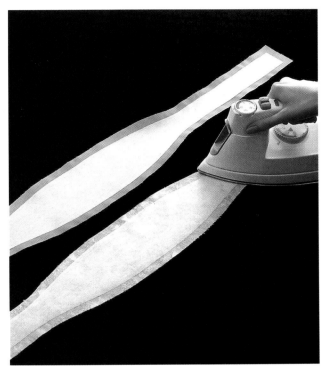

2) Apply one piece of fusible web to one piece of interfacing, according to manufacturer's directions. Fuse interfacing to wrong side of belt. Repeat for facing.

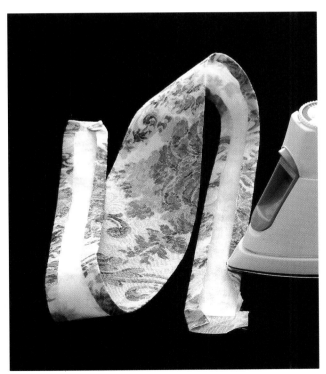

3) Fold ½" (1.3 cm) seam allowance on long edges of belt over interfacing; press. At corners, notch seam allowance and press at angle. Pink seam allowances, if desired. Repeat for facing.

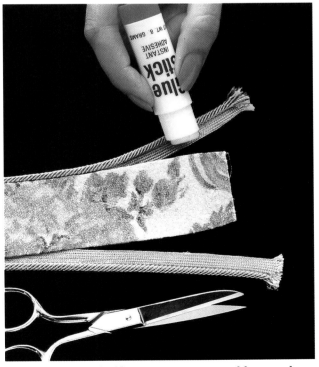

4) Cut piping in half. Baste to upper and lower edges of belt, on wrong side, using glue stick. Trim ends of piping even with raw edges.

(Continued on next page)

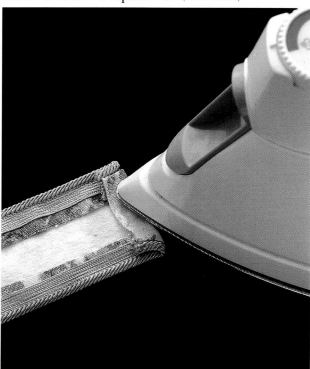

5) Fold ½" (1.3 cm) seam allowance at short ends of belt over interfacing; press. Repeat for facing.

6) Stitch loop side of hook and loop tape to belt facing, 1" (2.5 cm) from one end. Cut 1½" (3.8 cm) strip from hook side of tape; stitch to right side of belt, 1" (2.5 cm) from other end.

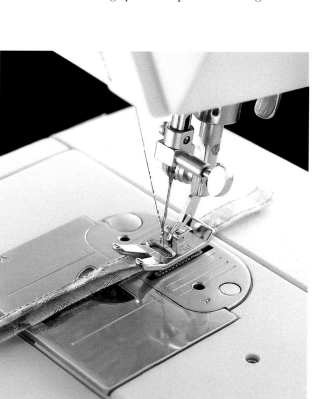

7) Fold ¼" (6 mm) to wrong side on long edges of belt carrier; press. Fold carrier in half lengthwise; press. Topstitch on both long edges.

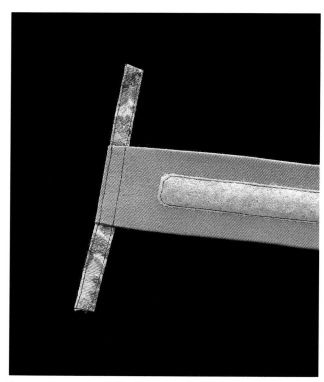

8) Center belt carrier on wrong side of belt facing, at end with loop tape; topstitch in place.

9) Align wrong side of belt facing to wrong side of belt; glue-baste in place.

10) Topstitch belt close to long edges, using zipper foot.

11) Slipstitch belt facing to belt at short ends.

12) Fold belt carrier around other end of belt; adjust length of carrier, as necessary, so end of belt slides through it easily. Handstitch ends of carrier securely.

Scarves

Scarves are easy to make, and they complete ensembles, from blue jeans to a cashmere jacket to an evening suit. A first-time sewer can complete a fringed scarf or muffler easily or, with the help of a rolled hem on the overlock machine or serger, make a professionally finished silk or rayon scarf. For a silk or rayon scarf, use a lightweight to mediumweight soft woven fabric. If you are using the serger to roll the edges, choose a lightweight fabric. Use a metallic holiday fabric for a rolled hem scarf, or make a soft wool muffler for everyone on your gift list. You can make four mufflers with 1¼ yards (1.15 m) of fine, 60" (150 cm) wool.

✂ Cutting Directions

Wool muffler: Straighten ends by pulling a cross thread and trimming evenly along pulled threads. Draw cutting lines on fabric, 15" (38 cm) apart, parallel with selvages. Cut four strips, each 15" × 45" (38 × 115 cm).

Silk or rayon square scarf: Cut a 36" or 45" (91.5 or 115 cm) square, depending on fabric width. Make sure threads are on the straight grain.

YOU WILL NEED

Wool muffler: 1¼ yd. (1.15 m) of 60" (152.5 cm) wide fabric (makes 4 scarves).

Silk or rayon square scarf: 45" (115 cm) of 45" (115 cm) wide fabric or 1 yd. (0.95 m) of 36" (91.5 cm) fabric.

How to Make a Wool Muffler

1) Zigzag with a short, narrow stitch close to each long edge and across each short end at top of desired fringe depth.

2) Fringe short ends by pulling away cross threads up to stitching.

How to Make a Silk or Rayon Square Scarf

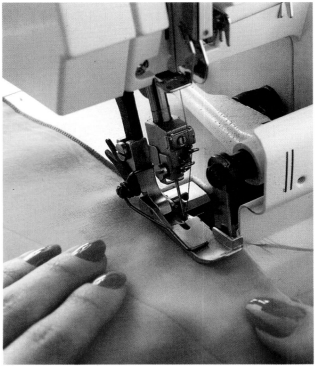

Square scarf with rolled hem. Set serger for rolled hem and finish all four edges of scarf. Fray-check each corner of scarf.

Square scarf with fringed edge. Pull threads to create fringe. A ¼" (6 mm) fringe on silk or rayon is more desirable because it doesn't add weight.

Ponytail Wraps

For ponytails, add a touch of color with simple-to-make elasticized ponytail wraps of grosgrain ribbon or fabric. The ribbon ponytail wraps are embellished with inserted trims like cording, decorative thread, or narrow ribbon.

When making ponytail wraps, vary the cut length of the strip according to the weight of the fabric or ribbon and the desired fullness. Generally, the length of the strip is about 30" (76 cm). A lightweight fabric, such as silk or chiffon, may be up to 36" (91.5 cm) in length. A shorter length may be used for heavier fabric or ribbon. Choose braided elastic of good quality for maximum stretch and recovery.

YOU WILL NEED

60" (152.5 cm) length of grosgrain ribbon, 1½" (3.8 cm) wide, and 3-yd. (2.75 cm) total length of desired trims, for ribbon ponytail wrap.

¼ yd. (0.25 m) fabric, for fabric ponytail wrap.

8" (20.5 cm) length of braided elastic, ¼" (6 mm) wide.

How to Sew a Ribbon Ponytail Wrap

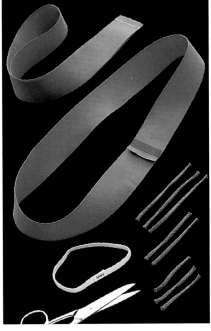

1) Cut two 30" (76 cm) lengths of ribbon. Stitch ends of each ribbon strip together; stitch the ends of the elastic together. Cut desired trims into lengths ranging from 2" to 4" (5 to 10 cm).

2) Place the ribbons wrong sides together. Stitch ribbons together on outer edge, inserting trims to form overlapping loops as desired.

3) Insert elastic between ribbons. Stitch ribbons together along inner edge, bunching ribbon as you stitch. Do not catch elastic in stitching.

How to Sew a Fabric Ponytail Wrap

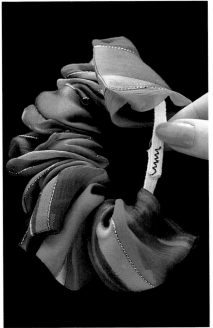

1) Cut 4½" (11.5 cm) strip of fabric to desired length. Fold fabric in half lengthwise, right sides together; stitch ¼" (6 mm) seam on long edge.

2) Turn fabric tube right side out. Insert elastic through tube; stitch elastic ends together securely.

3) Fold under ¼" (6 mm) on one end of fabric; lap over opposite end. Slipstitch; do not catch elastic in stitching.

Headbands

Use fabric scraps to make custom headbands. Inexpensive plastic headbands or plastic headband forms, available at fabric and craft stores, are easy to wrap with a bias-cut strip of fabric. If desired, the top of the headband may be padded with ¼" to ½" (6 mm to 1.3 cm) polyurethane foam. For a professional finish, gimp is glued to the inside of the headband.

For best results, use a firmly woven fabric; avoid slippery fabrics that are difficult to handle. Mediumweight to heavyweight fabrics are easier to wrap around headbands that have been padded with ½" (1.3 cm) polyurethane foam.

YOU WILL NEED

Fabric scraps.

Plastic headband form.

Polyurethane foam, ¼" to ½" (6 mm to 1.3 cm) thick, for a padded headband.

Spray adhesive, for a padded headband.

Thick craft glue.

½ yd. (0.5 m) gimp.

How to Make an Unpadded Headband

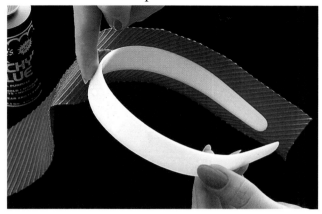

1) Cut a bias strip of fabric at least twice the width of the headband and about 2" (5 cm) longer. Spread a thin layer of glue on outside of the headband. Center headband on wrong side of fabric strip; secure.

2) Trim fabric so edges extend one-half the width of the headband; round fabric strip about ⅜" (1 cm) beyond ends of headband. Clip fabric at ends, and glue to inside of headband.

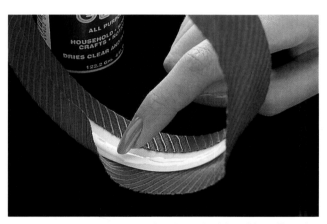

3) Glue one long edge of fabric to inside of headband, applying glue to the headband; work in sections, keeping fabric smooth. Repeat for opposite side.

4) Glue gimp, centering it on inside of headband and turning under ends.

How to Make a Padded Headband

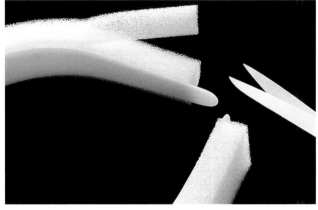

1) Spread a thin layer of glue on outside of headband; secure to strip of polyurethane foam. Cut foam even with edges of headband. If using ½" (1.3 cm) foam, trim foam ½" (1.3 cm) shorter than ends. Clamp ends of foam with clothespins until glue dries.

2) Follow steps 1 to 4 above, applying a light layer of spray adhesive to foam, to secure fabric; wrap the headband with fabric, pulling it taut to round the edges of the foam.

Embellishing Headbands

By embellishing headbands with trims, you can create a number of different styles. Depending on the look you want, combine dramatic fabrics with embellishments that sparkle, or use sportswear fabrics and sporty trims.

Most items can be glued in place, using a craft glue or hot glue. If trim will be wrapped around the headband, attach it before securing the gimp on the inside.

1) Twisted cording, applied in a diagonal wrap, is threaded with decorative beads to create a headband that is one of a kind.

2) Coordinating fabrics are wrapped in three or four separate sections. Wrap a decorative ribbon around the headband to conceal the raw edges where the fabric sections overlap.

3) Faceted stones highlight the fabric of this padded headband. For best results, secure the faceted stones with a gem glue.

4) Decorative ring embellishes a plain headband. Secure cording to the ring with larkspur knots, and glue in place. Wrap the ends of the headband with a narrow trim to conceal the ends of the cording.

5) Decorative buttons, glued in a row, provide a simple embellishment. Remove the shanks from the buttons, using a wire cutter.

6) Gold chain, woven with a narrow strip of synthetic suede or leather, adds a unique embellishment. Weave the suede or leather strip through the chain before gluing it in place.

Beaded Barrettes

Make beaded barrettes using vinyl cross-stitch canvas. Chart a design on graph paper, in 11 rows of 47 squares or 12 rows of 48 squares, depending on whether an odd or even number of squares is desired. Or apply the beads in a random design. The finished barrette is about 1" × 3½" (2.5 × 9 cm).

Use a short beading needle and a single strand of cotton-wrapped polyester thread. Allow at least ⅜" (1 cm) of cross-stitch canvas around the edges of the design for finishing the barrette.

YOU WILL NEED

Vinyl cross-stitch canvas, 14 count.

Seed beads; short beading needle; cotton-wrapped polyester thread.

Spring barrette clip, about 3" (7.5 cm) long.

Leather or synthetic suede scrap, for backing.

Thick craft glue, or hot glue gun and glue sticks.

How to Make a Beaded Barrette

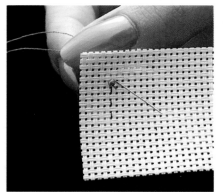

1) Weave needle through canvas to anchor thread, bringing needle up at upper left corner of design. Take diagonal stitch down through bead and to the right. Bring needle up at upper left corner of next square.

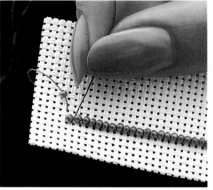

2) Continue to end of first row; bring needle down to wrong side at last bead. Turn canvas upside down for second row, so stitching will be in same direction. Repeat to complete all rows; secure thread.

3) Trim vinyl ⅜" (1 cm) from edges of design; trim corners. Fold under edges; glue in place, using craft glue or hot glue. Cut backing to size of design; glue to canvas. Glue barrette clip to backing.

Tulle & Ribbon Hair Bows

Feminine, romantic hair bows can be made from layers of tulle, ribbons, and decorative trims. Select trims in black and gold for a striking evening accent, or in soft pastels for an ingenue look.

The tulle, available in many colors, provides a full background for the ribbons and trims. Layer lengths of any dominant ribbons or trims, and accent them with several layers of narrow trims, such as ribbons, decorative cords, or strands of pearls or beads.

YOU WILL NEED

Tulle, two pieces about 6" × 40" (15 × 102 cm) each.
Ribbons and trims as desired, in 1⅛-yd. (1.05 m) lengths.
Spring barrette clip, about 3" (7.5 cm) long.
Beading or millinery wire.

How to Make a Tulle and Ribbon Hair Bow

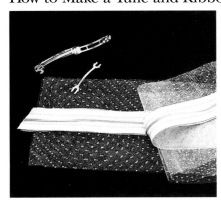

1) Cut and layer two 6" × 40" (15 × 102 cm) strips of tulle. Layer trims over tulle as desired, placing narrow trims on top. Open spring barrette clip, and remove tension bar.

2) Gather trims 4" (10 cm) from one end; secure to barrette clip with wire. Gather trims 6" (15 cm) from secured wire, forming loop; secure to barrette clip.

3) Continue to gather and secure four more loops, leaving tail at end. Replace tension bar. Fan out trims and ribbons, alternating sides.

Chiffon Hair Bows

For a classic hair bow, make either a looped-style or a circular-style bow from chiffon. Other lightweight sheer or silky fabrics, such as China silk, georgette, or charmeuse, may also be used.

Both styles of bows are easily made by wiring a single strip of fabric to a spring barrette clip; a narrow hem finishes the edges of the fabric. If desired, a circular bow may be embellished with artificial flowers.

YOU WILL NEED

⅜ **yd. (0.35 m) fabric,** such as chiffon, China silk, georgette, or charmeuse.

Spring barrette clip, about 3" (7.5 cm) long.

Beading or millinery wire.

Hot glue gun and glue sticks.

How to Make a Looped-style Hair Bow

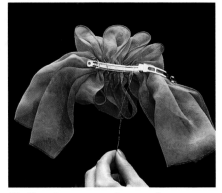
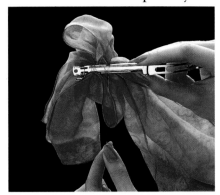
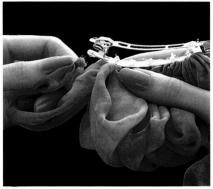

1) Hem long edges of 10" × 36" (25.5 × 91.5 cm) fabric piece as desired. Open barette clip; remove tension bar. Gather fabric 6" (15 cm) from one end; secure to clip with wire. Gather the fabric 6" (15 cm) away, forming loop; secure to clip.

2) Continue to gather and secure loops at 6" (15 cm) intervals, leaving 6" (15 cm) tail at end.

3) Gather one end of fabric piece; secure gathers with thread or wire. Fold under end of fabric, forming loop; secure to end of clip with hot glue. Repeat at the opposite end. Replace tension bar.

How to Make a Circular-style Hair Bow

1) Hem the long edges of 7½" × 34" (19.3 × 86.5 cm) fabric piece for the bow as desired. Press 2" × 4" (5 × 10 cm) fabric strip in half lengthwise for center wrap. Open strip; fold and press raw edges to center fold to make ½" (1.3 cm) strip.

2) Stitch short ends of fabric piece for bow, right sides together, in narrow seam. Position tube, right side out, with seam centered on bottom. Open the barrette clip, and remove tension bar. Gather fabric by hand, starting at center of one folded edge.

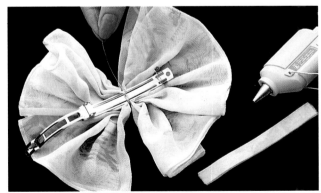

3) Secure gathered fabric to center of barrette clip, using wire. Wrap fabric strip around center of bow, securing with hot glue on back of barrette; trim excess fabric strip.

4) Glue fabric to ends of barrette clip. Glue fabric at folded edges together, just above and below center strip. Replace tension bar.

Fabric-wrapped Bracelets

Use leftover fabrics to make bracelets that coordinate with your garments. These fabric-wrapped bracelets are quickly made, using inexpensive bangle bracelets and two narrow strips of fabric. The strips are torn, adding texture to the bracelet. You may want to make a set of bracelets, reversing the order in which the strips are wrapped or combining different fabrics.

Choose soft, lightweight fabrics that can be torn into narrow strips. Sueded silks and rayons work well and add subtle color shading. When wrapping a bracelet, stretch the fabric strips taut to prevent the fabric from shifting when the bracelet is completed.

YOU WILL NEED

Fabric scraps.

Plastic or wooden bangle bracelet with rounded surface, at least ¾" (2 cm) wide.

Decorative rayon cording.

Fabric glue or thick craft glue.

How to Make a Fabric-wrapped Bracelet

1) Tear one 1" × 36" (2.5 × 91.5 cm) strip of fabric for first layer; tear one ½" × 36" (1.3 × 91.5 cm) strip of contrasting fabric for second layer. Glue wrong side of one end of 1" (2.5 cm) strip to inside of bracelet, positioning fabric at an angle.

2) Wrap fabric around bracelet, angling fabric and overlapping edges; trim excess fabric, and glue end to inside of bracelet.

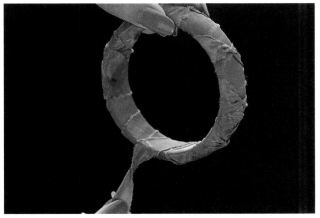

3) Glue wrong side of one end of ½" (1.3 cm) strip to inside of bracelet, with fabric angled in opposite direction from first fabric. Wrap strip at an angle, twisting fabric once or twice on outside of bracelet. Trim excess fabric; glue end to inside.

4) Wrap rayon cording around bracelet as desired. Glue ends of cording to inside of bracelet.

English Smocking

The technique of smocking refers to gathering material into folds and creating designs by hand-stitching through one pleat at a time. It is used on many household items as well as on yokes, bodices, pockets, sleeves, and waistlines of clothing such as nightwear, children's wear, blouses, and dresses. There are many smocking stitches that allow for countless patterns and endless creativity, but with only two basic stitches many patterns can be created.

A decorative pattern results from the use of smocking. In addition, smocking gives shape to the garment. It provides an elasticity that pleats and tucks do not give. For smocking, a lightweight, crisp fabric is best. Lightweight polyester and cotton blends, batiste, broadcloth, calicos, or soft flannel are suitable because they will gather into pleats. Embroidery floss is used for the decorative stitching. A size 7 or 8 (55 or 60) needle is most often used with three or more strands of floss. Use a finer thread for batiste.

Smocking is done before the garment is constructed. The fabric should be preshrunk. The piece to be smocked should be at least three times larger than

the finished area, because smocking decreases the size of the fabric. If a desired commercial pattern does not use smocking, it may be adapted in a pattern with gathers. A basic pattern that involves a small area to be smocked will give best results. When you are working with two identical pieces such as collars, cuffs, or bodice fronts, it is helpful to complete them simultaneously to maintain uniformity.

Before the fabric is smocked, it must be gathered into pleats. A pleating machine may be preferred at this step to accommodate today's busy life-style. It provides a fast and efficient way of gathering the fabric. Since buying a pleating machine can be quite costly, one can simply take the fabric to a quilting store and have the piece pleated. The fabric is fed into the machine, which consists of 16, 24, or 32 needles. The needles are threaded with quilting thread because it is stronger, less likely to tangle, stays in the fabric better, and makes pleats that are fuller and more rounded. The result is evenly pleated fabric that is ready to be smocked. Before smocking, count the pleats, and mark the center so that symmetrical designs will balance.

The look of the finished pattern will depend on which stitch, or combination of stitches, is selected. A wide variety of stitches may be used. They are completed by working from left to right. Two of them are the cable stitch and the trellis stitch. The cable stitch is used often and is easy to learn. It is a compact stitch with a basket-weave appearance. The trellis stitch is versatile and can vary in the number of stitches that compose it. It gives a zigzag effect and can be worked to any height. Two pleats are worked at a time. Stitches are made in a steplike fashion.

The creativity involved with smocking comes into play during the planning of the design. Drawing a sketch of the design on paper before working on the fabric helps to eliminate uncertainty. Choose a dominant color for the theme, and use compatible colors or accent colors suitable for the fabric or design. Using dark, medium, and light colors enhances the design even further.

Pleating machine. Fabric is wound on a dowel, and the fabric end is inserted between two rollers. Fabric is fed through by turning a handle at the side of the machine.

How to Make a Cable Stitch

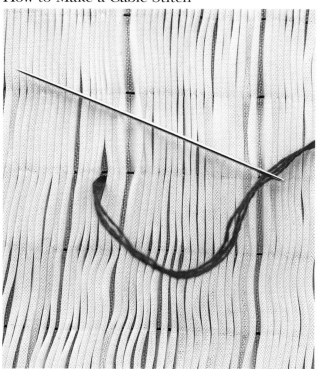

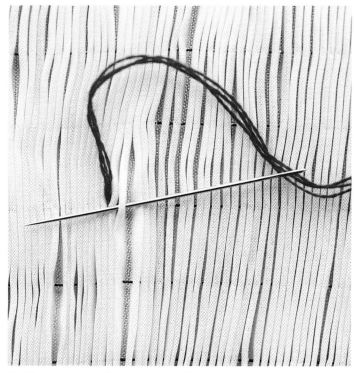

1) Bring the needle through the first pleat from the underside.

2) Place thread above the needle, and stitch under the second pleat.

How to Make a Trellis Stitch

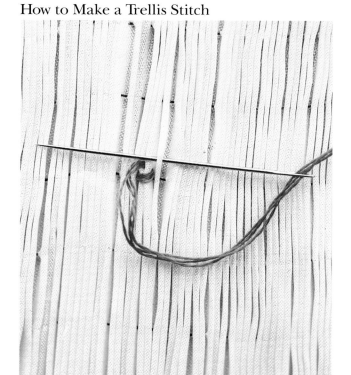

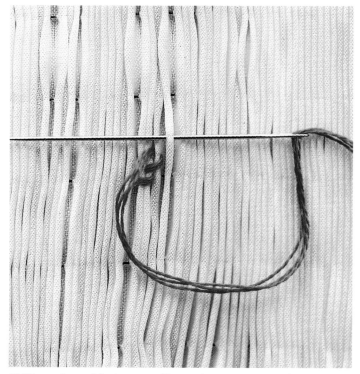

1) Start with bottom cable, bringing the needle through the first pleat from the underside. Placing thread below needle and moving up a quarter of the way between rows 1 and 2, stitch the next pleat.

2) Keep thread below needle, and move up another quarter space to halfway point between rows 1 and 2; stitch the next pleat.

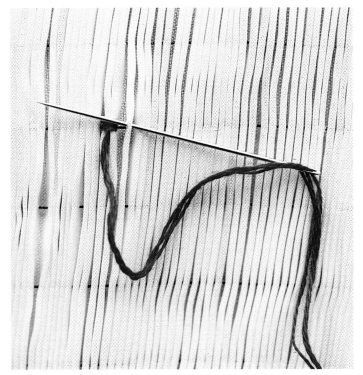

3) Place the thread below the needle, and stitch through the third pleat.

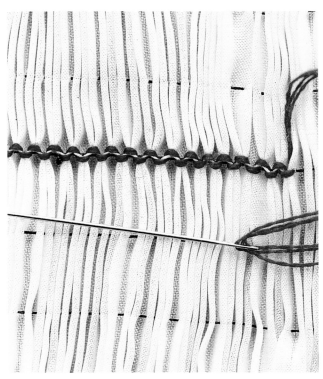

4) Alternate this way until the row is complete. Repeat the procedure for the remaining rows.

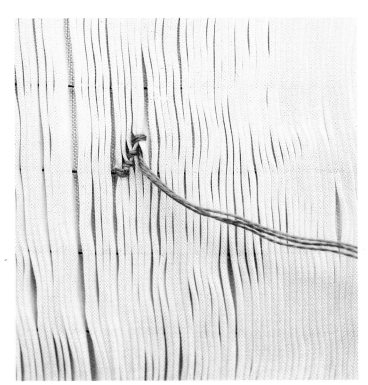

3) Place thread above needle, halfway between rows, and stitch the next pleat, making cable at top of trellis. This stitch completes first half of trellis.

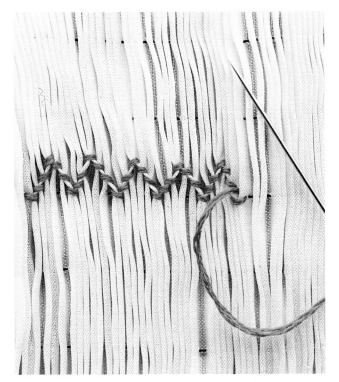

4) Keep thread above needle, and move down a quarter space; stitch next pleat. Repeat. With thread below needle, stitch the next pleat, making cable at bottom of trellis. Repeat steps 1 to 4 as necessary.

Smocked Christmas Ornaments

Smocking can easily be used to make Christmas tree ornaments or decorative eggs, or be inset into a variety of projects, from home decorations to accessories. This 2" (5 cm) ornament is an excellent beginning project, because it is fast and easy.

Combinations of the two basic stitches on pages 312 to 313 can make a variety of patterns for your projects. Read pages 310 to 313 for basic smocking information.

YOU WILL NEED

Mediumweight fabric, 4½" × 22½" (11.5 × 57.3 cm).

Styrofoam® ball, 2" (5 cm).

12" (30.5 cm) satin ribbon, ¼" (6 mm) wide.

3" (7.5 cm) satin ribbon, ½" (1.3 cm) wide.

Embroidery floss and needle.

How to Make a Smocked Christmas Ornament

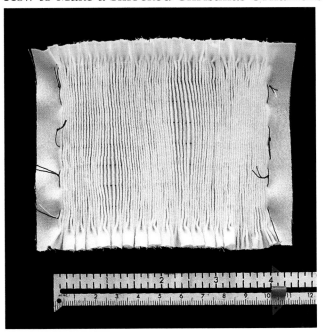

1) Pleat a piece of fabric 4½" × 22½" (11.5 × 57.3 cm) into 9 rows (page 311). Spread pleats to a width of 4" (10 cm). Tie the gathering threads into pairs with an overhand knot.

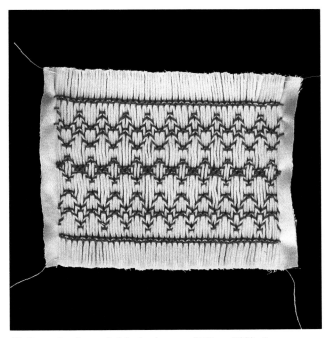

2) Smock pleated fabric (pages 312 to 313). Leave one pleat on each side for seam. Trim fabric ⅛" (3 mm) above gathering row 1 and below gathering row 9. Remove gathering threads from rows 2 to 8. (Other threads are used to pull rectangle into ball shape.)

(Continued on next page)

315

How to Make a Smocked Christmas Ornament (continued)

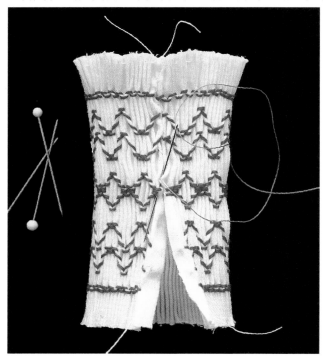

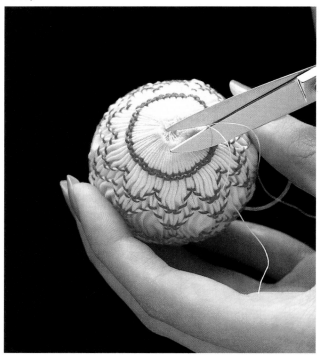

3) Turn under one side edge, matching smocking design. Pin and slipstitch. This makes a tube. (Pins were removed and contrasting thread was used to show detail.)

4) Slip Styrofoam ball into tube. Center design on ball and pull up gathering threads on rows 1 and 9, as tightly as possible. Clip threads.

5) Cut ⅜" (1 cm) ribbon into 9" (23 cm) and 3" (7.5 cm) lengths. Make 3 loops with 9" (23 cm) piece, and secure to top with a pin. Form loop with 3" (7.5 cm) piece for hanging, and pin to top with 2 decorative pins.

6) Use 3" (7.5 cm) piece of ⅝" (1.5 cm) ribbon to form a loop. Flatten loop, and pin to bottom of ball with 2 decorative pins.

Ideas for Smocking

After learning the smocking techniques and stitches on pages 310 to 313, you can make a variety of projects. Try the projects on this page, or create one of your own.

Beaded Christmas ornament is easy to do, using the cable stitch. Beads are added after the first stitch of a cable, as on page 312, step 1. Finish ornament, as in steps 3 to 6, opposite.

Smocked tieback with piping adds an original touch to this curtain.

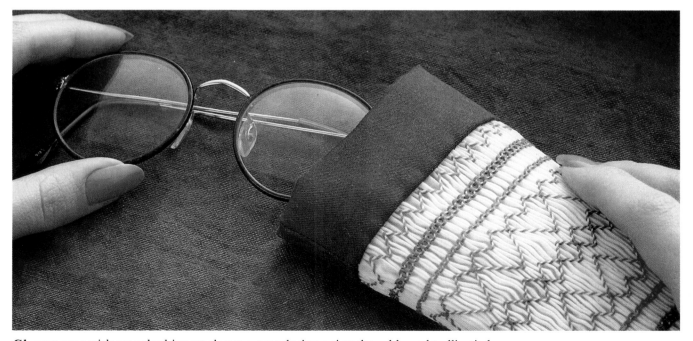

Glasses case with smocked insert shows a new design using the cable and trellis stitches.

Index

Cy DeCosse Incorporated offers
sewing accessories to subscribers.
For information write:
  Sewing Accessories
  5900 Green Oak Drive
  Minnetonka, MN 55343